Roman Social History

D0219651

This lively and original guidebook is the first to show students new to the subject exactly what Roman social history involves and how they can study it for themselves.

After presenting a short history of the development and current position of the discipline, the author discusses the kinds of evidence that can be used and the full range of resources available. Two case studies provide practical examples of how to approach sources and what we can learn from them.

Clear, concise and accessible, with all text extracts translated into English, this is the ideal introduction to an increasingly popular subject.

Susan Treggiari is Anne T. and Robert M. Bass Professor in the School of Humanities and Sciences, Stanford University. Her previous publications include *Roman Marriage* (1991, 1993), a chapter in *Cambridge Ancient History X* (1996) and *Roman Freedmen during the Late Republic* (1969, reissued 2000).

Classical Foundations

The books in this series introduce students to the broad areas of study within classical studies and ancient history. They will be particularly helpful to students coming to the subject for the first time, or to those already familiar with an academic discipline who need orientation in a new field. The authors work to a common brief but not to a rigid structure: they set out to demonstrate the importance of the chosen subject and the lines of recent and continuing research and interpretation. Each book will provide a brief survey of the range of the subject, accompanied by some case studies demonstrating how one may go deeper into it. Each will also include guidance of a practical kind on sources, resources and reference material, and how to pursue the subject further. When complete, the series will comprise a critical map of the whole field of ancient studies.

The series is planned to include:

Early Christianity
Greek History
Greek Literature
Greek Philosophy
Late Antiquity
Latin Literature
Roman Social History
The Roman Empire

Books currently available in the series:

Latin Literature
Susanna Morton Braund

Roman Social History
Susan Treggiari

Roman Social History

Susan Treggiari

London and New York

First published 2002
by Routledge
11 New Fetter Lane, London EC4P 4EE

Simultaneously published in the USA and Canada
by Routledge
29 West 35th Street, New York, NY 10001

Routledge is an imprint of the Taylor & Francis Group

© 2002 Susan Treggiari

Typeset in Times by
Florence Production Ltd, Stoodleigh, Devon

Printed and bound in Great Britain by
TJ International, Padstow, Cornwall

All rights reserved. No part of this book may be reprinted
or reproduced or utilised in any form or by any electronic,
mechanical, or other means, now known or hereafter
invented, including photocopying and recording, or in any
information storage or retrieval system, without permission
in writing from the publishers.

British Library Cataloguing in Publication Data
A catalogue record for this book is available from the
British Library

Library of Congress Cataloging in Publication Data
Treggiari, Susan.
  Roman social history/Susan Treggiari.
    p.cm. – (Classical foundations)
  Includes bibliographical references and index.
  1. Rome – Historiography. 2. Rome – History – Study
  and teaching. 3. Rome – Social conditions.
  4. Social structure – Rome. I. Title. II. Series.

  DG205. T74 2001
  937'.007'2–dc21   2001034794

ISBN 0–415–19521–7 (hbk)
ISBN 0–415–19522–5 (pbk)

Matri Nepotibusque

Elizabeth Mary Franklin

Jasmine Emily Rajagopalan

Thomas Arnaldo Rajagopalan

Contents

Preface

I am grateful to Richard Stoneman for inviting me to write this book and for the constant help and encouragement he has given. It has been an unalloyed pleasure to work with the team from Routledge.

This book is intended to help a student make a start in specialised work on Roman social history. To some extent, it represents the tips I would like to give or to have given to each of my own students at an appropriate moment. In part, it is what I would have liked to know when I started out about forty years ago. Often I have stated what will appear obvious to many readers, in the hope that it might make things more accessible to others. Most of us have odd and often embarrassing gaps in our knowledge. It must be emphatically stated that this is not all you will need to know. We always have to learn.

Some of the material has been used for Stanford classes, but my debt to Stanford and Ottawa students is more general. I have taught a variety of courses on Roman social history during the last thirty years and hope I have learned in the process. I owe an especial debt to those graduate students with whom I have worked (or just talked) and who chose to write on topics which involved social history: particularly David Cherry, Leonard Curchin and Roberto Melfi at Ottawa; Andrew Bell, Paul Chénier, Nicholas Cofod, Cynthia Damon, Lesley Dean-Jones, Judith Evans Grubbs, Peter Hunt, Margaret Imber, James Rives and Richard Westall at Stanford; Cristina Calhoon of Irvine and Leslie Shumka of the University of Victoria. Krista Pelisari, who took part in an undergraduate seminar at Stanford in Oxford in the winter of 2000, kindly read Chapter 4 and made helpful suggestions. There are many others, whom I have met over the years, to whom I feel warm gratitude. The debt to my own teachers can never be repaid.

Translations are (except where indicated) my own, with the important exception of those in Chapter 4, where the excerpts from Cicero's correspondence are drawn from D.R. Shackleton Bailey. I regret that Professor Bailey's Loeb edition of Cicero's *Letters to his Friends* (2001) appeared after this book had gone to press, so that I was unable to profit by it.

The bibliography is intended to be highly selective and merely to suggest lines of approach for English readers. Omission implies no negative judgement.

Because I find it works to dive into the middle of the subject and to learn by doing, I have given little space to worries about the philosophical basis of history or to theoretical methodology, but I have directed the reader to some of the literature on such topics. I also confess a non-theoretical cast of mind.

I thank friends and colleagues in the field of Roman history for the inspiration of their work. This book is not for them. Each would have written it differently and better. Keith Bradley proved this by reading the whole typescript more rapidly than a man with heavy administrative responsibilities could possibly be expected to do and by giving me the benefit of his bibliographical and scholarly expertise, sharp editorial eye and critical acumen.

The dedication is to an older and younger generation of our family in gratitude and without the expectation that they will read it. As always, I thank all my family for their love, support and society, and especially my husband, for making it possible for me to research and write on the Romans and for constant inspiration.

Abbreviations

Abbreviations of the names and works of ancient authors are normally those listed by the *Oxford Classical Dictionary*, with a few exceptions given below.

A	Cicero *Letters to Atticus*
AJP	*American Journal of Philology*
ANRW	*Aufstieg und Niedergang der römischen Welt*
APh	*Année Philologique*
App. *BC*	Appian *Civil War*
Ars P.	*Ars Poetica*
c.	*circa*, about (to give an approximate date)
c.	century
CHGL	P.E. Easterling and B.M.W. Knox (eds) (1985) *Cambridge History of Greek Literature*, Cambridge: Cambridge University Press
CHLL	E.J. Kenney and W.V. Clausen (eds) (1982) *Cambridge History of Latin Literature*, Cambridge: Cambridge University Press
Cic. *A*	Cicero *Letters to Atticus*
Cic. *F*	Cicero *Letters to Friends*
Cic. *QF*	Cicero *Letters to his brother Quintus*

CJ	*Code of Justinian*
CTh	*Code of Theodosius*
Coll.	*Mosaicarum et Romanarum legum collatio = FIRA* ii.543 ff.
cos	consul
CV/EMC	*Classical Views/Echos du monde classique*
D	*Digest of Justinian*
ead.	Same author (female)
F	Cicero *Letters to Friends*
FIRA	S. Riccobono *et al.* (eds) (1940–1, repr. 1968–9) *Fontes iuris Romani antejustiniani*, Florence: Barbèra, 3 vols.
Iav.	Iavolenus
id.	Same author (male)
inst. div.	*Divinae institutiones*
Jacoby *FHG*	*Fragmenta historicorum graecorum*
JRA	*Journal of Roman Archaeology*
JRS	*Journal of Roman Studies*
Just. *Inst.*	*Institutes of Justinian*
Kleine Pauly	*Der kleine Pauly. Lexikon der Antike*, Stuttgart: Druckenmüller, 1964–75
Lab.	Labeo
LTUR	E.M. Steinby (ed.) (1990–) *Lexicon topographicum urbis Romae*, Rome: Edizioni Quasar
Mod.	Modestinus
MRR	*Magistrates of the Roman Republic* ed. T.R.S. Broughton i (1951), ii (1952), iii (1986)
Neue Pauly	*Der neue Pauly. Enzyklopädie der Antike*, Stuttgart: Metzler, 1996
OCD	*Oxford Classical Dictionary* (3rd edn) Oxford: Clarendon Press, 1996
Pap.	Papinian
Paul	Paulus
Pomp.	Pomponius
pr.	(in *Digest*) principium, the beginning of an excerpt (which precedes '1')
QF	Cicero *Letters to his brother Quintus*

RE	*Real-Encyclopädie der classischen Altertumswissenschaft*, ed. A.Fr. von Pauly, rev. G. Wissowa *et al.*, Stuttgart, 1894–1980, now Munich: Druckenmüller.
Res Gestae	see Brunt and Moore
RhM	*Rheinisches Museum für Philologie*
SB *A*	D.R. Shackleton Bailey 1965–70
SB *F*	D.R. Shackleton Bailey 1977
TLL	*Thesaurus linguae Latinae*
TvR	*Tijdschrift voor Rechtsgeschiednis*
Ulp.	Ulpian
Vocabularium	*Vocabularium iurisprudentiae Romanae*
XII Tab.	*Twelve Tables* (see Crawford 1996b ii 555–721)

Chapter 1

Introduction

> . . . memorable, but probably non-existent and therefore perhaps
> less important historically . . .
>
> (W.G. Sellars and R.J. Yeatman, *1066 and All That*: 18)

History, historiography, historians

Social history is part of history. The social historian needs general historical understanding. Anyone setting out to study Roman social history will do well to get a general grasp of the history of the ancient Romans first of all. To study history is to study human beings in the past. Everything that concerns the lives of individuals or groups of people may interest the historian.

Definitions

The word 'history' is used in English in two main senses. First, it denotes what has happened in the past: in this sense 'history' means much the same as 'the past'. Second, it describes the study of that past and the writings produced by the student of the past, the historian. To Greeks and Romans the distinction would be clearer. For the first sense, they could talk of what human beings had done, as Herodotus at the beginning of his book talks of the 'deeds' (*erga*) of the Greeks and the Persians, or a Roman might say '*res gestae*', the things done. But such expressions may suggest a focus on events, which is too narrow to describe the human past as it is now understood. For the second sense, Herodotus ('the Father of History') uses '*historiai*' (plural), investigations or researches. Coming through Latin 'historia' and French 'histoire', this word was brought into English, by the fourteenth century, to mean, not so much the researches, as the written or oral 'narrative of past events, account, tale, inquiry' (*Oxford English Dictionary*). It then comes to mean also 'that branch of knowledge which deals with past events' and 'the aggregate of past events in general: the course of events or human affairs'. We may use 'historiography' to describe the writing down of the results of historical research, the text produced by the historian. The titles conventionally given to works of history may highlight either the subject matter (The Peloponnesian War) or the process of research (Histories, Studies) or the form in which the narrative is cast (Annals, Chronicles).

The historian will usually put his or her own name to a work. Herodotus begins with his own name in the possessive case 'Herodotus the Halicarnassian's'. Then comes *historiēs*, also possessive, and finally *apodexis*, 'exposition'. So we have great emphasis on the agent and his research. In English we might paraphrase 'The book in your hands is the exposition (or showing forth) of the research (or investigation) of Herodotus of Halicarnassus'. He explains that his purpose is to prevent the great deeds of both Greeks and foreigners from being forgotten and to give the reasons why they fought what we call the Persian War.

To put it simply: something happens; a person (a historian or someone who becomes a historian in the process) thinks this something worth recording, investigates it and writes down the results of the research so that others may read them. People – and therefore human error, uncertainty and failings – are involved at every step of the process.

Time

How should we define the past? We may raise interesting theoretical questions about the exact chronological limits within which a historian may operate. The origins of the human species are in practice left to anthropologists with scientific qualifications, while preliterate human societies are the province of archaeologists. At the other end of the chronological span, where today becomes yesterday and tomorrow becomes today, a historian may be sharing territory with sociologists, specialists in politics and economics, and journalists. Historians write, for example, biographies of people who are still alive, and may speculate on what they will do in the future. But most historians will think about a period which is clearly 'past'.

Until recently, history as a subject in schools and universities tended to have a stopping-point several decades earlier than the birth-date of their students. A distant viewpoint gives the viewer a chance to see things in relation to each other, without being confused by unnecessary detail or being himself or herself part of the scene. Objectivity, hard as it is to achieve in practice, remains the ideal for all historians. But to stop a class abruptly in 1900 or 1914 or 1945 frustrates students' desire to understand what has more immediately shaped their own world.

Such sharp breaks are artificial. As we look back from the commanding position of AD 2000 (or thereabouts), it is natural for us to help ourselves make sense of the human past by dividing history up into 'periods'. The date in the form 'AD 2000' immediately suggests a division of history into the pre-Christian and Christian eras. Periods are often marked by the beginning and end of a war or the accession and death of rulers. This is a convenient and tidy way to study history, but we must not be misled into missing the continuities. The impact of Christianity in human terms did not begin in AD 1. The Christian system of dating (BC 'before Christ' and AD, *anno Domini*, 'in the year of the Lord') does not come naturally to non-Christians. But it is commonly recognised and is used by most English-speaking Roman historians. (It will be used here. The student will also come across books which use the same reckoning but refer to the 'Common Era': BCE, 'before the Common Era' and CE, 'the Common Era', rather than BC and AD.)

Like this big division of time, our division into centuries or decades ('the swinging Sixties') or by dynasties or rulers (the Tudor period, the Victorian age) is crude and can hinder analysis. The divisions of time conventionally used for political history may be particularly unhelpful when we study social history. Each defined subject which a historian undertakes to study will confront him or her with problems about where to start and stop. Do we begin a biography with the birth of the subject, or must the parents and family be described? Do we end with the person's death, or did he or she have a continuing influence which should not be ignored? A historian of a war will usually, like Thucydides, examine its roots in the past. Ronald Syme, writing *The Roman Revolution* (1939), about the changes in the Roman state associated with Augustus, went back to 70 BC and the domination of Pompeius, but forty years later told a meeting of the Association of Ancient Historians in North America that if he had the task to do again he would have started a decade earlier, with the civil war and the domination of Sulla. In considering a topic in social history, we may find that different facets of our subject require different chronological divisions.

Space

Similarly, geographical limits may blinker us. It is obvious that you cannot investigate the foreign policy of a nation state without looking at the countries with which it comes in contact. It is equally true that the life of the smallest village must be studied in relation to neighbouring villages, to the county and wider area, as well as the state, in which it is set.

History involves time and space. The social historian usually begins his or her historical education with a broad training in history, which gives a chronological and geographical overview and a basic grasp of politico-military history. The Roman social historian may also have a background in Latin literature.

Social history

Definitions

The term 'social history' denotes the study of people in relation to each other. Such a broad definition would embrace political and military history, and even constitutional history, since the systems set up to run states are developed by and for people. But we generally use the term to mean 'not political or military or constitutional or diplomatic or legal history'.

Peter Burke has recently written:

> G.M. Trevelyan's notorious definition of social history as 'history with the politics left out' is now rejected by almost everyone. Instead we find concern with the social element in politics and the political element in society'.
>
> (Burke 1991: 19)

His statement encapsulates the truth that the material of the historian should not be divided up into neat and watertight compartments. How politics were organised for a particular group may have a major impact on social life. Economic forces and law can scarcely be ignored. So the study of politics, legal history and economics may be part of the job of the social historian. It is a question of emphasis or focus. We focus on how individuals and groups relate to each other. The physical environment will be important: land, sea, climate, plants, animals; what people have made of their environment: the development of hunting, fishing, stock-keeping and cultivation, manufacture and trade; the demography of the human population: life expectancy, fertility, diseases; the institutions people developed: whether they lived in isolated houses, or villages or cities; at what age they married, how they treated their property, what customs or laws they set up. It is clearly hard for one individual fully to comprehend such a variety of topics even for a society narrowly defined in time and space. In practice, the themes selected by historians will be chosen in the light of their own interests and competence and the availability of material to study.

A 'society' is a grouping in which human beings have something in common. The Latin common noun *socius* from which the abstract noun *societas* (and related adjectives) derived means 'partner, sharer, ally'. In studying social history we shall usually focus on one society at a given time or over a given period. Societies come in many shapes, forms and sizes. We might want to explore how society was structured in England in the nineteenth century (and perhaps compare it with Scotland) or how people interacted with each other in the villages which circle the old common of Otmoor in Oxfordshire or how dukes married and had children. England as a society is defined by shared experience, geography, law and politics; Otmoor villages lie around what was a low-lying common, forming a geographical group; dukes, a select group of individuals, are defined by rank. We might want to look into the society formed by one family or household, or children playing in one street, or a soccer team or a learned society of social historians. We investigate how people within a given society relate to each other socially.

Roman history

In picking any such topic, we might find it directly relevant to our own experience. But the social history of Rome may well seem remote. The value of an intellectual pursuit should not be measured by its direct application to a practical purpose. Research in 'pure' science, intended to expand human knowledge, may eventually produce practical applications (useful or harmful to humanity). To learn more about how human beings have behaved in the past extends our understanding of the human condition.

Roman history offers much of intrinsic interest. With many cultures and periods to choose from, many find that Rome is endlessly fascinating.

The traditional justification for studying it relies on twin arguments: the legacy of Rome and the gap between Romans and ourselves. Rome, by virtue of its expansion into an empire which controlled the Mediterranean and north-western Europe, acted as the conduit for Greek culture and for the transmission of Graeco-Roman culture to mediaeval western Europe and hence to all the areas of the world colonised by Europeans. Rome left us the Latin language (transformed later into the Romance languages) and a great body of Latin literature (which inspired all the later European literatures); Roman law (the basis of church and civil law and an effective model for common law); the structures of the western church, and a fruitful heritage in art and architecture. Rome is part of the ancient history of anyone descended from those reared or partly reared in this tradition. In saying such things, one does not intend to ignore the immense contribution to western thought and culture of the Greeks, spread and transmitted by the Romans, and continuing in the eastern 'Roman' (but no longer Latin-speaking) empire, influencing the Islamic world, and to be more fully and immediately experienced in the West from the Renaissance onwards. The religious thought and scriptures of the Jews were part of the amalgam of Christianity from the beginning. The legacy of Rome is part of a complex web.

I have spoken so far of the most obvious influences. They are obvious because Jews, Greeks and Romans left written records which survived. Others contributed too through folk customs, art, religious sensitivities, technological know-how: the Celts are one example. Because being Roman was not a matter of ethnicity but a matter of legal definition (the Romans were relatively generous in conferring citizenship on foreigners), theirs was a diverse and complex society.

The Romans are among our spiritual ancestors. They are also remote enough in time for us not to 'identify' with them and different enough to provide a contrast. Ideally, we can treat them more objectively than those whom we regard as our own recent ancestors. Historians aspire to represent objective truths and to control their own prejudices, although it is agreed that no-one can fully achieve this aim.[1]

In exploring Roman history we may find much that is alien and much that may appear familiar. It has often been said that it seems easier to enter into the thought-processes, joys and sorrows of people in the Roman period than into those of our mediaeval precursors. Although the Romans lived before the industrial and scientific revolutions, in a society in which the institution of slavery was of major importance in law, in the economy and in shaping people's conceptions of themselves, the ways in which individuals reacted to their world strike chords with us. Cicero is as accessible as Addison, Caesar as the Duke of Wellington. We should beware of thinking any of them immediately accessible to us. But they are easier for most of us to understand than Francis of Assisi or Henry V of England.

The development of scholarship in Roman history

Because they wrote books, chiselled inscriptions, built stone buildings, struck coins, made statues, the Romans have left us material with which to study them. Because Church and State in the Middle Ages needed men who could read, use a pen and draft documents and therefore saw to it that they were trained in reading appropriate works of classical Latin literature, some people had a familiarity with at least some literary texts. From this developed an interest in historical and antiquarian matters. The ancient texts were quarried for material of contemporary relevance. Moral and constitutional ideas (as well as literary inspiration) could be extracted from the classical authors. The Renaissance, marking a breaking-away from mediaeval patterns of thought and the exciting rediscovery of texts which had not engaged the attention of monkish scholars, meant that thinkers, polemicists and rulers engaged with the ideas of Cicero or Tacitus. They became familiar with the texts and used them for their own purposes. (For Cicero see, e.g. Clarke 1965; for Tacitus see especially Ronald Mellor 1995. In general, see L.D. Reynolds and N.G. Wilson 1991. For transmission of individual authors, down to Apuleius in the second century AD, see L.D. Reynolds 1983.) Professional scholars edited and commented on texts. But they were the common 'classics' of all educated men (and a few women) in western Europe. High standards for research and exposition were set by masterpieces such as Gibbon's *Decline and Fall of the Roman Empire*.

As History became a subject of study for schoolchildren and undergraduates in the nineteenth century and research became institutionalised (a development led by Germany) and expected of university teachers (but happily never yet reserved for them), the study of Roman (and Greek) history advanced. Essential research tools were developed. Not only did the production of more accurate texts and the commentaries which help us understand them proceed. But the late nineteenth and early twentieth centuries saw the publication of collected inscriptions, papyri, coins, works of art; the creation of dictionaries, thesauri and encyclopaedias; the collection of laws and legal documents. Work on Roman history was, in the aftermath of the First World War, on a proper scientific footing. Few areas of history can boast such effective coverage in printed books. In recent decades, material available on CD-ROM and the Internet has begun to serve the scholar effectively. Bibliographies can be searched more effectively. Word-searches on literary texts and inscriptions can be performed electronically as well as through printed indices or by the patient labour of the individual. Illustrations of sites or works of art or the collections of the great museums can be tracked down on the Web. Discussion groups make it possible for us to submit questions on points which puzzle us to a huge group of international experts.

During the last century, people who classify themselves as ancient historians (the phrase in English, rather invidiously, is used chiefly of ancient Greek and Roman historians) have come to mark themselves off from 'classicists' in general. (There are exceptions – 'ambidextrous' scholars who work in both literature and history.) Because the teacher of ancient history at the university level must be competent in Greek and Latin, ancient historians have usually been trained in Classics before specialising in history. Nevertheless, university disciplines were set up partly as an accident of history, partly as an administrative convenience. In any department or faculty, people need links to kindred departments. It is the usual (but not invariable) practice in UK and Commonwealth universities for Roman historians to be placed in departments of Classics. In the US they may more commonly be found in departments of History, and may have studied for their doctorates in such departments. This makes a difference to their training, orientation and teaching responsibilities. There are advantages and disadvantages to both arrangements. Ancient historians whose primary affiliation is to Classics need to reach out to other kinds of historian; those who are in History departments need to liaise with those who deal with Roman material from the literary or art-historical point of view. This is the major responsibility. But an individual historian may have many others. For instance, it will be important for a Roman social historian to be alert to the work of Roman archaeologists and historians of Roman law, and perhaps of sociologists and anthropologists working in other periods. The ideal Roman social historian would be learned in many fields. But we cannot all achieve everything. Much can be learned from the work of practitioners who derive inspiration chiefly from several, but not all, potentially relevant fields.

Roman social history

Some ancient writers of history were keenly interested in social relations, in the components and customs of a human society. Herodotus was the Father of Anthropology as well as of History. Livy asked his reader to pay attention to the way of life and customs, the individual men and the skills in war and at home which had made the empire possible (*Preface* 9). Antiquarians collected rituals and curious practices. Biographers took an interest in the personal lives of their subjects as well as their military and political achievements. Modern writers until recently fell into similar categories, discussing the social context when it was relevant in histories of the state; collecting data on 'everyday life', religious cult, dress, the organisation of the army, the lives of women and such matters; including 'private life' in biographies of great men.

In what follows, I shall indicate important contributions to specific topics or methodology which seem to me to make good starting-points for those coming new to the field.

Since the 1960s, there has been striking expansion in Roman social history. (Background and earlier bibliography are discussed in Treggiari 1975.) While some older work aimed only to collect information, contemporary scholarship aims at a critical understanding of how society worked. Fields include demography, living conditions, slavery and the family. Such topics overlap. Studies of slavery led the way: a subject clearly of great interest to Marxist historians. English-speakers should now start with Bradley 1994, 1984/7.

Methodological inspiration for study of various groups (e.g. Wiseman 1971 on senatorial 'parvenus') came from the technique of prosopography (study of groups based on meticulous compilation of the known facts about members of the group, e.g. senators) already exploited by Syme (e.g. 1939) to explain the power and tendencies of members of the ruling élite. Collection and analysis of data on a definable group (often, in Roman terms, an 'order', such as the senators or the *equites*) makes it possible to examine social mobility (up or, worse attested, down). For groups below the ruling classes, the evidence is largely epigraphic or papyrological. Here we can cite successful studies of, e.g. lower-class families in Rome by Wilkinson 1966; the slaves and freedmen who supported the emperor's public work by Weaver 1972; wetnurses by Bradley 1986 and 1991: 13–36. Epigraphy and papyrology allow statistical surveys on, e.g. age at marriage (Saller 1987; Shaw 1987; Parkin 1992; Bagnall and Frier 1994). Exploration of law, founded on juristic sources, also engages with literary texts (Gardner 1986, 1993, 1998).

To examine a theme, the scholar casts the net wide. Data on the manpower available during the Republic (Brunt 1971a), on patronage (Saller 1982; Wallace-Hadrill 1989a, b), on the continuity of senatorial families (Hopkins 1983), on Roman mothers (Dixon 1988) or the elderly (Parkin 1997), on wills (Champlin 1991) come from all types of source. Similar inclusiveness is also characteristic of scholars working in more recent periods. Traditionally, ancient historians are specific in referring to the exact passage of a text on which they base an argument. Where necessary, they will quote the actual words if citation of paragraph is insufficient for them to make themselves clear. This precision is meant to enable the reader to verify their points conveniently. Peppering one's text with references is done not to impress, but to assist.

For some subjects, careful argument from other periods in part substitutes for direct evidence (e.g. J.K. Evans 1991; Golden 1992; Scheidel 1995–6). To read through the bibliography of any recent book is to admire the methodological alertness, thoroughness and eclecticism of social historians.

They are affected by broader trends, by what they read and whom they talk to. Each selects what is helpful or inspiring. Methods and theories may sometimes be adapted. Marxist and feminist scholarship, anthropological and sociological approaches, historiography of other periods, new trends in literary criticism have all had an impact.

Cross-fertilisation from other fields is especially clear in demography, where theories worked out for better documented epochs can be applied (Scheidel 1994; Saller 1994). In family studies the work of scholars like Lawrence Stone (e.g. 1986) has been influential, in slavery work on the New World (e.g. David Brion Davis 1970; Orlando Patterson 1982). Scholars as diverse as Fernand Braudel, Jack Goody, Eric Hobsbawm, Peter Laslett or Max Weber have had a major impact. Ideas may derive from those circulating in other fields, theories proposed elsewhere may be tested for our data. Comparison with better-documented societies may suggest possibilities.

> Reports from other cultures cannot in themselves replace missing data for Greece and Rome, but they can be useful all the same in providing models of the working methods of investigators into other cultures, in developing hypotheses, in identifying patterns from scattered scraps, in refuting generalizations.
>
> (Golden 1992: 311)

Deliberate attempts to encourage debate between specialists have been sought: one such workshop and resulting volume is Kertzer and Saller 1991, which brought together ancient historians, mediaevalists and anthropologists to discuss the family in Italy. Journals such as *Past and Present*, *Mediterranean Archaeology* or *Journal of Mediterranean Archaeology* are interdisciplinary.

Fields are constantly changing: there is, for instance, a trend for family historians to move out from Rome of the central period to studies of Italy (Rawson and Weaver 1997) and the provinces (Cherry 1998) and of the later Empire (Evans Grubbs 1995; Arjava 1996), two areas in which the ground has been prepared by scholars not primarily interested in social history. In the study of sexual life, the pioneers were often literary specialists: a historical breakthrough has now been made by T.A.J. McGinn 1998, using juristic evidence. The physical setting has long been recognised as essential (e.g. D'Arms 1970, 1981). But it is likely that efforts to exploit archaeology (especially as younger historians are now more likely to be 'ambidextrous' in archaeology) will bear new fruit. Studies of buildings, especially private houses, are a case in point. Along with that, will go increased use of works of art (cf. Fantham *et al.* 1994; Rawson 1997; Bradley 1998). Cultural inter-action is no longer treated as 'Romanisation', where the influences are assumed to be in one direction only: indeed it is questioned how we could define a Roman or an item of Roman cultural baggage (e.g. Woolf 1998). Another area which looks like expanding is 'mental-ities'. For instance, Lendon 1997 has explored how honour oiled the wheels of imperial administration; Bannon 1997 has investigated rela-tionships between brothers and Flower 1996 ideas about ancestors. Religious history is being treated with ever-increasing attention to socio-historical questions (e.g. Rives 1995). All these topics interact.

Our primary concern, in exploring and writing about questions in our fields, must be with what the sources can tell us.

Chapter 2

Evidence

> Historians are concerned and committed to offer the best and most likely account of the past that can be sustained by the relevant extrinsic evidence. Let us call this statement about the historian's commitment the "reality" rule.
>
> (Hexter 1971: 55)

Finding sources

A source is a piece of evidence. ' "You must not tell us what the soldier, or any other man, said, Sir," interposed the Judge, "it's not evidence" ' (Dickens 1986: 531 [ch. 34]): so the opinion of a modern writer is not evidence. Our sources are material which survives from the Roman world. They vary in quantity, quality and immediacy.

Because of the distance in time and because much material which once existed has been lost, the sources on specific periods or questions of Roman history are often limited. The same sources are usually studied, and have for centuries been studied, by everyone. The level of debate among scholars is intense, since the sources are in the common domain. A beginner, taking the sources into full consideration, may arrive at an opinion as worth considering as that of the oldest scholar. In one way, the sources are accessible and 'manageable'. Texts are available in published, printed form (whereas a modern historian may need to delve into manuscripts and private archives). This is particularly true of the periods which have been most commonly studied at school and university, periods which offer interesting political or military history and for which classic literary sources exist. Examples include fifth- and fourth-century BC Athens, and Rome in the first century BC and first century AD.

In another way, they may not be accessible to everyone who is interested. Only large, scholarly libraries contain the whole written output of classical antiquity. Reliable translations of texts are not always available. Many works of interest to the historian lack the careful textual work which gives us an edition as close as possible to what the author originally wrote. More still lack detailed commentaries to explain the text and supply cross-references to other evidence. The problem is especially severe for those working on the later Roman Empire, where sources are extremely rich and complex.[1]

Exciting new texts and documents are made accessible with commendable speed and thoroughness. We have, for instance, hundreds of wooden tablets of the late first to early second century discovered from AD 1970 onward, at the military base at Vindolanda (on the Stanegate, just south of the line of the future Hadrian's Wall). These include administrative documents and private letters and give a vivid impression of frontier life (Bowman and Thomas 1994). Or there are the bronzes (found with metal-detectors in Spain) which record the senatorial decree about Cn. Piso, who committed suicide in AD 20 during his trial on a charge of treason and of having poisoned the emperor Tiberius' adoptive son Germanicus (M. Griffin 1997, Damon and Takács 1999, etc.). The decree is a rich source for social conventions.

Archaeological evidence takes special training to assess. The beginner should start with evidence which he or she can handle with relative confidence. Good examples of how to handle the material are given by practising archaeologists who tackle historical questions and by historians with hands-on knowledge of archaeology (e.g. Dyson 1992; Wells 1992; Wallace-Hadrill 1994; Wiseman 1981/94).

Much of the human past is inaccessible to us. We experience this in our own lives. The most indefatigable diarist will only record a tiny percentage of the events, thoughts, feelings, experiences of one day. Anyone who has been for a walk with friends, or needed to give evidence as an eyewitness of a crime or accident, will be aware that different people observe and recollect different things. The account one can give straight after seeing an event will be different if one is questioned a week, or a year, or ten years later. A car crash really happens: the various results of the impact can be observed and assessed objectively by doctors or mechanics and insurance assessors. Perhaps experts can even reconstruct with fair hope of accuracy what happened, and how, and why. But the ability of the eyewitness to express in words 'what actually happened' will be affected by physical facts (what was his angle of vision?, how good was his sight?, was he looking?), and by the state of his mind (was he attending to something else?), and possibly by preconceptions (did he hate motorists?) and by what he heard from other witnesses and subconsciously incorporated into his own impressions. Even re-running one's own account of an event may lead to selection of features to remember, discarding of others, and generally 'improving the story'. We often don't notice we are doing it. Similar processes affect our recollection of the whole course of our life: occasions of strong emotion may stay with us; routine daily life is often hard to recall, even with the aid of photographs, visits to remembered places, conversations with friends who shared our experiences, the accidental hearing of an old tune or the smelling of a familiar smell. We may also find difficulty in converting our thoughts, impressions and recollections into language which others can understand.

Our own memory may make sense of such patchy sources on our own life. But it will be more difficult to reconstruct our grandparents' lives from their photograph albums, a few surviving letters, a ration-book, the tea-set and the electricity bills, even though we live in a society which is continuous with theirs. These are the sort of sources which a social historian might use. In fact, social historians working, say, on what life was like in the London Docks during the Blitz would have a wealth of private and public written documents on which to draw: maps, newsreel films, newspapers, what is left of the area and its buildings, the recorded reminiscences of those who lived through that period. They would also have the accumulated historiography of more than half a century. But for many periods and areas sources are few or non-existent. A society for which no sources are preserved is happily no business of a historian.

The Roman historian has a sizeable total mass of sources, but their distribution in time, space and type means that for many questions he or she would like to ask there is no direct evidence.

It will be useful at this point to sketch a hierarchy of sources. What one most wants is first-hand witnesses to an event or state of affairs (cf. D. Potter 1999: 22–9). Just as the independent testimony of several witnesses of an accident might help us get closer to the truth, so we would like to have several witnesses, with different points of view, to tell us what happened, for instance, at the meeting of the Senate in Rome on 15 March (the Ides) in 44 BC and to tell us immediately after the event.[2] The topic could interest a social historian as much as a student of politics.

Killing Caesar

Contemporaries

Who saw it, what happened, why did they think it happened and what were their reactions? Caesar could not tell us; Brutus and Cassius do not; Mark Antony was outside; Cicero was probably present. His later remark to Atticus that he had had 'happiness through his *eyes* by the death of a tyrant' (to translate *A* 14.14/368.4, 28/29 April, very literally) suggests that he saw the killing and not just the corpse. Antony later, accusing Cicero, said (according to Cicero) 'When Caesar was killed, Brutus *at once*, raising his bloody dagger high in the air, called on Cicero by name and congratulated him on the recovery of freedom' (*Phil.* 2.28, with SB *F* ii p. 462; cf. Cass. Dio 44.20).

If we take 'at once' literally, Brutus' appeal took place in the meeting-room, and it would have much more point if Cicero were physically present. He was certainly in consultation with the assassins at their meeting on the Capitol later in the day (*A* 14.10/364.1, 19 April, cf. 14.14/368.2, 28/9 April; *Phil.* 2.88–9). But there is no surviving letter of Cicero's for several weeks. (*A* 14.1/355, dated 7 April 44, is probably the first letter from Cicero after the murder.)

Cicero talks of the murder as 'a fine deed but half done!' (Antony should have been killed too), but does not describe the scene (*A* 14.12/366.1, 22 April 44; cf. *F* 10.28/363, to Cassius, ?2/3 Feb. 43). Occasionally, he remarks a specific detail. Caesar is alluded to as 'the man whom Brutus wounded' (*A* 14.22/376.1, 14 May). In February 43 he recalled to Trebonius that it was he who had drawn Antony aside (*F* 10.28/364.1; cf. Plutarch *Brut.* 17.1; App. BC 2.117). He applauds the deed as tyrannicide, but laments the inability to follow it up: with his close friend Atticus he could be frank about all this.[3] Obviously, the murder of Caesar was talked about a great deal. But the surviving references by contemporaries take the unfolding of the action at the foot of Pompey's statue as generally known. They were caught up in the aftermath, the changed and changing political situation (e.g. *F* 11.1/325, from D. Brutus to M. Brutus and Cassius, ?*c.* 22 March; *A* 14.13a/367a, from M. Antonius *c.* 22 April).

The next level of source might be recollections of eyewitnesses some time after and in a document meant for a less restricted readership than are the private letters of Cicero to like-thinking friends or the guarded diplomatic correspondence between opponents. Again these are very slight. Cicero in his little book on divination writes of pathetic deaths. Caesar, he says, was killed beside Pompey's statue under the very eyes of men he had appointed to the Senate. Slaughtered by noble citizens whom he himself had promoted, he lay dead – and no one, friend or slave, dared approach to attend to his body. This sounds like the account of an eyewitness, but we have to allow for Cicero's purpose of evoking pity, as he had just done for Pompey himself, murdered on a foreign shore (*On Divination* 2.23).

Some of the talk about how Caesar was stabbed is reflected in a third level, formal accounts by contemporaries with access to oral informants. So Nicolaus of Damascus (a Greek polymath born around 64 BC, who in the 30s was tutor to the children of Antony and Cleopatra in Alexandria), in his life of the young Augustus, transmits various titbits about who stabbed Caesar in which part of his body, including the information that Minucius Basilus accidentally wounded a fellow-conspirator, not surprisingly since the assassins planted their daggers in thirty-five places in Caesar's body (*Life of Caesar Augustus* 24 = Jacoby *FHG* III: 445; Jane Bellemore 1984).

Later authors

The canonical figure was twenty-three wounds, mentioned by Livy, writing under Augustus, for whose Book 116 we have only a short paragraph compiled by a later (?4th century) abridger.[4] Valerius Maximus, the compiler of examples of virtues and vices, writing in the 20s and 30s AD, gives Caesar high marks under 'Modesty' for having, despite the twenty-three wounds, used both hands to ensure that his toga fell decently over his lower body as he collapsed.[5] Moralising, already present in contemporaries, had by now a firm grip on the tradition.

Our main narrative accounts come from authors of biography and historians much further removed in time: Plutarch and Suetonius, Appian and Cassius Dio. It is clear that by the time of the first three of these (late first/early second century AD), the oral and written tradition had been much worked over. The rights and wrongs of what Brutus and Cassius had defined as noble tyrannicide had been debated.

In the interval between the event and our formal written narratives, Caesar's nephew, the future Augustus, had sworn to avenge him and in the process had eventually succeeded to Caesar's despotism, so that the concept of tyrannicide remained a hot potato. In the circumstances, it is unsurprising that the Augustan poets played down the details. One of them, Horace, had fought on the side of the tyrannicides at Philippi.[6]

So we move from immediate witnesses to ancient writers who derive their information from a line of informants. A Plutarch (Greek but a keen student of things Roman) or a Suetonius (a Roman administrator who, as Hadrian's secretary, studied the emperor's archives) were much more in touch with the Rome of 44 BC than we can be. They had access to historians who have not survived for us. But the event they describe had been embroidered by rhetoricians and moralists and neither of their discrepant blow-by-blow accounts can possibly be taken as accurate by a modern historian who evaluates them as sources.[7]

What this illustrates

The five minutes or so of the 'history of events' (*histoire événementielle*) which I have taken as an example has been used to flag two dangers: the remoteness of an ancient source from what is described, and the introduction of distortion. The more an event affects people and continues to affect them, the more likely it is to be embroidered and falsified. An ancient literary source can be ignorant or tendentious.

We should always find out as much as possible about the author we are reading, especially about his sources of information and his overt biases. Standard works of reference, such as *The Oxford Classical Dictionary* (use the third edition) will provide the known facts of an author's life and work, as well as guiding us to recent bibliography. Many authors have been supplied with excellent historical commentaries, with introductions to equip us to approach the text and cross-references, citation of other evidence and scholarly discussion to guide us on specific passages. The historian needs to have such up-to-date editions constantly to hand.[8]

Other sources?

Given the scrappiness of the literary record, the historian – or the producer of Shakespeare's *Julius Caesar* or a film-maker – might want want to recreate the physical setting. What can archaeology tell us of the Senate's meeting place in the huge and imposing complex of the Theatre of Pompey? What do we know (from coins or sculpted portraits) of what the great men looked like? What other men were usually present at Senate meetings and what were the procedures? What were the pen-cases in which daggers were concealed? The historian must use knowledge and imagination to bring things to life.

> What interests me is the discipline, the bent of mind. Get the tangible and visible universe right, and everything else will shine through. That seems to me the notion. It demands the cultivation of a habit, I take it, of seeing what is really there – the whole of what is really there

as the fictitious detective, Appleby, says in Michael Innes' novel *Death at the Chase* (Innes 1970: ch. 20; Penguin edn, p. 179).

If such a famous event as Caesar's murder is hard to reconstruct in any detail, we may expect that the sources for events in the lives of less famous individuals and for the social institutions of the Romans will also present many different problems.

The whole range of sources comprises different genres of literature (historiography, biography, plays, poetry, private letters, novels, forensic, political and other oratory, technical writings, philosophy, etc.); the corpus of Roman law (attested in literature and through inscriptions and papyri); collections of published inscriptions, papyri, coins; archaeological reports and the artefacts and sites themselves. Among modern guides to the sources and how we use them, M. Crawford 1983, Wells 1992, Goodman 1997 will be found especially helpful.

Literary texts

Latin

The texts mentioned as sources for Caesar's death included various types of writing by his contemporary Cicero (letters, a pamphlet in the form of a spoken invective against Antony, a philosophical book) and later historians and biographers. Our sources include a wide range of literary genres, in both Latin and Greek.[9]

Most of these are available in translation in the Loeb Series published by Harvard (with facing texts in the original, bound in green for Greek and red for Latin). Recent paperback translations, especially from Penguin and Oxford, have useful notes and aids to study.[10] Some older translators produced readable versions which are inconveniently 'free' for the reader who wants to know exactly what the text says. For advanced work, it is essential to be able to read the original. But a great deal can be done without that skill.

In the following sketch I will highlight some of our more useful Latin and Greek sources for social history down to the end of the Principate in AD 235: a date which marks the beginning of a half-century of extreme disruption. It is likely that the beginning social historian will find topics within this period, which is that usually studied for literature and political history.

The author's background and interests will be sketched where relevant to our topic. I refer also to books about genres or individual authors which will serve to orientate the reader and to works which exploit the texts for social history.

It is a well-worn observation that many writers of Latin were not natives of the City of Rome but natives of other parts of Italy or, later, of Roman or Italian stock from overseas or aliens or slaves who had acquired the citizenship. Italy and the Latin-speaking provinces of the West were a mosaic of races and cultures. But the culture represented in Latin writings, though not monolithic and not immune from temporal change, is consistently recognisable as Roman.

Historical sources must not be confused with Roman historiography, the formal written history of authors such as Livy and Tacitus. Many other types of literature must be exploited as well. (D. Potter 1999 gives a fuller account.)

Republican texts: c. 240–44 BC

Written Latin literature begins with verse. Of the surviving fragments, drama and satire (rather than epic) offer most. The fragments of comedy and (less useful for our purposes) tragedy give some sense of ideas about society, which emerged from that society and in turn helped shape it. Roman citizens of all ranks met in the theatre. (See *Remains of Early Latin* (Loeb). cf. Horsfall 1996; Wiseman 1998.) The complete comedies of the Umbrian Plautus (especially, produced *c.* 205–184) and the African ex-slave Terence (160s), despite being adapted from Greek originals, reflect ways of life and thought common to Greek and Roman, and Plautus added much original material which is specifically Roman, especially on law. (For Plautus used as a source on law see, for example, Watson 1967; McDonnell 1983.) The upper-class satirist Lucilius (? 180–102/1 BC) gives some lively material in the remaining 1400 lines of fragments, while the sententious one-liners of the mime-writer Publilius (a Syrian freedman of the first century BC) illustrate avowable moral views.

In prose during the Republic we have fragments of historians and orators (the former usually and the latter always upper-class) from the second century onwards (collected by Peter 1914–16 and Malcovati 1930, but not translated). These include substantial excerpts from the elder Cato (234–149 BC), who had a major impact on the life of his time as censor (185) and as an excoriating critic of the morality of his contemporaries. We also have his handbook on how to make a profit from farming.

The first century BC saw the development of personal poetry, which reached maturity with Catullus of Verona in the 50s. He transmuted his experience into poetry of love (for home, brother, friends, and lovers, both women and boys) and hate (e.g. for Caesar and his lieutenant Mamurra). Lucretius' great Epicurean *On the Nature of the Universe* (50s BC) contains some reflections of ordinary human life. Politicians advertised their exploits in verse, by professional poets or by themselves.[11]

In prose, Cicero adopted the practice of recording, polishing and circulating his speeches, both those given in the lawcourts and those addressed to the Senate or People. (Cf. D. Potter 1999: 26–8.) Fifty-eight survive; forty-eight are lost (fragments and testimony in J.W. Crawford 1984, 1994). For five of the speeches, including two lost ones, we have the invaluable commentary of Asconius, written AD 54–7 (cited conventionally by the pages of the edition of Clark: Asc. 1C(lark), Asc. 2C etc.) Unfortunately, the speeches of Cicero's contemporaries survive only in fragments.

Cicero also gave thought to preserving at least some of his voluminous correspondence. Probably thanks to the efforts of at least two of his correspondents, his most intimate and trusted friend the *eques* Atticus and his much-loved former slave and secretary Tiro, over 900 letters, chiefly from Cicero but including some from others (but not Atticus or Tiro), were collected and transmitted. They span the period 68–43 BC. The collection known as *Letters to Friends* include twenty-seven to Tiro and twenty-four to Cicero's wife Terentia; the rest are to men of senatorial or equestrian status. The 'Letters to Atticus' include confidences on politics and Cicero's state of mind, as well as documenting his literary work, movements around Italy and abroad, domestic finances, family quarrels, friendships and much else. The letters to his brother Quintus cast further sporadic light on family matters. Those to M. Brutus are chiefly political. The work of D.R. Shackleton Bailey has made this unrivalled source accessible to English readers as never before.

Cicero's third gift to posterity was treatises on oratory and philosophy, both cast in the form of dialogues, often with a historical setting which illuminates generations before his own, sometimes given a vivid contemporary context at a villa where his own friends meet to talk. Both are a source for considered views really held on Roman society, as the speeches are for debating points.

Caesar's war commentaries provide biographical data for his officers, illustrate logistical facts, and, in his description of non-Roman cultures, imply judgement on Rome. His works on the Gallic and the Civil wars were completed by his officers (the author of the *Spanish War* clearly less educated than his predecessors).

Several forms of technical treatise are important for us. The great scholar Varro (116–27 BC), Cicero's older contemporary, who lived to see Caesar's heir in control of the Roman world, produced a new handbook on farming (37 BC). His treatise on the Latin language is full of useful data. The social historian must mourn the disappearance of most of his book *On the Life of the Roman People* (Riposati 1939) and the fragmentary state of his *Menippean Satires* (Cèbe (ed.) 1972–) and his forty-one lost books of researches on 'things human and divine'. Varro was a great collector of information on religious ritual, mined for anti-polytheist point-scoring by later Christian apologists.

The period also saw the development of juristic scholarship, launched by Aelius Paetus (*cos* 198). Excerpts from the writings of Q. Mucius Scaevola (*cos* 95) and of Cicero's friend Ser. Sulpicius Rufus (*cos* 51) survive in the *Digest* of Roman law.

Between Republic and Principate: 44–27 BC

In the period of transition between the assassination of Caesar in 44 BC and the confirmation of his great-nephew in supreme power as Augustus in 27 BC, Sallust (probably 86–35 BC) produced *Histories* on the period from 78 BC to some date after 67 BC (of which we have substantial excerpts (McGushin 1992, 1994) and monographs on the conspiracy of Catiline of 63 (*c.* 42/1) and on the Jugurthine War (*c.* 41/0) at the end of the previous century. Cornelius Nepos (*c.* 110–24 BC) wrote a laudatory but illuminating biography of his friend Atticus (110–32 BC; Horsfall 1989). Vitruvius (formerly engineer to Caesar) writing on architecture, was conscious of the people who would use the buildings he described.

The late works of Varro and the early works of the Augustan poets fall in this period.

The principate of Augustus: 27 BC–AD 14

Another literary golden age is launched by Vergil (70–19 BC, from a village near Mantua), whose *Eclogues* (pastorals), *Georgics* (overtly on farming and the land of Italy) and *Aeneid* (the epic which became the quintessential expression of the tradition on the mission of the Roman People and the glory and pain which accompanied it) provide some insights for social history, as well as primary evidence for the political and imperialist mood of his times. His friend Horace (65–8 BC, a freedman's son from Venusia), writing lyrical *Odes* on politics and morality, also crystallised the Augustan spirit. The odes by their nature allow more personal expression and many may be crudely categorised as poems of love, friendship and wine. Scholars have disputed how much they derive from literary sources (especially Greek models) and how much they reflect real Roman life of the period. Although we need not believe that everything that Horace reports as from his own experience really happened exactly as he said it did, I accept him as accurately reflecting facets of reality and the *mores* and attitudes of his society. (See on social realities J. Griffin 1985. D. West's running commentaries on *Odes* i (1995) and ii (1998) are invaluable for English readers.) The early *Epodes* and the 'more realistic' *Talks* (*Satires*) and *Letters* (*Epistles*) in 'prosaic' hexameters are also excellent.

Propertius and Tibullus wrote elegies on love and religion. Their younger contemporary, Ovid (43 BC–AD 17, from Sulmona, a senator manqué), rivalling their learning and their ability to evoke timeless scenes of Mediterranean life, is a major source for the first half of the ritual year (in the *Fasti*, partially revised during his exile) and, in the

Amores (second edition no earlier than 16 BC), explores the possible evolution of a love-affair, including variations such as exchange of messages at a dinner-party or suspicion that the male protagonist has been sharing his favours with the woman's maid. Darker themes such as abortion occur. *The Art of Love* (*c.* 1 BC), in the vein of hunting manuals, is a witty guide to ensnaring members of the opposite sex in a city, helpfully remodelled by Augustus to provide ideal venues. Such highly readable works failed to back up the 'moral regeneration' of society which the emperor had legislated: the poet was sent to the Black Sea (AD 8) and his use as a source for social history (except for prosopography) declines markedly.

Under Augustus, the Elder Seneca (of Roman stock from Spain) documented the speeches given on fictitious (and often fantastic) but fascinating cases invented for rhetorical exercises. A typical 'controversy' sets out an imaginary law, such as 'A girl who has been abducted may choose either marriage to her ravisher without a dowry or his death'. The invented scenario follows: 'A ravisher demands that the girl he abducted be brought before the magistrate. The father refuses' (*Controversies* 3.5). The historian Livy (?59 BC–AD 17), of whose 142 books from the foundation of Rome to 9 BC, thirty-five survive, is particularly valuable as a witness to contemporary attitudes to events in the past. He draws attention (in his Preface, soon after 31 BC) to the qualities and customs which had made Rome great.

Under later emperors: AD 14–c. 235

Valerius Maximus, in the time of Tiberius, collected historical anecdotes under headings, so that an orator need never be at a loss for an example of *fides* (loyalty) or *pudicitia* (sexual purity). (An English translation is to appear in 2001.) Velleius dedicated a brief history of Rome, moralistic and conservative, to M. Vinicius (*cos* AD 30). Celsus, under Tiberius, produced another reference tool, an encyclopaedic work: we have the section on medicine.

Imaginative prose is represented by a picaresque novel, *Satyrica*, attributed to Nero's Arbiter of Taste, Petronius (AD ?20–66). The story is set in Campania and the most famous and substantial fragment, *Trimalchio's Dinner*, mocks the pretensions of wealthy, vulgar freed slaves. Like any novel, this vivid and memorable piece of writing is to be used with caution.

Also under Nero, the Younger Seneca (*c.* AD 4–65, *cos suff.* 55/6; see M. Griffin 1976) wrote a number of philosophical books (as well as tragedies): the 124 *Moral Letters* include some vivid pictures of contemporary life and individual monographs, e.g. on *Clemency* and *Anger*, deploy anecdote and example. Columella wrote a new DIY book on agriculture for the landowner (*c.* 60–5). The Elder Pliny (Gaius Plinius Secundus, AD 23/4–79), whose research methods are detailed by his nephew (*Letters* 3.5), compiled an encyclopaedia, *The Natural History*, in thirty-seven books ('published' AD 77) on astronomy, meteorology, geography, mineralogy, zoology and botany, with digressions on human inventions and institutions (Book 7). It is here that we may learn that Cornelia, mother of the Gracchi, bore twelve children, with the sexes alternating (57) or that Julius Caesar could listen and dictate simultaneously, dictating to four secretaries at once (91). Quintilian (*c.* 35–*c.* 100) wrote on the education of an orator. *The Minor Declamations* (ed. Winterbottom 1984), attributed to him but probably written later, are full-scale displays of rhetorical technique in fictitious cases, full of illustrations of Roman attitudes if not of real legal contexts.

Tacitus (*c.* 56–not before 118, *cos suff.* 97) wrote an eulogistic biography of his father-in-law Gaius Julius Agricola (AD 98), monographs on Germany and on oratory, and major historical works on the periods AD 14–68 ('the *Annals*'; much is lost; there are commentaries by Goodyear 1972, 1981; Woodman and Martin 1989, 1996) and on AD 69–96 (the *Histories*: the extant sections cover only 69–70; commentaries by Wellesley 1972; Chilver 1979; Chilver and Townend 1985), the most important literary sources for the politico-military history described, but also full of data for social history. (Cf. Syme 1958, 1979–91 for much detailed work on prosopography, an essential reference tool.)

The biographer Suetonius (*c.* 70–*c.* 130) covers much of the same ground on Julius Caesar and the eleven earliest emperors, but he was more receptive of gossip and more curious about the private lives of his Caesars. His interest extended to the less eminent: those of his lives of the poets which survive (garbled) and his section on eminent teachers and rhetoricians give short but valuable biographies. (See commentary by R.A. Kaster 1995. The newly revised Loeb translation, with an authoritative introduction by Keith Bradley, includes a fresh translation of the lives of teachers and rhetoricians by G.P. Goold which takes account of Kaster's findings.)

The Younger Pliny (Gaius Plinius Caecilius Secundus, *c.* 61–*c.* 112), a senator and orator like his friend Tacitus, left a panegyric of Trajan, telling for the personality the emperor wished to present, a volume of his (not re-worked) correspondence with the emperor (98–110 and especially from the time he spent cleaning up the province of Bithynia *c.* 110–12, important as a view of provincial life from the top); nine other volumes of collected letters to a variety of addressees. Unlike those of Cicero, these (influenced by the verse letters of Horace and the philosophical letters of the Younger Seneca) were heavily revised for publication: each presents one theme and shows Pliny as he wished to be seen by contemporaries and posterity. (See commentary by A.N. Sherwin-White 1966. On the processes by which literary texts came into the public domain see D. Potter 1999: 23–35.) Nevertheless, they are an unrivalled source and have been ably exploited by historians (e.g. Duncan-Jones 1974; Bradley 1998).

The epigrammatist Martial (*c.* AD 40–before 104) and the satirist Juvenal (? 60–after 127; commentary by Courtney 1980) have been mined for information on social realities in the late first and early second centuries, but the usual caveats apply (e.g. Carcopino (1956) is uncritical and should be avoided).

Later in the second century, Marcus Aurelius' tutor and friend Cornelius Fronto (*c.* 95–*c.* 166) left genuine, if self-conscious, letters which charmingly portray the simple or learned pleasures of the imperial family. (The Loeb Fronto is based on an out-of-date text. The current edition is the Teubner, edited by M.P.J. van den Hout (1988). Champlin 1980 puts Fronto in his context.) The North African Apuleius (*c.* 125–after 170) wrote a number of prose works, including a novel set in Greece, *The Golden Ass,* perceptively discussed for its historical content by Millar 1981b. He also wrote a speech (*Apology,* AD 158/9; old translation by H.E. Butler (1909); new translation forthcoming in Oxford's World's Classics) in which he defends himself on a charge of magical practices (which had enabled him to marry a wealthy widow!), which is now yielding a harvest for Tripolitania like Millau's for Greece (Bradley 1997). The Christian (later heretical) Tertullian (*c*. 160–*c*. 240; monograph by Barnes 1971) polemicises on female conduct (from a north African Roman's perspective) as on more strictly theological themes.

Greek

It is a question how far Greek texts reflect the society and customs of Rome itself. Each author should be assumed primarily to exemplify the culture in which he lived, under Roman rule or influence. This was not the Greek culture of Athens of the fifth century BC, however strong the impact of a classical education. Polybius and Plutarch came from mainland Greek cities with a strong local culture and both had first-hand experience of Rome. Many of our other authors come from outside Greece, usually springing not from the ancient Greek colonies of western Asia Minor or Sicily, but from groups of Greek and Macedonian followers planted by Alexander or his successors in areas long settled by people of different races and cultures. They spoke and wrote Greek, but their environment and no doubt some of their ancestry had other roots as well. Many of them acquired or inherited Roman citizenship; some lived part or most of their lives in Rome; some had a career in Roman administration at the equestrian or senatorial level. The more they participated in the privileges of Roman citizenship and office, the more they can be taken to represent the Roman part of their make-up. The Greek authors (from the late first century BC on) are certainly evidence for the society of the hellenized eastern Roman Empire. The Empire was a multicultural and complex world. Social historians have mostly, so far, tried to grapple with the problem of defining how things worked for Roman citizens, and although these were present all over the Empire, they have focussed on Rome and Italy (themselves a complicated mix). This has meant that – with notable exceptions – they have not fully exploited Greek texts for what they can tell us about specific enclaves at specific times.

The Greek poetry which chiefly needs to be taken into consideration is the epitaphs and occasional verses, such as dedications, party invitations, poems to members of the imperial family and love poems, collected in the *Greek Anthology*.

The Greek historiographers relevant to Roman social history include Polybius of Megalopolis in Achaea, who expounded the expansion of Rome in the Mediterranean, especially for his first-hand acquaintance with the ruling class in the mid-second century BC; Diodorus Siculus (the Sicilian; monograph by Sacks 1990), whose universal history down to 60 BC (fifteen out of forty books survive), an essential source for the Sicilian slave-revolts, was 'published' *c.* 30 BC; Dionysius of Halicarnassus *Roman Antiquities* (the surviving section goes down to 441 BC; the author was in Rome *c.* 30 BC); Josephus, the hellenized Jew, historian of the Jews and of their war with Rome (born 37/8) for Romano-Jewish interaction; Appian of Alexandria (late 1st century AD–160s; for republican wars and interest in socio-economic questions); Cassius Dio (*c.* 164–after 229; monograph by Millar 1964) a consular whose huge Roman history in 80 books partly survives and is, for instance, the major narrative source on the late Republic and Augustus (commentary by Reinhold 1988; discussion by Gowing 1992).

The biographies of great men by the Chaeronean Plutarch (before 50–after 120; start with C.P. Jones 1971 or Russell 1972) are important, and much antiquarian information is stored in his *Moralia*, particularly illuminating for life in Roman Greece. Geography is represented by Strabo of Amaseia in Pontus (*c.* 64 BC–after AD 21), another participant in the lively intellectual life of the Augustan period. (See now K. Clarke 1999.)

Philosophy continued to flourish and to be written in Greek even by Roman citizens and native speakers of Latin. Musonius Rufus (an *eques* from Volsinii, before AD 30–before 101/2, conveniently translated by Lutz (1947)) and Epictetus (an ex-slave, *c.* AD 55–*c.* AD 135) taught Stoic ethics and exemplify enlightened views on slavery and the capabilities and duties of women. The emperor Marcus Aurelius' '*Meditations*' (*To himself*) contain some material on his life (AD 121–80) as well as on his thought and ideals as a ruler.

The efflorescence of professional rhetoricians in the second century AD gives us Dio ('Chrysostom') of Prusa (*c.* AD 40/50–after 110; monograph by C.P. Jones 1978; cf. P.A. Brunt 1973 for his deployment as a source for socio-economic conditions) and the witty Lucian of Samosata in Commagene (*c.* 120 until after 180; study by C.P. Jones 1986), whose *De mercede conductis* and *Apology* are especially interesting on the status of a dependent intellectual, as well as Aelius Aristides, celebrated for a eulogy of Rome as the mother-city of the world. Such works were presented orally to an enthusiastic audience.

Medical writers such as the prolific Galen of Pergamum (AD 129–?199/216) and Soranus of Ephesus (AD 98–138), or Artemidorus, also from Ephesus, (mid/late-second century; S.R.F. Price 1986 provides the way into this text) who wrote on how to interpret dreams, provide information about beliefs and practices. For instance, Artemidorus 1.64: 'If a man enters the baths with his clothes on (sc. in a dream), it signifies sickness . . . For the sick enter the baths clothed'. Pausanias wrote an authoritative guide to the monuments of Greece. (There are monographs by Arafat 1996, focussing on Pausanias' reactions to Romans who had a major impact on Greek cities, and Habicht 1998.)

The Greek novels, a form of literature with wide appeal to the literate classes, can usually not be precisely dated (*CHGL* 684), and have a timeless quality, often seeming to presuppose a Greek world scarcely touched by Roman dominance. They have been little exploited by social historians, but the great upsurge in scholarly attention promises possible future advances (Reardon (1989) for translation; Stephens and Winkler (1995) for fragmentary novels; Harrison 1999 for recent scholarship; Reardon 1991 for the framework in which the novels may be understood.).

Among Jewish theologians, Philo(n) of Alexandria, enormously prolific and attuned to Greek philosophy, is significant for us for ethical treatises and for his vivid account of an embassy to the emperor Gaius in Rome (AD 39/40; Loeb x). Like the novels, the early Christian writings such as *The Shepherd of Hermas*, the New Testament and the narratives of the deaths of martyrs bring us into contact with classes scarcely touched by the writings of senatorial and equestrian Romans or the members of the ruling class of Greek cities. They provide a vivid picture of provincial society and of Roman administration seen from below.

Some tips

The social historian must always consider who, what, when, where, why, and to whom when assessing a literary source. Commentaries on the specific text and monographs about the author are an invaluable aid. Reference tools such as *OCD* or *CHLL* will lead you to the most important of these.

Works of creative literature often allow us to see what an author regarded as feasible rather than what actually happened to named individuals. The historian is interested in what the author takes for granted, his assumptions about how the world is or should be. In schools of rhetoric, Romans learned to use the same set of facts to argue in contrary directions. As Asconius told his young sons, who were studying Cicero's oratory:

> I don't want you to miss the point that it is a privilege of the cleverness of orators, when need arises, to exploit the same facts on both sides or from contrary points of view.
>
> (Asc. *Corn*. 70C)

Excursus: adorning the facts

Romans' rhetorical training practised them in adding verisimilitude to an otherwise bald and unconvincing narrative. How much credence should we attach to Cicero's circumstantial account of the young Antony's quasi-marital but mercenary affair with Curio, quaestor 54 (*Philippics* 2 (late 44 BC).4, 44–5)? (Antony was born about 83, quaestor 51. The affair would be supposed to date to the late 60s.) No holds were barred in invective. This pamphlet burned Cicero's boats: reconciliation with Antony or his wife, Fulvia, would be difficult. Curio and his father were safely dead. The Elder Curio was not there to say he had never thrown Antony out of the house, that he had no knowledge of Antony getting in through a hole in the roof. Who could rebut the pathetic picture of a scene when the father lay grieving in his bed and the son writhed on the floor at Cicero's feet, weeping and saying he could not live without Antony? Cicero suggests that he was the only eyewitness and claims that Antony was another who knew about it! The historicity of the scene is in doubt. Some historians will credit a close friendship between the two young aristocrats, who, if Cicero here contains a grain of truth, may have got into a financial embarrassment together in youth and later (50–49 BC) shared political ties to Caesar. After Curio was killed in the Civil War in 49 BC, Antony had married his widow, Fulvia. Others will accept that there was a sexual relationship. If we believe Cicero on Antony's sex-life, we should be prepared to believe the incest of Cicero with his daughter (part of the Antonian attacks on Cicero), Clodius with his sisters, Nero with his mother, information transmitted by orators, Roman historians and biographers. Nothing alleged by political enemies can be ruled out as impossible: that is what made the attacks effective.

Anecdotes may illustrate current ideas rather than facts. The story is shaped to make a point or a joke; good stories are attached to famous people (e.g. the witty remarks attributed to Augustus and his daughter Julia and recounted in the late source Macrobius' *Saturnalia* 2.4.19–5.9) and possibly switched to a more recent famous person as fashions change. (See Saller 1980.)

Juristic texts

Law prescribes, but some legal texts also describe what happens in real life. The considerable bulk of Roman legal writings is a vitally important source for social history (O.F. Robinson 1997).

Statutes are documented in literary sources or by inscriptions. Laws of the Roman People and decrees of the plebs (which from 287 BC had the force of laws) have been collected, translated and annotated (M. Crawford 1996b).

The most important body of technical writings is undoubtedly jurisprudence. Learned lawyers wrote commentaries on statutes and other forms of legal rules, and on the commentaries of their predecessors. These – 1,500 books, all dating before AD 300 – were eventually reduced to 5 per cent of their volume by a 'scissors and paste' method by a committee working for three years (AD 530–33) at the order of the emperor Justinian, to produce the *Digest* in fifty books, which then had legal force. (The jurists' original books were discarded.) Some two-fifths of the excerpts are drawn from Ulpian of

Tyre and one-sixth from Paul (both flourished late second to early third century AD). Arranged under headings (e.g. in a book dealing especially with rights and duties of landowners, we may find sections on drains, acorns, rivers) the excerpts, which generalise, theorise, argue and cite actual or hypothetical cases or questions, document both what the law prescribed and the context in which Roman citizens lived in the heyday of the Empire. Scholars have worried about texts being revised or reworked to bring them into line with sixth-century legal practice. Modern social historians tend to hold that this is rarely an issue, especially given the limited time in which the committee worked. It is more important to watch out for lively disagreement between jurists and to be alert to the difference between what appear to be real problems presented to them by clients and to the often abstruse intellectual puzzles they set themselves in a spirit of 'what would happen in the (unlikely) event that such and such was the case?'

The *Institutes* of the second-century Gaius (adapted later by Justinian, AD 533) are an unsurpassed introduction for students of law. The *Code* of Justinian (second edition promulgated 534) documents the emperors' replies to a wide cross-section of society who petitioned them on legal problems. This includes a little material from the second century, a great deal from the third. We now have up-to-date translations of *Digest* (Watson 1985) and *Institutes* of Justinian (Birks and McLeod 1987).

Other legal texts, including documents such as wills and juristic writings other than those mentioned above, may be found in various collections (e.g. *FIRA*, Bruns (1909–12) (not translated)). Much work remains to be done on socio-legal history, although these sources have never ceased to be pondered by practising lawyers and students of legal history. The social historian will profit from the latters' expertise but will focus, not so much on what the law was at any given date and what it prescribed, but on what the legal sources can tell us of how people behaved, reacted to law and lived with it.

Archaeological data and artefacts

What can archaeology tell us? It rarely documents an event known from a literary source, such as the eruption of Vesuvius in AD 79 (Pliny

Letters 6.16, 20), which drew a line across Roman habitation at Pompeii and Herculaneum. Everything discovered below the volcanic debris there had been there in AD 79 and cannot be dated later: we thus have a *terminus ante quem* (latest possible date) for all buildings, artefacts and animal remains. Pliny gives us the exact year and the narrative of what he observed; excavation rounds out the narrative of the eruption and tells us almost all we know of life in the towns before the disaster. Elsewhere, sketchy literary data on, for example, Augustus' campaigns in Germany can be fleshed out by results of scientific excavation of early military sites (in what had been an area free of Roman intervention: here the Augustan advance of 12 BC onwards provides an earliest possible date, *terminus post quem*, for Roman camps (Wells 1972). The beginnings of a foreign influence can be detected through material remains and fairly precise dates given because of the intersection of written evidence and datable sites. But often the archaeological evidence stands alone and tells us more about the material circumstances of life over a period than about one day or one decade.

Continuity of occupation has preserved structures above ground: Hadrian's Pantheon, turned into a church to enshrine cartloads of bones from the Catacombs, or the Colosseum, Arch of Titus and Mausoleum of Hadrian, all used as fortresses. Similar processes have worked the other way: the Colosseum could be used as a handy source of cut stone, lime or metal (from the clamps which bound the stones). Hadrian's Wall went to build local farmhouses. Some sites were abandoned (Ostia), others buried by later buildings (London). We are lucky to have cities (with their normal complement of forum, temples, theatre, amphitheatre, baths, latrines, markets, shops and houses), sanctuaries, military installations, harbours, roads, aqueducts, villas and farmsteads and tombs of various kinds uncovered by excavation or sometimes preserved standing above ground. They give a vivid sense of the background to Roman life. The historian must cultivate a sense of place and use imagination and the conclusions of experts to weigh the evidence about how far what he or she sees represents what would have been there in the past. Before you go to an area, guides such as those in the series '*Exploring the Roman World*' will give you an overview. Guidebooks (including many local publications to be acquired on the spot) are essential as you try to understand a site.[12]

Much archaeological work focusses on material less obvious to the traveller: evidence for wooden structures such as humble dwellings and temporary buildings, for land-use and for engineering works such as water-siphons (below ground). We usually find out about such things by reading specialised reports or works of synthesis. For the history of settlement patterns and of agriculture, not only excavation, but the combination of survey and excavation have greatly increased our understanding. Aerial photography can pin-point ditches and pits or walls and roads. (Crops grow lush where a ditch or pit has been filled in, parch more easily where their roots are shallow above a wall.) Systematic field-walking by a team can locate fragments of pot or tile brought to the surface by ploughing and suggest where there have been settlements or isolated houses. Terracing or field boundaries can be observed. Metal-detectors pin-point metal below the surface; archaeologists also use magnetometers and resistivity surveys to give them a picture of what is underground. Such soundings are a prelude to full-scale excavation, which ideally explores the evolution of a site and its whole geographical context. For the proper investigation of a major villa-site, for instance, it would be necessary to excavate both big house and farm-buildings, to determine what cultivated and wild plant-material and animal remains are present, to survey the land related to the villa and to form as precise an idea as possible of the whole geographical context (e.g. nearby and distant markets). Many universities run excavations and will welcome their own students and others. There are also 'training digs', which make a good place to start before you can aspire to being a valued member of a team.

For artefacts, a historian need usually look no further than the local museum for a range of objects in everyday use, such as coarse-ware cooking pots, dinner-ware in red fine pottery, jewellery, surgical instruments, metal fittings of harness, weapons, tomb inscriptions, coins. With luck, you might find a leather sandal, a portrait-bust, or a set of presentation silver toilet-articles or dinner-ware. A sample of finds from local sites will often be meticulously displayed to illustrate their history and how the excavators arrived at their conclusions. Pottery is vital for dating strata and provides data for socio-economic history (Peacock 1982; Peacock and Williams 1986; Hayes 1997). Books such as Wells 1992 (where first-hand knowledge of, for instance

North Africa, illuminates the discussion of life in the provinces) and, in more detail, Alcock 1993 (dovetailing literary, epigraphic and survey data to explore the socio-cultural history of Greece), show how to call in archaeology to redress the balance of the evidence.

Finer artefacts may be regarded as 'Art'. Art historians have brought the study of sculpture, painting, mosaic, metal-work, coins and, of course, architecture, to a high degree of sophistication. Increasingly, they relate their results to the sort of questions about the aspirations of whoever commissioned or lived with the works of art which a social historian would want to ask. They may also be interested in the social status of the maker or in how fashions change and develop. (See, e.g. Zanker 1988; Ling 1990; Dunbabin 1999.) Portraits of individuals, even if unidentified, sculpted in the round or in relief (especially on sarcophagi), painted on mummy-cases or represented on mosaics, often give a vivid sense of a person, as do even the idealised portraits, in sculpture or coins, of members of the imperial family.

Coins combine art-work and superscriptions, both intended to convey a message. Numismatics are a recognised sub-discipline. The imagery on Roman coins (not the only currency in circulation in the Empire) was decided in the Republic by junior annual officials (who might commemorate how an ancestor had served the state), later in the emperor's name and highlighting his achievements. We may draw conclusions about what was expected to appeal to those who handled the coins: Liberty, Concord (usually after civil war), or the allowances given to children by Trajan and subsequent emperors. Coins have chiefly been exploited for political and economic history (Howgego 1995; Harl 1996).

Epigraphy and papyrology

Political propaganda also occurs on public inscriptions (on stone or bronze). Augustus ordered that his account of his achievements should be displayed in cities throughout the Empire (Brunt and Moore 1967). The recently-discovered senatorial decree on the alleged poisoner of Tiberius' destined successor was also copied and displayed (M. Griffin 1997), as were statutes. (See Documents under Translations, pp. 130–2.)

There are many other kinds of inscription, from marks on items of common use to advertisements and graffiti on walls, from dedications on temples, votive offerings or statues to discharge certificates for soldiers or written spells (valuable introduction by Millar 1983). Epitaphs of the dead form the most numerous category and have been most exploited for social history (e.g. Treggiari 1975b, 1980). Latin tomb inscriptions are accessible in the huge *Corpus inscriptionum latinarum*, through national compilations such as Collingwood and Wright 1967 and Frere and Tomlin 1990–94 for Britain, on CD-ROM and the Web, and through annual updates (*Année épigraphique*) and regional journals. The reader with rudimentary Latin can soon learn how to understand most of them. Not all inhabitants of the Empire caught the Roman 'epigraphic habit' (a term invented by MacMullen 1982) or could afford to commemorate their lives. Those who did leave a record may give a bare name, but others detail age at death, job or family relationships. There are a recent studies of the use of epigraphic evidence by Keppie 1991 and Bodel 2000.

Other records are the domain of papyrologists. Documents such as business records, wills and letters were written with a pointed instrument on wax tablets on folding wooden boards. Ordinarily, the wax does not survive, but, if the stilus penetrated the wax and scratched the wood beneath, the text can sometimes be restored and read. Such texts survive from Pompeii and Herculaneum. Elsewhere, writing in ink on wooden tablets (preserved in damp conditions) may give us correspondence, lists etc. from northern provinces such as Britain (Bowman and Thomas 1994).

The most prolific source is on papyrus, manufactured in Egypt and preserved in arid conditions in Egypt and the Near East (Bagnall (1995) gives a lively and inspiring account). The Egyptian documents are a precious source for administration and the economy and have recently been used to study demography (Bagnall and Frier 1994). Conclusions based on Egyptian evidence cannot necessarily be applied to other areas under Roman rule. There are opportunities for specialised training in epigraphy and papyrology.

Using evidence

How do we evaluate and use our evidence? Learn from the examples of leading practitioners. (Morley 1999: 53–95 has some illustrations.)

All the evidence must be weighed for what it can tell us. While you can be forgiven for not knowing even the useful observations of modern scholars, you must attempt to collect and consider all the ancient data relevant to a given topic. Content analysis should be thorough. 'Whatever ideological considerations guide my research, I shall be judged by my use of the evidence' (Momigliano 1984: 54). Because it is easy to make a mistake over one possibly ambiguous item of data, we run checks with other types or items:

> Against the misinterpretation of evidence, there is, as Ramsay MacMullen has put it, 'safety only in numbers: *many* facts, of which one may be wrong without destroying the argument'.
> (Cherry 1998: ix, quoting MacMullen 1990: 12)

We must be alert to our own blind spots. Have we mistranslated, misunderstood the context, jumped to conclusions, made an assumption based on modern conditions, been blinded by prejudice or ideology, or (like Dr Johnson) by pure ignorance?[13] Momigliano again:

> I have good reason to distrust any historian who has nothing new to say or who produces novelties, either in facts or in interpretation, which I discover to be unreliable. Historians are supposed to be discoverers of truths. No doubt they must turn their research into some sort of story before being called historians. But their stories must be true stories.
> (Momigliano 1984: 50–51)

The only way to avoid false novelties is to do the homework thoroughly. It is vitally important to consult good and, if possible, recent commentaries when you read a literary text, so that you are aware of problems and have cross-references at your finger tips. Standard reference works and monographs will save you from error.

Focusing on a particular theme or set of problems (as one must), the historian may inadvertently press the evidence too far. We must not claim to have proved what we have merely shown to be plausible. Speculation has its place, but it must be labelled. The opposite trap is proving the obvious. 'He said much that was new and true. But what was new was not true and what was true was not new.'[14] Let us hope we can avoid both these faults.

You may start with a theory, but you must not stretch or distort to fit it whatever facts can convincingly be deduced from the evidence. As a well-read publisher wrote about another field of scholarship:

> I much prefer the old-style critics who tried to get inside their authors, find out what they were driving at and interpret accordingly. Nowadays, they attempt to force their authors into some preconceived theory of their own.
>
> (Hart-Davis 1978: 35)

Taking courage in both hands, do your best to assess the data and state what you believe to be true. The editors of a French series of books entitled *Histoire* (Paris: les Belles Lettres) call for us to develop a historical sense in order to recreate:

> a picture which, though it cannot be impossibly exact, tends towards the possibility of exactitude. It matters little what is the object of study – battle, ideas, 'mentality', structures, cultures etc. – it is the vision of the author, a vision which is subjective, involved, partial, simply human, which gives this object a historical value achieved by the rigour of the enquiry, familiarity with sources and absolute freedom in exposition.
>
> (My translation)

They want the historian to be free from fashionable dogma and to strive constantly to cast light on people of the past for the reader of today. This is the ideal practised also by the anglophone social historians to whom I shall be drawing your attention in the chapters which follow. They differ from each other on many points but they all make a serious effort to get at truth.

Different scholars will legitimately interpret the same data differently. We must guard against fallacies of argument (Fischler 1970), but must claim the responsibility of making up our own minds as best we can. Others will judge if our conclusions are persuasive and illuminating.

The aim must be to deal with significant topics of more than antiquarian interest. For some valid and interesting questions, the data can unfortunately provide no answer.

Chapter 3

A sketch of
Roman society

> To fulfil the bargain with my father, I acquired a working know-
> ledge of Roman law, and, after a year, I knew how to manumit
> a slave, adopt an elderly senator or contract a marriage by the
> ceremony of 'brass and scales', skills which I have never found
> of great service in the Uxbridge Magistrates Court.
>
> (John Mortimer, *Clinging to the Wreckage* [1982] 57)

To understand Roman society, it is essential to have some knowledge
of the course of Roman history and the main developments. The expansion of the power of the Roman People (*imperium populi Romani*) from
humble beginnings in a grouping of villages in the plain of Latium to
an empire controlling the countries of the Mediterranean and north-
western Europe is an enormous fact which must be explored. We should
have maps constantly before our eyes. Succinct and up-to-date accounts
of many matters can be found in *OCD* and in standard textbooks. The
make-up of the people in various periods cannot be understood without tracing the expansion of the citizenship as the Romans absorbed or
formed alliances with their neighbours (first the Latins, who shared
their language and culture and the Sabines, who did not; later all
the other peoples of Italy, including the Etruscans, the Greeks of the
South and the Celts of the North) and gradually extended the full

Roman citizenship to them (a process completed by the late 1st century BC), granted citizenship to those freed by individual citizens from legal slavery, enfranchised individuals and eventually communities elsewhere in the empire, gave citizenship to non-citizens who served in the army, and sent their own citizens to live abroad, first in Italy, in newly-founded cities or as individual landholders, and later all over the empire (cf. Sherwin-White 1972, M. Crawford 1996a).

The area in the power of the Roman People was a patchwork. (Millar 1981a is a clear and vivid introduction.) Some of it consisted of provinces, directly ruled and taxed, overseen by a governor (who during the Republic had previously been elected to high office by the people – during the Principate the emperor strongly influenced both election and appointment of governors). Within the provinces, cities (*urbes*) enjoyed various privileges and internal autonomy. Outside the provinces there were client kingdoms, often the less urbanised areas, which we might regard as 'protectorates'. Those on the eastern frontier were buffers against the only other great power in contact with Rome, Parthia. (China and India were on the fringes of Roman consciousness, though there were trade-links.) The normal frontiers of empire were marked (with some variations over time) by deserts in the Near East and North Africa, by the Atlantic and the Irish and North Seas (and the English Channel before southern Britain was annexed in AD 43), by the Rhine and Danube, and by the Black Sea. Roman influence spread beyond these frontiers and they were not impervious to people and influences from the outside. (Millar 1981a makes a good starting-point. See also Balsdon 1979; Whittaker 1994.)

Inside the empire, the city was the focal point for the life of a citizen. The Greeks had exported the city-state, with its varying political, religious and social customs, from mainland Greece to Asia Minor, Sicily, southern Italy and southern France. Later Alexander spread the same model around the Near East and Egypt. Roman foundations continued the tradition in Spain, France, Britain and among the Greek cities elsewhere. Although the vast majority of the population of the empire as a whole lived as farmers, stockbreeders and hunters (e.g. Dio Chrys. *Euboicus*), Roman-citizen countrymen would usually 'belong' to a city and have voting rights there. In the wild hinterlands of the provinces, there would be few citizens and tribal loyalties continued to function as they had from time immemorial. These people were characterised as belonging to *gentes* (races, tribes), not *urbes* (Horace *Odes* 1.35.10). Here the chiefs gradually obtained the Roman citizenship, but the mass of the population was relatively untouched by Roman or Greek culture or language. Villages and small towns had their own local cultures.

Greek was the common tongue (*koine*, the language of the New Testament) of the eastern provinces (though it was expected that Roman citizens could function in Latin), Latin of North Africa and the West. Other languages continued to be spoken.

It is estimated that in the time of Augustus (27 BC–AD 14) about 10 per cent of the population of the empire were citizens. The census of AD 14 claimed 4,937,000 citizens. (For a recent survey see Nicolet 1994: 600–8.) None of those could have claimed that all their ancestors were Romans from the little town on the Tiber, traditionally founded in 753 BC. The blue-blooded aristocrat had to claim pre-eighth century forebears from one side or the other in the Trojan War: Greeks or Trojans, and, more remote still, some god or goddess. The myth was of mixture and assimilation. There was historic intermarriage between tribal groups and Italian towns. Tacitus could report the argument that many senatorial families had freed slaves in their family-tree (*Annals* 13.27.2, on AD 56): in practice it was difficult for most people, as for us, to trace ancestry back over more than three generations, especially to identify women.

> I have not been able to find out who was Piso's mother-in-law, obviously because historians have not transmitted the names of women in houses and families as they have of men, unless they were distinguished.
>
> (Asc. *Pis*. 10C)

Ex-slaves in the historic period intermarried freely with the free-born of the lower classes, especially those who were themselves only one generation away from slavery. Marriage with non-citizens presented problems: marriage with citizens of foreign origin did not.

What distinguished the citizen was not blood but possession of a bundle of rights. The adult male could vote, stand for office and fight for Rome. A male and female citizen could marry each other (provided they were of legal age and not within forbidden degrees of relationship; Augustus introduced further restrictions). They could make contracts and wills valid in Roman law. The slave owner could free a slave and pass on the citizenship to him or her. The citizen's life was governed by the rules of the Roman legal system (Gardner 1993). He or she could expect to be protected by Roman officials. How law worked in practice in all areas of life has been explored in fascinating detail by Crook 1967.

There is something more important even than the context of the Roman empire and the framework of Roman law for defining how a citizen could live. That is the demographic regime which operated at the time and in the place in which he or she lived. Scholars are able to postulate what this was only in terms of what they think applicable to the empire in general over centuries. They suppose that Rome resembled modern pre-industrial societies (for which we have statistics and model life tables). If we conjecture that expectation of life at birth was twenty-five, then we can calculate a number of other probabilities (Parkin 1992; Saller 1994: 12–73). Such a figure means, not that the individual could expect to die at twenty-five, but that almost one-third of all babies died before the age of one, about half by the age of ten. Those who survived the dangers of the first few weeks, weaning, childhood illnesses, accidents and malnutrition and reached their tenth birthday, would then have almost a fifty–fifty chance of reaching the age of fifty. Under one-sixth of those who reached ten would see their seventieth birthday (Saller 1994: 24–5. For standards of hygiene see Scobie 1986.) These figures represent a hypothetical stationary population, where the birth-rate is equal to the death-rate, over a long term. A stable population is one where these rates do not balance each other, but the 'shape of an age distribution' is unchanging, though the total numbers may go up or down (Parkin 1992: 73–5; Saller 1994: 42). They give a rough idea of Roman realities. By adding the hypothesis (based on Latin inscriptions to the dead) that women of the middling class which put up epitaphs tended to marry in their late teens and men in their late twenties (Shaw 1987 and Saller 1987 are the break-through articles), Saller 1994 (with the aid of the Cambridge Group for the History of Population and Social Structure) has offered computer simulations of the kinship universe of Romans at various ages.

The student will examine the social structure of the Roman citizen body. The Romans saw their society as consisting of 'orders' (*ordines*: e.g. the senatorial and equestrian), with a large and amorphous mass of plebs at the bottom of the hierarchy (Frier 1996; Treggiari 1996). The emperor (*princeps*, leading citizen) took his place at the top of this system, which was based partly on service to the state. The economic classes into which moderns divide the citizens (Cartledge 1996) roughly correspond. The emperor was by far the wealthiest Roman; the richest senators (minimum capital 1,000,000 sesterces; richest known 400,000,000) came next. Some *equites* (minimum capital 400,000 sesterces) were richer than some senators. The wealthiest known imperial freedman allegedly had 400,000,000 sesterces. (All such figures are suspect.) The local dignitaries came next to *equites*; below were small landowners, craftsmen/shopkeepers, and then the propertyless masses, day labourers. Soldiers had annual pay and, if they survived to retirement, might be prosperous. Slaves were usually allowed to accumulate their own resources; freed slaves belonged to all economic groups up to the senatorial. So did women. For the common people, one might begin now with Purcell 1994.

We can see 'fault-lines' in the society (male/female; slave/free, poor/rich, country/town, hellenized/unhellenized). There are also cross-class links (patronage, manumission, moral and legal obligations). Upward mobility was possible, especially over several generations, as we see, e.g. with the family of Vespasian. Privileged ex-slaves of privileged patrons had a headstart; a soldier could work his way up to the centurionate. It could be said that senators were recruited from soldiers and emperors from senators (Tacitus *Histories* 1.84). Downward mobility is sometimes documented.

Reciprocal obligations might link citizens. Relationships, such as contracts or marriage or friendship, involved trust (*fides*). (Schulz 1936: 223–38 remains essential.) Friendship, ideally between equals and based on liking, was expected to involve exchange of kind acts of various sorts (Brunt 1988b). The unequal relationship of patron and client (which includes that of manumitter and ex-slave) was presented often as friendship between 'a powerful friend' and a social inferior: this too involved reciprocal acts, as when a literary patron gave an estate which provided an income to a poet, and the poet wrote poems to celebrate the patron. Although the political importance of patronage in the late Republic has been overstated (for the correction see Brunt 1988c), its social importance is everywhere. The republican dynasts and later the emperor were founts of patronage, their clients might, in turn, be patrons of lesser people. Not every citizen was a client or patron, nor were clients limited to one patron, but networking involved the various elites and the upwardly mobile. Honour, services, material goods were given and repaid. (The primary modern treatments are Saller 1982, 1989; Wallace-Hadrill 1989a, 1989b, 1996).

What difference did sex make? Biology dictated important parts of the pattern of women's lives. In law, Roman women were citizens, but lacked the public rights of adult males to vote, hold office and serve in the army. In private law, some distinctions were made, but on the whole women's legal rights in property and the family compare well with those of women in other historical periods down to the twentieth century. Class shaped the lives of women: the aristocrats Claudia Pulchra or Caecilia Metella lived very differently from a peasant or a tavern-keeper. The subject was pioneered by the entertaining and informative book of Balsdon 1962. For a recent introduction, one might start with Fantham *et al.* 1994.

The social historian needs an understanding of the economic basis of life (which applied to everyone; see, e.g. Nicolet 1994) as well as of the framework of law (which applied to citizens). Understanding of how the economy worked has made great strides recently (W.V. Harris 1993). Farming methods have been intensively studied (e.g. K.D. White 1970; Spurr 1986). The Romans' understanding of the profitability of farming has been scrutinised by Dennis Kehoe (e.g. 1997). For commerce, begin with D'Arms 1981. We may also need to think about technological realities. On all these areas, Brunt 1971b: 20–41 gives a stimulating introduction.

Religion pervaded social and political life. The starting-point now will be Beard, North and Price 1998. Polytheists could recognise alien gods as corresponding to their own: many, like Cybele and Isis, were partially naturalised in Italy. Priests (except in some of the imported cults) were not a caste apart. Office-holders and senators who were members of the great priestly colleges led sacrifices on behalf of the Roman People. The *paterfamilias* and *materfamilias* led worship in the household. Slaves and freedmen had their own role in the worship of the household gods at the hearth and, along with the free poor, of the tutelary spirits at crossroads where the boundary paths of four blocks of land met. Recent work has focussed on what people did; more needs to be done on what they believed.

The chronological limits of this book are those of the 'central period' of Roman history, from the time when usable primary sources become available in sufficient supply, *c.* 100 BC, to the breakdown of the Principate, *c.* 235 AD, when a fifty-year period of upheaval changed lives and commemorative practices. This choice of period means that a great, but scarcely documented time of innovation in the earlier centuries of the Republic is ignored (though some sources have been briefly mentioned), and so is the social engineering which took place after the Empire was consolidated by Constantine in the fourth century. But the Empire in which the emperor's religion was now Christian was in many ways a very different place. To see, for instance, what can be discovered about the family of the late Empire, look at Evans Grubbs 1995 and Arjava 1996.

Anyone moving on from a basic grasp of politico-military history to thinking about Roman society might start with the lucid, critical and up-to-date survey by Garnsey and Saller 1987. My students tell me (and I discovered it for myself) that much of what they want to find out about daily life is in the original and highly readable compilation by Balsdon 1969 (which inexplicably never became a paperback).

Chapter 4

Case study I: Tullia

It is important to approach the ancient world with questions and directions of research in mind, since mere accumulation of material or parallels is rarely rewarding. In this context, one can go far beyond the largely moral categories of explanation common in antiquity, though one must always be careful not to impose modern categories or preconceptions on a very alien world. This caution is particularly important where our suggested explanation involves the attribution of motives; the thought structure of the ancients was very different from our own.

(M. Crawford 1983: xi)

Approaches

Ancient historians, to put it crudely, fall into two groups, those inspired by their material and those inspired by questions. But even the former will have questions in mind which may dictate their choice of material to study and must put questions to themselves about the material, and the latter must get to grips with the evidence. In this chapter we will take a manageable body of material, study it as critically as we can and see to what sort of questions it might provide answers.

I have chosen a body of material which will support a partial reconstruction of the private life of one woman of the senatorial class. The public life of an individual man may be documented by so much evidence that a full-scale book is possible: Cato the Elder, Cicero, Caesar, many of the emperors, Seneca and so on. But not even for these, not even for the best documented do we have the kind and variety of sources needed for a complete biography of the sort which may be written on a twentieth-century politician: Cicero, for instance, is seen chiefly from Cicero's point of view, and he also dominates the contemporary evidence on Caesar's activity in civil life in Rome. Less rounded studies may be attempted for lesser politicians (Crassus) or women of the imperial family (Livia, Antonia, Agrippina the Younger). At the other extreme, individual women attested only by their epitaphs will only yield a paragraph or so (on job, marriage or children, perhaps), with a few exceptions such as the anonymous wife eulogised by her husband for her behaviour in the civil wars and in private life (*Laudatio 'Turiae'*). So I have chosen to discuss Tullia, the daughter of Cicero. She has been the focus of study in her own right (especially in recent years) as well as an ancillary figure in discussions of her father.

The demographic regime, socio-legal framework, economic context and physical environment of the mid-first century BC are well known. We must keep in mind the general situation of women as it will have affected Tullia. In turn, the specific experience of Tullia is part of the evidence for women of her class and time. The obvious dangers of circularity and of arguing from the general to the particular and from the particular to the general cannot be entirely avoided. Only if we had a larger sample of senatorial women, with comparable documentation, could we feel secure.

These are my practical considerations. Another motive is that the letters of Cicero, which will form our main source, are endlessly fascinating, and unique among all our sources for Roman social history. Thanks to the work of Shackleton Bailey, they can be handled by the beginner with confidence as well as enjoyment.

The translations which follow are his (Bailey 1988, 1999). Because of the size and variety of Cicero's extant writings, and especially because he was relatively frank in his letters to his closest friends and members of the family, he is the best documented Roman of the classical period. Family life has frequently been explored from his point of view, especially in the modern biographies.

Apart from the intrinsic interest of the source – and students who have read, say, Cicero's self-righteous and carefully calculated first speech against Catiline as a Latin set-book are often amazed to find he was a human being – there is the interest of attempting to find out about an individual woman. Men as well as women seem to find this attractive.

In the last quarter of the twentieth century, serious attempts have been made to reconstruct, as far as possible, the experience of women from written sources predominantly produced by and for men. The effort parallels work on slavery and the lower classes. Women (obviously) belonged to all social classes and socio-economic status determined what sort of life was open to them. Literary evidence allows us to explore the lives of the richer classes, chiefly the women of senatorial and equestrian families. How far did a *paterfamilias* control his daughter-in-power (*filiafamilias*)? How were marriages arranged? What motives did people have in agreeing to a particular marriage? What property might a woman own and how did she administer it? How and where did people live at different periods of their lives? What were a mother's duties to her children? How did high infant mortality affect mothers' attitudes to babies? What were the ideals for affection between married people and blood relations? How did the legal availability of divorce to both husband and wife work out in practice? What feelings did people have when a relative died and what were the social conventions governing the expression of grief? Questions can be asked about law and practice, about physical realities, about ideas and emotions. These are the sort of questions which have been asked in books and articles about the Roman family: the material we shall look at will suggest some answers specific to Tullia.

To understand the general context of family life, you might begin by looking at Dixon 1992. The three conferences held at Canberra, resulting in volumes of papers, have been influential for family history (B. Rawson 1986, 1991; Rawson and Weaver 1997). On specifics such as engagement or divorce, various sections in Treggiari 1991 might give an idea of social norms.

The method here is that of content analysis. For successful examples compare the acute study by Bradley 1993: 246–50 on Pliny and Bradley 1991: 177–204 on Cicero's relationship with his brother and nephew. We aim to take account of the whole body of evidence and assess what it can tell us.

The evidence

Finding and collecting data

If we want to find out about Tullia, we shall first need to assemble the data. There are two ways of doing this. One can read through the relevant writings of Cicero in chronological order and collect the references to her. This has the important advantage that we always see her in a context of her father's writings and preoccupations at a given time. We ought not to fall into the errors which occur when we rely on snippets of text. Having read everything that Cicero has to say about her, we could trawl through other Greek and Roman literature. Since she is unlikely to be mentioned except in such works as Plutarch's *Life of Cicero* or in attacks on her father by his contemporaries (reflected in Cassius Dio and Ps.-Sallust), this procedure is inadvisable, unless Tullia is merely part of a larger project – say, on the subject of Roman women of the senatorial class. It happens that I have collected the evidence on Tullia in this manner. But I shall assume here that this is not the way you would want to do it. For a research paper or short thesis a student would take a different line.

Standard reference works will direct you to the main sources outside Cicero. For instance, Ernst Badian in the *Oxford Classical Dictionary* says that Cicero's *Letters* and Plutarch's *Cicero* are the main sources. Groebe's article in *RE* (*s.v.* Tullius 60) adds sources on Tullia's husbands and puts Tullia in context. *Kleine Pauly* has a column (*s.v.* Tullius 21), with a selection of references to Cicero's correspondence. *Neue Pauly* had not reached the Tullii at the time of writing. The older Drumann-Groebe 1929: vi 614–28 deals with Tullia thoroughly.

For the far more informative Ciceronian evidence, first recourse should be to the three *Onomastica* (name-lists) for Cicero's writings compiled by D.R. Shackleton Bailey (1992, 1995, 1996). In the volumes on the speeches and letters, under Tullia there is a rich but still manageable haul of references. The passages in the former can be found in any reliable text or translation (the Loeb volumes will be the most accessible to English readers). It will be advisable to pay attention to the context of each passage and to know why and in what circumstances each speech was being delivered. Bailey's list of references in the speeches (with the titles written in full and dates added) is reproduced in Appendix 1.

Bailey's references to the letters are given in traditional form. But it is inadvisable to exploit the letters without paying the strictest attention to his own commentaries. We also want to read the letters in the order in which they were written, as far as possible. So the first chore is to look up the numbers which Bailey himself gives the letters in his editions. The concordances will be found in *A*, *F*, 1980, 1988, 1999: iv. Once that is done we have a list, of which a sample (all the citations from Book 1) would look like this:

> *A* 1.3.3 = 8
> 1.5.8 = 1
> 1.8.3 = 4
> 1.10.6 = 6
> (1.18.1) = 18

Bailey also refers us to *mulieres* ('the women'), a word which Cicero uses to refer to two or more of his and Atticus' female relations, Terentia, Tullia, Pomponia and Pilia. We can excise those irrelevant to Tullia.

These letters then need sorting into chronological order (as far as that can be determined). One may adopt the dating of Bailey, which commands invariable respect and usually assent. Here we should follow the revisions given in the 1988 second edition of the translation of *Letters to Friends* and *Letters to his brother Quintus and to M. Brutus* and in the 1999 Loeb translation of the *Letters to Atticus*. It is still a tedious job, but in the doing of it we can improve our familiarity with the source. With this additional information, the consequent reshuffling of the data and the details on who wrote the letter (Cicero, unless otherwise stated), to whom, from where, we have a list which I give in Appendix 1.

The dates are those of writing: the letter might be received considerably later. We now have a workable list of the letters where Tullia is referred to by name or by some descriptive noun or adjective. By reading other letters near these, or by following up the cross-references in commentaries, we should pick up other evidence on e.g. the problems with her dowry.

Difficulties

Various problems at once present themselves. The absolute number of letters Cicero wrote varied at different periods of his life. Correspondence with specific individuals fluctuated with need. He did not usually write to Atticus if they were both in Rome and able to meet (Bailey 1965: 4, 6, 12, etc.). His twenty-four extant letters to Terentia, though sparse, cluster during their separations: the period of his exile (58–7 BC), the time of the civil war when they were often apart even while he was still in Italy (49 BC) and from the time he left for Greece until he returned to Rome after a long period of living in Brindisi (when Plutarch says she failed to visit him (*Cic.* 41.2)). None survive from the other long separation of his provincial governorship in Cilicia (51–50 BC), except one from Athens on his way home.

Then there are the problems of survival. No letters to Tullia alone exist in the collection which has come down to us. (She is named in the headings to 14.1/8 and 2/7, as Tulliola; in 14.3/9, 4/6, 14/14, as Tullia, and in 14.18/144 as *filia* (daughter), but these are all primarily addressed to Terentia.) There are references to Tullia in correspondence with fellow-members of the senatorial class when circumstances made it necessary, but confidential information (on marriage and financial arrangements) and hints of the intimacies of family-life are almost entirely restricted to the correspondence with his wife and with the friend who was also a member of the family (by the marriage of his sister and Cicero's brother) and a trusted financial aide. In public pronouncements, Cicero alludes to his daughter to well-calculated rhetorical effect.

The nature of the evidence does not permit a rounded biography of Tullia. Space does not permit us to analyse all the snippets. But a reading of the texts may allow us to highlight certain features of the father–daughter relationship. I am deliberately sparing with comment on what we know from other evidence, since the object is to see what this restricted collection of texts tells us directly. I hope this will give you some sense of discovery, though nothing substitutes for exploring the evidence for yourself. I have cited the specific evidence for each statement I make, and have given the dates of letters when it seemed useful for you to have them in front of you. It is important in historical argument to substantiate statements. This results here in a high density of sources in parentheses. You will be able to check the source quite quickly if you want to do so. You will find in what follows that the same text may be used to illustrate different specific points. The technique of skimming lightly over the citations (whether in parentheses or in footnotes) should be cultivated. But if you want to look at the evidence first hand for any particular point, you will be able to do so easily.

Known biography

Family background

The salient facts of Tullia's life are briefly listed. Her parents were Cicero and his wife Terentia (about whose natal family tantalisingly little is known: she brought a good dowry and had as cousin or half-sister a patrician Vestal Virgin called Fabia). Tullia's birthday was 5 August (Cic. *A* 4.1/73.4), but we do not know the year of her birth. Her parents could have married 80/79 BC, before Cicero left in mid-79 to study oratory and philosophy in the Greek East, or after his return in mid-77. If she was born 5 August 79, that raises questions about Cicero's solicitude for wife and unborn child. Many scholars, therefore, choose the later date (e.g. Sumner 1971: 258), putting her birth about 75 BC and the marriage to Piso in 62 or late December 63. If he married on his return, she was born at earliest 5 August 76, perhaps not until 75. Some find this date involves us in difficulties about the date of her first marriage. The only loophole that offers is that Cicero might have taken his bride on his tour and she might have borne her child abroad. Other Ciceronian evidence suggests that senatorial women travelled more routinely than scholarship has recognised.

First marriage

Tullia's engagement to C. Calpurnius Piso Frugi (*RE*: Calpurnius 93; quaestor 58, from a high-ranking plebeian family and son of an ex-praetor) is announced by her father at the end of 67 BC (*A* 1.3/8.3; on the later dating of her birth, she was just at an age when she might understand). We cannot be sure that she married him as early as 63, though Cicero calls him his son-in-law (*Cat.* 4.3; see Treggiari 1991: 128 n.17, *pace* SB *F* 1977: i. 285- 6). Sumner's conjectural dating to after Cicero's speech in 63 BC or to 62 may still be too early, since he takes 12–15 to be the normal age for first marriage of girls among the upper classes. Many, following Shaw 1987, would now think 12–14 uncommonly early. The marriage must have taken place before Cicero was driven out of Rome in 58. Piso died during his father-in-law's exile in 57, after supporting him bravely (*F* 14.4/6.4, 14.2/7.2, 14.1/8.4, *On his return, to the citizens* 7; *Sest.* 54; *Pis.* fr. xiii Nisbet).

Second and third marriages

She was engaged and probably married to Furius Crassipes (*RE*: Furius 54) in 56 BC (Bailey 1965: 2.186–7, but see also P. Clark 1991, who argues that the marriage perhaps never took place) but divorced perhaps in 52 or early 51: in any case, she was again on the marriage-market when her father left for Cilicia in May.

On 1 July 50 she married the patrician (but later adopted by a plebeian so that he could hold the tribunate) P. Cornelius Dolabella (*RE* Cornelius 141; Drumann-Groebe 1902: ii 486–97; tribune 47) perhaps aged now about 25 or 26, so very much Tullia's own age, in my view. A premature boy, born May 49, did not long survive. They divorced in 46, a few months before Tullia was delivered of another boy in January 45 (Lentulus), who probably died in babyhood. She herself died of complications in February.

Content analysis

Tullia's girlhood

In the earliest reference, in the published but never delivered second part of the prosecution of Verres in 70 BC, Cicero, attacking a decision of Verres which went against a daughter, makes out that he and his auditors, as devoted fathers, are equally shocked. He emphasises the affection he feels for 'my daughter' and the duty all fathers feel to do their best for their daughters. Cicero strikes this note repeatedly: he aligns himself with a norm of fatherly love and plays on the sympathies of his audience (whether judges or senators or the People).

The letters of the 60s, with frequent references to 'little Tullia' (*A* 1.5/1.8, 1.3/8.3, the name he usually gave her down to 57 (Bailey 1995: 99)), affectionate epithets like 'darling' (*deliciolae*, 1.8/4.3) and small private jokes about her interaction with Atticus (1.8/4.3, 1.10/6.6: it is easier to think of an eight- or seven-year-old here than of an eleven-year-old), make it clear that the paternal affection was genuine. We cannot say that the enthusiasm Cicero shows at the belated birth of his son in 65 BC (*A* 1.2/11.1) would not have been paralleled when Tullia was born.

In the published version of his heroic speech on what to do with the confessed conspirators in 63 BC, Cicero claims he is ready to risk his life and happiness to save those of his audience and their wives and children: still, he is not hard-hearted enough not to be moved by his brother (present in the Senate) and the thought of his fainting wife, terrified daughter and little son at home, and the sight of his son-in-law (standing outside) (*Cat.* 4.3).

Tullia is again part of the close family group in which Cicero delights in early 60 BC (*A* 1.18/18.1: it is not clear whether she is by then a married woman ? in her mid-teens). In April 59, she was apparently accompanying Cicero on all or part of a spring tour, planned to include a three-day festival at Anzio which she wished to attend (2.8/28.2).

Her father's exile and her life with Piso

In the crisis of 58–7 BC, Cicero wrote emotional letters to Terentia and family, giving a prominent place to 'Tulliola' (*F* 14.2/7.1). His exile and the confiscation of his property imperilled her married status and reputation (*F* 14.4/6.3; Bailey suggests her dowry had not yet been fully paid) and Cicero was worried about her and blamed himself.

> To you and our Tulliola I cannot write without many tears, for I see that you are very unhappy – you, for whom I wished all the happiness in the world. I ought to have given it to you, and should have done so if I had not been such a coward.
>
> (*F* 14.2/7.1)

In the subsequent letter, he wallows in apologies for his mistakes and their suffering:

> And to think that our Tulliola should be suffering so much grief on account of her papa, who used to give her so much pleasure!
>
> (*F* 14.1/8.1)

Cicero continues to use affectionate diminutives (e.g. *F* 14.4/6.3,6) and, when he tells his brother in a highly emotional passage, how much he is missing his family, gives a lightning sketch of her: 'the most loving, modest, and clever daughter a man ever had, the image of my face and speech and mind' (*QF* 1.3/3.3). The egocentric note is unmistakable, but so is the affection (cf. *A* 3.10/55.2). He is confident that her uncle will regard her and her brother as his own children (*QF* 1.3/3.10); similarly Atticus is asked to look after them (*A* 3.19/64.3). Public figures are later credited with having defended them (*Sest.* 144; *Planc.* 73; *Mil.* 100). In public Cicero laments the 'solitude' of his children and the ruin of his family (*On his house* 96) and his own separation from them (*Sest.* 49, 145). Cicero's recall, in prospect and retrospect, is regarded as restoration to his family (*A* 3.15/60.4, *On his return, in the Senate* 1). His house was restored to him and his children (*On the reply of the haruspices* 16).

It is clear that, like her mother and husband, Tullia interceded on her father's behalf (*A* 3.19/64.2). Cicero claims that she and her husband went down on their knees to the consul Piso, who repelled his kinsman and relative by marriage with arrogant and cruel words

(*On his return, in the Senate* 17, not in the *Onomasticon*; for the son-in-law alone cf. *Sest.* 68). But later Cicero downplays the women's visibility to the People, since their grief and mourning-garments were observable indoors (presumably by influential members of the upper classes on whom or on whose wives and daughters Terentia and Tullia, with the pathetic seven-year-old Marcus, worked for Cicero's recall), while his male supporters could be seen in the forum (*On his return, to the citizens* 8). He also mentions their 'necessary journeys'. Where had they been? Elsewhere he claims that Tullia's grief and mourning garb excited general pity (*On his house* 59). Once Cicero claims that his children's lives were threatened (*Sest.* 54, cf. *Mil.* 87), but this may allude to Marcus (*On his house* 59). There may have been some real physical danger to Tullia, since the Palatine house was attacked and fired.

Her father's restoration and her widowhood

This completes the explicit mentions of Tullia during the exile. She was involved in her father's happy return, for she undertook the fairly arduous overland journey to Brindisi (360 miles (Bailey 1965: ii 166)) to greet him the day after the law to recall him was passed, which happened to be the birthday of the port-city as well as hers. She was given special treatment by the citizens and presumably by all the other deputations which fêted Cicero on the way back to Rome (although he does not mention her presence then: as so often, we must read between the lines) (*A* 4.1/73.4–5; the occasion is also triumphantly described in *Sest.* 131). Cicero evokes her to the Senate on 5 September when he claims that the passing of the law was like a birthday for him, his brother and his children (*On his return, in the Senate* 27). The Senate had conferred benefits on all of them (1; he says the same of the People). A few days later, he magnifies his sacrifice, as he had done earlier, prospectively, in the *Fourth Catilinarian*, and strikes the same note as in the *Verrines* (cf. also *Planc.* 69):

> What sweeter thing has Nature given to the human race than each man's children? My own, because of my love toward them and their own excellent character, are dearer to me than life. But

> I did not acknowledge them at birth with as much pleasure as
> now when they are restored to me. . . . The immortal gods gave
> me children; you have given them back.
>
> (*On his return, to the citizens* 2, 5)

Cicero, at the time of his recall, thought he could rely on the affection of his brother and daughter: there was apparently some
estrangement from Terentia (*A* 4.2/74.7, cf. 4.1/73.8). Tullia's loss of
her husband and her grief for him are directly mentioned only in
Cicero's allusion in court to their first poignant meeting on his return
(*Sest.* 131). A new marriage-alliance had to be sought without delay.
Finding the right eligible young man at the right moment was not
always easy: search and approaches might take some time.

Her life with Crassipes

On 4 April 56 BC, after some negotiation, Cicero betrothed Tullia (*QF*
2.4/8.2, 2.6/10.1) to the young, wealthy patrician and prospective senator Furius Crassipes (? quaestor 54 (Bailey *F* 1977: i. pp. 138–9),
which would make him about 26 now). On 6 and 8 April Cicero and
Crassipes gave dinners for each other (*QF* 2.6/10.2,3). It is not clear if
the future bride was invited. The engagement elicited correct congratulations from at least one political ally (*F* 1.7/18.11). Apart from the
relationship between the two men (e.g. *F* 1.9/20.20), the marriage itself
leaves no trace in the correspondence. But mentions of Tullia in the
late 50s are sparse in the extreme: we find her hoping that Atticus'
young wife Pilia will visit her at Anzio (*A* 4.4a/78.2), but other details
of her life escape us. We can only speculate on the luxurious life-style
which her husband could command for her and on a social circle in
which she should now have been an accepted figure.

The search for a third husband

On Cicero's departure for his province in late spring 51 BC, when
letters to Atticus resume after a break since November 54, arrangements for Tullia's remarriage after the divorce were on the front burner.
He and Atticus must already have had face-to-face discussions. The

surviving evidence gives us their interchanges on possible candidates and their pluses and minuses. Although Cicero wanted Atticus to sound out various possibilities and keeps urging him on (*A* 5.4/97.1, 5.13/106.3, 5.14/107.3, 5.17/110.4, 5.21/114.14, 6.1/115.10, 6.4/118.2, 7.3/126.12), it is clear that Tullia's consent was essential (5.4/97.1), and he later claims that he had left the decision to her and her mother (*F* 3.12/75.2–3). We lack letters to Terentia, though of course Cicero was writing to her (*A* 6.1/115.10). Other people too were involved (5.17/110.4): again no letters survive. (See further Treggiari 1991: 127–34.) The engagement to Dolabella was made without Cicero's knowledge (just when he had decided to recommend Nero (*A* 6.6/121.1, cf. 6.4/118.2)), and he had to think away what he knew of the man's character and record when responding to other people's congratulations or more negative reactions (*F* 8.13/94.1, *A* 6.6/121.1, *F* 2.15/96.2, 3.12/75.2–4, *A* 6.8/122.1, 7.3/126.12). He hoped all would turn out well for Tullia and himself (*F* 3.12/75.2).

Life with Dolabella and civil war

Writing from Athens on his way home, Cicero was anxious for Atticus to report on the match (*A* 6.9/123.5) and sent affectionate wishes to the women (*F* 14.5/119.1–2). Dolabella's unsteadiness in sexual and political life were to outweigh the charm he exuded both for Tullia (*A* 6.6/121.1) and for Cicero (*A* 7.3/126.12) and eventually to wreck the marriage. To judge from the annual date for paying instalments of the dowry, the wedding took place on 1 July, in Cicero's absence (Treggiari 1991: 133 n.36, *pace* SB 1977: i. 435–6). Cicero met the new couple apparently near Trebula on his journey back in early December (*A* 7.3/126.12).

Dolabella would soon be leaving Tullia for active service. Caesar invaded Italy on 11 January 49. Dolabella commanded a fleet in the Adriatic that year. In 48 BC he served under Caesar at Dyrrachium and Pharsalus, returning to Rome in the autumn to stand for the tribunate. In 47, holding that office, he was in Rome. (His activities were not approved by Cicero or, more important to him, Caesar.) He was again with Caesar in the new theatres of war, Africa in 46 BC and Spain in 45. So the marriage was interrupted by considerable absences. When Dolabella was in Rome as tribune, Tullia left him for a considerable time to visit her father.

The next cluster of references to Tullia belongs to the uncertain days of the civil war in the winter of 49 BC, after Caesar had crossed the Rubicon but before Cicero had finally committed himself to Pompey by leaving Italy. A major fact, known to Atticus and the family, remains unmentioned: Tullia was expecting a child. Because Dolabella sided with Caesar, Tullia had a foot in both camps and could expect protection (*F* 14.18/144; *A* 7.13/136.3). Should she and her mother stay in Rome? Would it be safe (*A* 7.12/135.6; *F* 14.14/145)? Would it look bad, reflecting on them and on Cicero (*F* 14.18/144; *A* 7.13/ 136.3; *F* 14.14/145; *A* 7.14/138.3)? What were other ladies of rank doing? He voiced his concerns both to them and to Atticus. The letters to the women are markedly affectionate and explicit about the problems. It appears that both were at the Palatine house, which was to be barricaded and guarded. Cicero felt that they would be safer at one or other of his villas, but he leaves it to them to discuss the matter with trusted advisers and make their own decision. He repeatedly consulted Atticus, who had also remained in Rome (e.g. *A* 7.13a/137.3, 7.16/ 140.3).

On 2 February, the women came to the villa at Formiae, intending to return to Rome soon (*A* 7.18/142.1, 7.20/144.2, cf. 7.22/ 146.2 and Bailey's detailed calendar in *A* 1968: iv 428–37 which plots Cicero's movements). Now it was their return to Rome which might be interpreted politically (*A* 7.23/147.2) That pressure could be exerted through Tullia is demonstrated by Antony's later appeal to Cicero not to join Pompey, where he reminds him of his fondness for Dolabella and 'that most admirable young lady your daughter' (*A* 10.8A/199A.1) and by Caelius' similar attempt 'in the name of your . . . children' (*A* 10.9A/200A.1), pointedly rebutted in a disingenuous reply (*F* 2.16/ 154.5). Tullia may have been back in Rome by 4 April *(A* 10.1a/191.1) but was with her father at the villa near Cumae by 7 May (10.13/205.1, probably having travelled with her mother: 10.16/208.5).

In the meantime, Cicero was pondering his own position, with occasional explicit reference to the interests of his children (*A* 8.2/152.4). The thought of them and Terentia, he claims, prevented him throwing in his lot with Pompey, although they wanted him to do so and thought it the more honourable course (*A* 9.6/172.4, 11 March). But his purpose constantly shifted.

By May, Tullia was urging delay, to see how the civil war went in Spain (*A* 10.8/199.1). But when Cicero left Italy to join Pompey in Greece, he later represented himself as having acted in obedience to members of the family (*A* 11.9/220.2).

> ... nothing ever needed writing more than this, that of all your many kindnesses there is none I have valued more than your tender and punctilious attention to my Tullia. It has given her the greatest pleasure, and me no less. Her courage and patience in face of public disaster and domestic worries is really wonderful. How brave she was when we parted! She combines natural affection with the most delicate sympathy. Yet she wishes me to do the right thing and to stand well in men's eyes.
>
> (*A* 10.8/199.9)

By 7 May, Tullia had rejoined her father at the villa near Cumae, where on 19th, she gave birth to a boy, two months premature. 'For her safe delivery let me be thankful. As for the baby, it is very weakly' (*A* 10.18/210.1). How would you assess the grandfather's reactions?

Cicero was waiting, not for the birth, but for a favourable wind. On 7 June, he wrote from his ship to bid Terentia farewell:

> All the miseries and cares with which I plagued you to desperation (and very sorry I am for it) and Tulliola too, who is sweeter to me than my life, are dismissed and ejected. ... I should give you words of encouragement to make you both braver had I not found you braver than any man.
>
> (*F* 14.7/155.1)

Then the practicalities: he would commend them to friends and he begged them to look after their health and to use the country houses (particularly those furthest from army units). If food prices went up, they should go to the ancestral house near Arpinum with the town-staff, if they thought fit. The child was dead and forgotten, no doubt. Another gap in our evidence follows. Cicero was busy until Pompey was defeated at Pharsalus in August 48 BC. At Caesar's invitation he returned to Italy and waited at Brindisi until Caesar authorised his return to Rome (September 47 BC).

From now on it is problems with Tullia's marriage which form the major theme in the references to her (though in the correspondence as a whole Cicero agonised over other political and private problems as well). Atticus, as usual, was deeply involved. Cicero had problems in 48 BC paying the second instalment on the dowry, due annually, and worried that Tullia's maintenance was not being paid (*A* 11.2/212.2, cf. 11.3/213.1,3, 11.4a/214, 11.4/215). He asked Atticus to intervene. All this made Cicero unhappy (*A* 11.3/213.3). For the details of what was going on, see Dixon's masterly reconstruction (Dixon 1984: 88–93, slightly abridged in 1986: 102–7), as well as Bailey's commentary. Here I underline Cicero's insistence that he had failed in his duty to his 'poor girl' (*A* 11.3/213.1). Cicero blamed his steward and may have held that Terentia was implicated (Bailey 1966: 5.266–7). Already, in spring 48, the alternatives were clear: to continue to invest money in the marriage or to bring about a divorce: Cicero left the decision to Atticus' 'friendship and good will, and to her judgement and inclination' (*A* 11.3/213.1). Any one of three people had the legal right to end the marriage unilaterally: Cicero, if he was, as we assume, the wife's *paterfamilias*; Dolabella, or Tullia herself. (If Dolabella's *paterfamilias* had been alive, he could have acted too.) From the point of view of social convention it might be more comfortable for Tullia if her father, on her instructions, took the initiative.

In May, Dolabella, making another effort to get Cicero away from Pompey, reported from Caesar's camp that Tullia was well, news he must himself have had by letter (*F* 9.9/157.1). After Pompey's defeat and his own return to Brindisi in about mid-October, Cicero heard from Atticus that Tullia was ill and weak (*A* 11.6/217.4) and expressed his 'agony' to Terentia (*F* 14.19/160). Soon after, news that Atticus was 'being pressed' apparently by Tullia's creditors, made Cicero weep and beg Atticus to intervene (*A* 11.7/218.6). And Tullia's continued illness worried him (*F* 14.9/161, 14.17/162). His own ruin threatened to deprive her of his presence and her inheritance (*A* 11.9/220.3).

Cicero deplored Dolabella's behaviour in 47 BC (*A* 11.15/226.3, 11.23/232.3).

When Tullia joined him at Brindisi on 12 June 47, he told Atticus:

> Her own courage, thoughtfulness, and affection, far from giving me the pleasure I ought to take in such a paragon of daughters, grieve me beyond measure when I consider the unhappy lot in which so admirable a nature is cast, not through any misconduct of hers but by grave fault on my part.
>
> (*A* 11.17/228)

He thought of sending her back to her mother as soon as she was willing (*A* 11.17a/229.1, but this was delayed [*F* 14.15/16, *A* 11.21/236.27]). To Terentia he says:

> She is so wonderfully brave and kind that it gives me even greater pain to think that through my carelessness she is placed far otherwise than befitted a girl of her station and so good a daughter.
>
> (*F* 14.11/166)

A 11.25/231.3, 5 July, when he asks Atticus to discuss Tullia's situation with Terentia, also conveys the flavour of his relationship with his daughter at this difficult time:

> This poor child's long-suffering affects me quite beyond bearing. I believe her like on earth has never been seen. If there is any step in my power which might protect her in any way, I earnestly desire you to suggest it. I realize that there is the same difficulty as formerly in giving advice (?). Still, this causes me more anxiety than everything else put together. We were blind about the second instalment. I wish I had acted differently, but it's too late now. I beg you, if anything in my desperate situation can be scraped together, any sum raised and put away in safety, from plate or fabrics (I have plenty of them) or furniture, you will attend to it (cf. *A* 11.24/234.1–2). The final crisis seems to me to be upon us. There is no likelihood of peace terms. . . .

Cicero thinks now that he had made the wrong decision in paying a fraction of the dowry on 1 July 48: he ought to have withheld it and perhaps proceeded to the second option, a unilateral divorce from Tullia's side. He blamed himself repeatedly for making a mess of providing for Tullia, on the occasion of her third marriage (Bailey 1977: i 502–3) and by making political decisions which imperilled the family's prosperity. It is striking that he never, as far as we know, blamed Tullia for choosing Dolabella.

> I implore you to think about this poor girl, both as to the matter on which I wrote to you in my last letter, how to raise something to keep the wolf from the door, and also as to the will itself (Terentia's). I wish the other thing too (marriage) had been taken in hand sooner, but I was afraid of everything. Certainly there was no better choice among evils than divorce. That would have been doing something like a man – whether on the score of the debt cancellation (Dolabella's proposals as tribune) or his nocturnal housebreakings or Metella (his adulteries) or the whole chapter of delinquencies. I should have saved the money and given some evidence of manly resentment. . . . Now he seems to be threatening it on *his* side. . . . Accordingly I am in favour, and so are you, of sending notice of divorce. He may ask for the third instalment (due 1 July 47), so consider whether we should send the notice when he himself takes the initiative or before.
>
> (*A* 11.23/232.3, 9 July 47; cf. *F* 14.10/168)

The next day, Cicero toned down these instructions, telling Terentia:

> As regards what I wrote in my last letter about sending notice of divorce, I don't know how powerful he is at the present time, nor how excited the state of popular feeling. If he is likely to be a formidable enemy, don't do anything – perhaps he will take the initiative even so. You must judge of the whole position and choose whatever you think the least of evils in this wretched situation.
>
> (*F* 14.13/169)

The matter remained in suspense: next summer Tullia was still un-committed (*A* 12.5c/241, 12 June (?) 46) and Cicero was maintaining dialogue with Dolabella (*A* 12.7/244.2), who returned from the African campaign and made his wife pregnant again.

A pregnant divorcee

In the meantime, Caesar had returned victorious from the East and permitted Cicero to leave unhealthy Brindisi and return to his house in Rome and his villas. Divorce from Terentia followed (46 BC (Dixon 1984: 92 = 1986 106)). Before the next reference to Tullia in the letters (*A* 12.1/248.1, 27 Nov. (where Cicero longs to return, after a brief absence, to Tullia's embrace and little Attica's kisses); *F* 7.23/209.4, Dec. 46), she and Dolabella were also divorced. This must have been some time after *A* 12.5c/241, 12 June (?) 46, probably in November (SB). We do not know who took the formal initiative, Dolabella, Tullia or her father. The divorce may even have been bilateral and consen-sual. She was apparently living chiefly in her father's house, though she may have given birth at Dolabella's as later, muddled accounts suggest (Asc. 5C; Plutarch *Cic.* 41.5). A letter to Lepta, an officer under Cicero in Cilicia, (dated to January by the reference to her) has the brief but frank mention:

> My Tullia's confinement has kept me in Rome. But even now that she has, as I hope, fairly well regained her strength, I am still kept here waiting to extract the first instalment out of Dolabella's agents.
>
> (*F* 6.18/218.5)

It was now the ex-husband's turn to repay the dowry.

Impact of her death

Tullia never recovered and the rest of our references deal with Cicero's grief at her death (? mid-February; at his Tusculan villa (*A* 12.44/285.3, 12.46/287.1)). Our list of references is lacunose, since in writing to Atticus, voluminously, about his own sorrow and his plans to commemorate her, Cicero only once uses her name. What can be gleaned about Tullia herself and about her life in all the letters which treat his attempts to control or conceal his grief (Treggiari 1998: 16–23)? Among the spate of letters of condolence which Cicero will have received (e.g. from Brutus: *A* 12.14/251.4; cf. Plutarch *Cic.* 41.5), the elegant literary/philosophical composition by the consular Servius Sulpicius Rufus (*F* 4.5/248; Hutchinson 1998: 62–77) argues that Tullia had little left to live for. Her father would have had difficulty finding her a worthy (new) upper-class husband to protect her among the modern generation; the political situation meant that children 'whose bloom would cheer her eyes' could not grow up with the expectation of freedom and intact inheritance or (for sons) the right of independence in a public career (3). In any case, she was mortal: it made little difference if she died young!

> Tell yourself that she lived as long as it was well for her to live, and that she and freedom existed together. She saw you, her father, Praetor, Consul, and Augur. She was married to young men of distinction. Almost all that life can give, she enjoyed . . . .
>
> (5)

Although Sulpicius could comment politely (6) on her love for Cicero (*amor*) and her dutiful affection (*pietas*) towards all her family, this is an outsider's view of the vicarious happiness she must have enjoyed through father and husband, and gives little sense of Tullia as a person. Cicero's deft reply (*F* 4.6/249) gives an insider's view, but an egocentric one:

> I had a haven of refuge and repose (from public troubles), one in whose conversation and sweet ways I put aside all cares and sorrows. . . .
>
> (2)

Bailey rightly comments 'This is what Sulpicius' letter ignores'. We could wish that the letters to Atticus, which resume several weeks after her death, after Cicero had had plenty of time to talk his heart out at Atticus' house in Rome (Bailey 1966: v p. 309) had more on this subject, but Atticus did not need to have it explained to him.

Cicero reiterates the theme that Tullia was all that made life worth living (*A* 12.23/262.1, 12.28/267.2; cf. *Tusculan Disputations* 1.84) and he claims that he is so changed that everything Atticus liked in him is gone for good (*A* 12.14/251.3). He regarded the intended shrine as a debt to be paid (*A* 12.18/254.1, 12.38a/279.2, 12.41/283.4).

What the data document

The relationship between Tullia and her father was slandered in antiquity by political enemies (reflected in ps.-Sallust *Against Cicero* 2, Cass. Dio 46.18.6). It was clearly recognised as particularly close, and the letters attest this. Observing the delight Atticus took in his small daughter, at a time when he had just seen Tullia after a year's absence, Cicero insists that parental affection is natural, as philosophers averred (*A* 7.2/125.4). We have repeatedly come across his conviction that he had a duty to secure his daughter's happiness. He never criticises her for any fault towards him (remarkable in so prickly a man) and the praise he bestows on her is heart-felt and unparalleled except perhaps sometimes in the warmth of his expressions about Atticus.

Cicero wanted to find his sons-in-law 'agreeable' (*F* 1.7/18.11, 2.15/96.2) and real members of the family, but in these marriages as in his own, it is striking how independently husband and wife operated (not only in financial matters), often separated by the husband's absence on public or private business, but often too in their leisure, for instance dinner engagements. Although married, Tullia continued to be her father's responsibility, and was almost certainly a daughter-in-power (Dixon 1984: 90 = 1986: 105). This would mean that Cicero could, in law, unilaterally bring about a divorce from Dolabella. It is clear that he would not have dreamt of doing it unless she authorised him. But her feelings would be spared if her family rather than she sent the notice of divorce.

I find nothing on Tullia's emotional relationship with her brother: affection is taken for granted. The same appropriate attitudes appear to characterise the interaction of mother and daughter. Cicero expects Terentia to look after her and be concerned for her (e.g. *F* 14.19/160, *A* 11.9/220.3) and disapproved of the provisions of Terentia's will (Dixon 1984: 96 = 1986: 110). When she helped Tullia financially in 48

BC, Cicero thanked her, too, in the correct but surely chilly words, 'As to what you say about our girl thanking you, I am not surprised that you should give her good reason to do that' (*F* 14.6/158; Dixon 1984: 90 = 1986: 104). As for Tullia's attitude, she was with her mother more than with her father, and to him seemed long-suffering. Tullia was said to be fond of her uncle Quintus (*QF* 2.4/8.2, mid March 56), who mentions her affectionately (*F* 16.15/44.1). She had known Quintus' wife, Atticus' sister, since childhood, but nothing indicates her reactions to that temperamental woman, or to her child, young Quintus, of whom Tullia must have seen a good deal in his childhood. Cicero reports on her whereabouts to Tiro (*F* 16.12/146.6), his confidential secretary who, after his manumission, was treated almost as a member of the family, and joins the name of Tullia, as well as of Marcus, Terentia and the Quinti, to his own, when all the family were together in January 49 and Tiro had been left behind sick in Greece (*F* 16.11/143).

The relationship between Tullia and Atticus seems to have been close and they often talked or corresponded (*A* 10.8/199.9–10, 10.13/205.1, 11.7/218.6, 11.17/228, 11.24/234.1). A particular friendship with his wife Pilia is indicated (*A* 4.16/89.4, 6.8/122.1, 12.14/251.4). Of her father's fellow-senators, Sulpicius claimed to be upset by her death (*F* 4.5/248.1). Of the younger set, Caelius knew her well enough in 50 BC to refer politely to her 'modest ways' (*pudor*) when congratulating Cicero on her new engagement (*F* 8.13/94.1). By 49 he is treated as a friend (*F* 2.16/154.7). She and Antony seem to have been acquainted. As Dolabella's wife, she must have been expected to entertain Caesarians, with their wives, when they came to Rome, and they would pay courtesy calls, as Hortensius did on her mother (*A* 10.16/208.5). We have a little vignette of her social interactions when she attempted to help a friend of Cicero's to buy a house and went to work through the potential vendor's wife (*F* 7.23/209.4). She had contacts and channelled news to Cicero and Atticus (*A* 10.1a/191, 10.2/192.2, 10.8/199.10)

Her father found her charming company. He attributes 'good sense' (*prudentia*) to her (*F* 2.15/96.2), tacitly emending Caelius' *pudor* (perhaps not because it was impertinent of Caelius to use the word, as Bailey seems to suggest, but because it was not for her father to claim such a virtue). In 54 BC he tells Atticus he refrained from speaking out at a trial, out of consideration for Tullia, who was unwell and afraid he might annoy Clodius (*A* 4.15/90.4). He discussed politics and the course of the civil war with her. In the *Consolation* which he wrote after her death, he claimed the right to consecrate her, with divine approval, like the heroes of old, as the best and most learned of all (Lactantius *inst. div.* 1.15.16–20 = Cicero 1904: iv 3.335). It is not clear how she was educated, but growing up in Cicero's household, with its books and shifting company of learned men and visitors, and talking to her father, must have had an impact, even if Cicero is generous in terming her 'learned'.

Questions

What questions can we usefully put to this evidence? We can ask for the salient events of Tullia's life, but they are few; vital ones (such as the date of her birth) are not covered; as far as they are recoverable, they are part of the standard reference works.

Attitudes

We can ask how Cicero reacted to those facts. Did he take the line we would expect, because of our personal experience of relationships between father and daughter? Or do we find that here 'the thought structure of the ancients was very different to our own'? It is, I think, undeniable that Cicero's love for his daughter was highly emotional. This is not usually called into question. But two strands of the relationship might surprise people who have heard about the legal power held by a Roman father and who have not read the letters. The first is the importance Cicero gives to his duty to Tullia (in looking after her well-being and happiness), a duty which continues even after her death. The other is the way in which he defers to her judgement and feelings, not only in matters such as her choice of her third husband or in the decision whether to divorce, but in his own practical and moral dilemma about whether to join Pompey. Almost certainly Tullia was a daughter-in-power, so that Cicero's consent was essential for her marriages and he could unilaterally have brought about a divorce from Dolabella. But it is unthinkable that Cicero would have crudely invoked his power. We have seen that he had no chance to give his formal consent to her marriage. His general instructions in advance, the fact that he did not signify lack of consent at the time of the wedding, and the fact that he acquiesced in the match and cordially accepted Dolabella as his son-in-law were enough to signify retrospective paternal consent. Similarly, if he did in fact initiate the divorce, it would have been at her bidding. His relations with her are characterised throughout by warmth and tact, not the legal power nor even the moral authority of the heavyweight father.

It is not surprising that frank, personal letters are full of Cicero's own reactions and feelings. This limits the questions we can ask. We wish for Tullia's own letters, which, like anyone's, must have been partly egocentric, and her diary (the Romans are not known to have invented this genre) or even her engagement book and household lists. But, even as seen through the eyes of her father and other men, she is an independent personality of whom account must be taken.

Circumstances of life

The other area in which snippets provide some evidence is the details of daily life. Where did she live? How and why did Tullia travel? Whom did she know socially? How far did pregnancy restrict her activities? Did she attend games?

Our evidence on Tullia forms part of the data which Suzanne Dixon exploited in 'a "case study" of the economics of Roman marriage' (Dixon 1984: 78 = 1986: 97), when she tried (successfully) to piece together a picture of the extent and function of a wife's contribution to the economy of a senatorial marriage, and to gauge the scope of her material obligations to the children' (Dixon 1984: 78 = 1986: 93). Such a study seeks the answer to specific questions rather than trawling for whatever comes up as this chapter has done.

Summing up

If you had performed the work I have outlined here, you would no doubt have come to conclusions different from mine. Krista Pelisari, for example, one of my Stanford students, was able to deploy the data in order to support the hypothesis that Cicero might have had what today would be seen as an unhealthy psychological dependence on his only daughter. Although the dead cannot be put on the psychiatrist's couch, she showed that Cicero's reactions are often consistent with habits which in our society would be regarded as dangerous for both parent and daughter, for instance a father's tendency to use a child rather than his wife as his main confidante. She rightly pointed out that, as the Cicero/Tullia relationship is much the most fully attested father/daughter relationship in antiquity, it is impossible to be sure if it transgressed Roman norms. Such fresh and thought-provoking views are a testimony to the continuing fascination exerted by our sources.

We end up with many unanswered questions. But the individual escapes from the stereotypes.

Chapter 5

Case study II:
How holy was
the house?

Scientific laws command assent only in so far as they cover all the known phenomena; once it is seen that they fail to do so, they must be discarded or amended. No hypotheses have been formulated with a like combination of simplicity, exactitude and exhaustiveness to make the phenomena of human behaviour in society intelligible. . . . Still, conclusions that arise from this procedure (sc. the application of general theories) must be tested by the whole body of relevant facts that the evidence discloses; they must at least be shown to be congruent with those facts, and they are susceptible, if congruence is lacking or incomplete, of refutation or modification; in the nature of things they can never be entirely verified, any more than scientific 'laws', which are no more than provisional hypotheses that account for the phenomena so far observed.

(Brunt 1988a: 87–92)

A theory and some questions

It is commonly held by classicists that the Romans thought of the home as somehow sacred. Scholars rely on their acquaintance with texts and on the rituals associated with private houses which are documented by students of religion. The point is well put (and substantiated by means of a selection of texts) by Richard Saller in a chapter developed from a seminal article on the semantic range of the Latin terms *domus* (house, family, lineage) and *familia* (household, staff, family):

> Since a man's *domus* was where he kept his *lar* (*Dig.* 25.3.1.2) the Roman house had a sacred aura, embodied in the *lares* or *dii penates*, that houses in more recent societies have not had.
>
> (Saller 1994: 89)

Saller presents the theory which we are going to test. We should start by considering what he means. It is often helpful to think of an author's definition of terms. However, he does not define precisely what he means by 'sacred aura', although we can get a strong hint from his clarification that it was made visible (or at least comprehensible) in the household gods, whose images might be physically present. So it must suffice for us to think about what we think it means. It might be paraphrased, perhaps, by 'religious atmosphere'. It must refer to the ideas and feelings which Romans had about their houses, not only their own but other people's, and what they sensed when they entered a house. Saller draws a deliberate contrast with contemporary western societies (again, without specifying further).

Imagine that our project is to examine this statement and explore its implications. We might start by following up references. The passage from Ulpian's commentary on the praetor's edict to which Saller refers us concerns the rule that a divorced wife who believed herself to be pregnant had thirty days to notify her ex-husband by sending a message to him or his *paterfamilias* or (failing that) to his house, *domum*. How was that house to be defined? It might be 'the place where they put the *Lar* for the marriage', which must mean the place which the couple regarded as the marital home.[1] We shall come back later to the importance of the household gods, the *Lares* and *Penates*. Already, by verifying one reference, we have found ourselves in a very specific context where what we would call law and religion intersect.

Saller's statement could simply be confirmed by citing further evidence about domestic cult.[2] But it will be more interesting to delve deeper. What is Saller's supporting evidence? What does he mean by his deliberately vague phrase 'sacred aura'? What were the effects of the 'aura'? How did the idea work out in ordinary life and discourse? Did the feeling that a home was sacred translate into action? Did sacredness attach to all homes? Did it make any difference if the house-holder or resident was a woman, and if the home was not a detached town-house (*domus*) or villa (also mentioned by Ulpian) but an apart-ment or a cottage? In short, what about socio-economic class and gender – or age, since sons-in-power of the upper classes seem often to have lived in smart rented apartments?

The very passage of Ulpian just paraphrased and quoted suggests such questions: Ulpian takes into account the lifestyle of the upper classes, of whom he primarily thought: such people would own town-houses, recreational villas, farmhouses, and lodges on roads they often traversed. They might also stay with friends. A married couple of this class, each owning property, would move around a great deal. But they might regard one particular house as their primary marital home. For a senator, despite loyalties to ancestral or particularly attractive villas, this would probably mean the house in Rome where he spent a good deal of his working life. For Cicero, for instance, from 62 BC when he bought it, it meant the grand house on the Palatine, 'his house', '*domus sua*' of the speech in which he defended his rights to it, *On his house*.

Having set yourself a question, you might browse in modern scholarship in order to find out if someone else had already come up with satisfactory answers. The question will be refined as you proceed and follow various leads. The browsing stage is important, allowing you to mull over the theme. Do not neglect the usual reference tools, such as *OCD*, where under 'House, Italian', Purcell 1996 gives an authoritative survey of how people were housed and encourages us by the verdict (italics mine):

> *Scholarship has concentrated on typology rather than function*, and has been given to making facile assumptions about standards of comfort, convenience and cleanliness based on modern cultural stereotypes. Despite the enormous quantity of archaeological explanation, *ancient domestic society still needs investigation*.
>
> (Purcell 1996)

Getting started

Setting the scene

At this point, it will also be useful to think what areas of life and types of evidence should be explored. For instance,

1 What legal rules affected houses and housing? Since practice (and not just theory) interests us, start with Crook 1967 on ownership. Specific detail can then be checked in such works as Schulz 1951, Watson 1968.

2 You will need a general idea of what Roman houses were like. The 'classic' town type is the old-style *domus* centred on the atrium. Our thinking tends to be dominated by this and by the range of possibilities represented by Pompeii and Herculaneum. But plenty of people lived in apartment-blocks (best known from Ostia). Then there was the rich man's house in a garden on the fringes of Rome (*horti* – not well represented archaeologically) and the villa in the country (examples all over the Roman world including Britain). Working farmhouses leave better traces than isolated cottages. To get an idea of the rich town-house, see Wiseman 1981/94, Wallace-Hadrill 1994, articles on *domus* in *LTUR* ii; there are further references in Treggiari 1999: 33.

3 Cult and religious belief will clearly be relevant: again, some background must be acquired.

4 Assumptions and idealisation in literary authors must be taken into account.

5 We may follow up Saller's 'recent societies' by consulting sociological encyclopaedias or anthropological or historical studies which might provide comparative material or hypotheses.[3] There has been fascinating work on the functions of certain types of house, for instance the English country house through the centuries by M. Girouard 1978 or the village houses of a dying Greek mountain community in the 1970s by du Boulay 1974. The use of the Roman town house as a focus of prestige and power and the place where a member of the élite did most of his work and received friends and lesser

people has been brilliantly discussed, in particular by Wiseman 1981/94 and Wallace-Hadrill 1994. The emotional attitudes of people to their houses have, however, it seems, been almost ignored in scholarship, although du Boulay recognises that 'the house is deeply linked with the identity of the family, for as the family is the principal and irreducible group of this society, so the house in which the family lives is the chief stronghold of those values which are basic to that society' (du Boulay 1994: 17). It is 'a sanctuary from the troubles which its members find in the outer community' (du Boulay 1974: 19, cf. 38). This exploration of the broad context of the phenomenon we are investigating is essential: the finished essay will be the 'tip of the iceberg' but must rest on a solid, unseen substratum.

Searching

The next step is to gather sources, beginning perhaps with those cited by the moderns and expanding the search, but also dipping into others which might turn out to be rich. For this stage you need the best accessible library. Reading of sources and moderns might proceed hand-in-hand.

No two people will conduct the exploration in anything like the same way. The account given here is not the best or classic recipe, but merely an account of how I proceeded on a particular occasion. It shows the false starts and the personal idiosyncrasies that you might expect.

It is in the nature of Roman social history that we have to go all over the place to find our sources. Our reconstructions tend to be a patchwork of all sorts of written texts from many periods and areas. (Saller 1994 is a good example.) We must be conscious of the risks involved. When can we believe a politician or advocate? Are lawyers telling us what the law said should happen or what actually did happen? Is a moralist giving us an observation of how people actually behaved, or is he inventing in order to preach an effective sermon? Or is he just repeating a moral point made ages before by a Greek philosopher? Does a statement by an early Christian writer tell the truth about polytheist practices and, if so, does it apply to his own time or centuries earlier? How much of Roman society gets a look-in in our upper-class literature?

'Always verify your references'

We might begin by following up the sources which Saller uses to substantiate his point. His other two *Digest* references show other contexts in which a lawyer might define 'house', *domus*. Alfenus Varus (*cos* 39 BC) considers the rule that a slave-owner might take slaves duty-free between Sicily and Italy if he was 'going home'. It would be necessary to consider whether he was a native of Sicily or Italy and his home might be defined as where he kept his records, administered his affairs and had his 'seat' (dwelling) (*D* 50.16.203, *vii digests*).

Ulpian at *D* 47.10.5. pr.-5, *lvi on the Praetor's Edict* is more to our purpose: he says the Sullan law on contempt (or insults and injuries) covers suits for forcible entry of the plaintiff's *domus*:

> By house (*domus*) we ought to understand not ownership of the house, but domicile (*domicilium*). So whether someone has lived in his/her own house or in a rented one or (sc. in someone else's house) free of charge or as a guest, this law will apply.

Now for some literary sources. In the fourth *Speech against Catiline* (delivered in 63 BC, reworked and circulated *c.* 60), in a highly-coloured pathetic passage alluding to the conspirators' attempts to murder him during his morning reception, Cicero refers to the *domus* as a universal refuge, *commune perfugium*, that is the place which was agreed to be the normal refuge for each individual.

> I am the consul for whom neither the forum . . . nor the Campus (site of elections) . . . nor the Senate House . . . nor house, the common refuge of all, nor bed, the place granted us for repose, nor this seat of honour have ever been free from ambush and peril of death.
>
> (*Cat.* 4.2)

Saller's other two Cicero references refer to a well-established principle of law. Cicero inveighs against Vatinius for having as tribune, sent a civil servant

> to drag Bibulus from his house by force (*domo vi extraheret*) so that a right which has always been observed for private citizens – that their house could be a place of exile – was not allowed to a consul when you were tribune.

> (*Vat.* 22)

This one takes a bit of disentangling. The reference is to an abortive attempt to put the consul in prison (Cass. Dio 38.6.6; Pocock (1967) 101–4; Wiseman 1994a: 371. This was an exercise of the tribune's right to coerce (Berger 1953 *sv. Tribuni plebis*; cf. Cic. *Laws* 3.20. For Vatinius' previous attempt see Millar 1998: 129–31)). Now, exile, *exsilium*, could be regarded as a refuge for avoiding the death penalty (Cic. *Caec.* 100: *perfugium*): I take it that Cicero means that a person who never left his house was as protected as one who had fled abroad to escape punishment or prosecution. *Exsilium* may be used concretely as a *place* of foreign exile (*TLL* v 2. 1490): Cicero's usage to describe a refuge in Rome remains bold. He claims that a tribune (or magistrate?) could not have brought such a citizen to trial. We may query this claim that there was an option of a sort of internal exile, given the source. For a trial-lawyer or a politician (Cicero was eminent as both) was trained to put a spin on facts, customs and laws. And the speech against Vatinius (56 BC) is an invective against a hostile witness delivered by a defending counsel in a highly political case, in which his own reputation was involved. So we may be inclined to be sceptical about Cicero's claim here. But we shall need to think about the author, nature, context and possible biases or reticences of all the bits of data we are looking at.

Saller's second citation, of the passage in Cicero's speech to the priests (57 BC) pleading for the restoration of his Palatine house (confiscated and razed to the ground and the site dedicated to the Goddess of Liberty by his enemy Clodius) again appeals to tradition:

> Did your splendid Goddess of Liberty cast my divine *Penates* and household *Lares* out so that she might move in as to a

captured dwelling? What is holier and more strongly fortified by all religious awe than the house of each and every citizen? (*Quid est sanctius, quid omni religione munitius quam domus unius cuiusque civium?*) Here are the altars, here the hearths, here the *Penates*, here the sacred things, reverence, rituals are contained. This refuge is so holy for everyone that it is never right (*fas*) to snatch anyone away (*abripi*) from there.

(On his house 109)

Now we have arrived at one of the two canonical texts for our theme. It is here that the standard commentary, Nisbet 1939:162, (citing also the 'less definite' *Cat.* 4.2) says:

What might at first seem to be only a rhetorical outburst has legal approval in Gaius, *dig.* 2.4.18. . . . Similarly the principle, 'A man's house is his castle' is not merely to be found in the fervid oratory of Pitt's speech on the Excise Bill ('The poorest man may in his cottage bid defiance to all the force of the Crown. . . . The storms may enter, the rain may enter – but the King of England cannot enter: all his forces dare not cross the threshold of the ruined tenement'.), but from the side of sober law has the support of Coke and (with qualification) of Blackstone.

(Nisbet 1939: 162)

This resonant passage from Pitt deserves to be followed up, or at least it was irresistible to me. (Chasing Nisbet's references, which lack the pointers which moderns find indispensable, took a disproportionate time, but was very enjoyable. The Elder Nisbet, writing before the Second World War, assumed that all his readers would know he meant the Elder Pitt (Lord Chatham), not the Younger. This was not immediately obvious to me.)[4]

Chasing concepts

Here, already, are a number of leads. We might categorise the themes so far as:

    i   definitions,

    ii   juristic contexts in which the house figures,

    iii religious ideas.

These are not watertight compartments: it should be said that law and religion are intertwined for Romans. In practice, a trip to the library may involve dipping into the evidence in all three areas. I present an artificially tidy account here, excising mention of books or articles which turned out to have nothing helpful for this project.

What is a house?

Definitions are of great importance in law, as in history. Jurists were concerned with the question 'What counts as a person's *domus*?' in various contexts, as we have seen in three texts. Other relevant passages may be found in the *Vocabularium* under *domus* and *domicilium*.[5] It is clear that the lawyers took *domus* in a broad sense as where someone actually lived. (See, for instance, *D* 11.5.1.2, 48.5.9 (8), Pap., on the law which made it a crime to provide a house for the commission of adultery; cf. *D* 39.2.4.5.)

    For people with more than one house, it was sometimes difficult to be sure which was the 'domicile'. In the Principate, senators who were also provincial magnates were held to have two, in their native country and Rome (Berger 1953 sv. *Domicilium*). Jurists might rule that the husband's house counted as the 'residence of the marriage', *domicilium matrimoni* (*D* 23.2.5 Pomp., cf. 25.3.1.2, Ulp.), so that would count for both husband and wife, but sons-in-power could have a domicile separate from the father's (*D* 50.1.3–4, Ulp.). Often the jurists are concerned with 'in which jurisdiction?' (*D* 50.1.3–10, 27; *CJ* 10.40 (39)) rather than 'which house?', but even so, the degree to which a house was 'equipped' might provide evidence of legal residence. In the Augustan adultery law (*c.* 18 BC), it was relevant if the father caught daughter in the act in his house (and irrelevant if the daughter lived there or not) or in that of his son-in-law: the father (with some further qualifications) could then legally kill the adulterers. But *domus* had to be understood as domicile, as in the Sullan law on contempt or insult. The daughter was committing a worse offence if she took a lover into the house where her father lived than into another which he merely owned (*D* 48.5.23 (22).2 Pap., 48.5.24 (23).2–3, Ulp.; *Coll.* 4.2.3). The husband might in some circumstances kill the lover (but not the wife) caught in the act in his own house (but not in that of his father-in-law) (*D* 48.5.25 (24) pr., Macer; cf. 26 (25).2, 30 (29) pr., Ulp.). The connection of father or husband with the house is important for their 'privileges'. No discussion survives on whether rented or borrowed accommodation qualified: I assume it did. Note that adultery was an insult and injury to 'the house', a word which might include family (*Coll.* 4.11.1, Pap.: 'iniuriam laesae domus').

Juristic contexts

Relevant material occurs in a variety of juristic contexts. All of these, despite the technical bias of the sources, offer a good deal of human interest. The cumulative effect is important for our exploration.

'Insult and injury'

Before Augustus' adultery law, the dictator Sulla's law on contempts or insults, of 81 BC (*lex Cornelia de iniuriis*) allowed prosecution of anyone who forced entry into your dwelling, as it did if he beat you up.

> The Cornelian Law on Contempts applies to the person who wishes to sue for contempts on account of the fact that he alleges that . . . his house was entered by force. . . . By house (*domus*) we ought to understand not ownership of the house, but domicile (*domicilium*). So whether someone has lived in his or her own house or in a rented one or (sc. in someone else's house; cf. 39.2.4.5, Ulp. *i on the Praetor's Edict*) free of charge or as a guest, this law will apply. What if someone lives in a villa or in a suburban park (*horti*)? The ruling should be the same. And if the owner (*dominus*) has let a farm and an attack is made on it, the tenant-farmer will sue, not the owner. But if entrance is made on a farm belonging to someone else which is cultivated

for the *dominus* (something may have dropped out here), Labeo says the owner of the farm does not have the right to sue under the Cornelian Law, because he cannot have his domicile everywhere, that is throughout all his villas. I think this law applies to every dwelling (*habitatio*), in which the father of the household (*paterfamilias*) lives, even though he does not have his domicile there. Let us postulate that he is spending time in Rome for the sake of study: he certainly does not have his domicile in Rome, but still it must be said that if his house is entered by force, the Cornelian Law applies. So the only places to which it will not apply are short-term rented rooms (*meritoria*) or overnight stopping-places (*stabula*, for travellers and their horses): it will apply to people who inhabit a place for more than a moment, even if they do not have their domicile there.

(*D* 47.10.5. pr.–5, Ulp. *lvi on the Praetor's Edict*)

There is also a Cornelian Act on Contempts. It introduced an action where the plaintiff had been struck or beaten or his home violently entered. The word 'home' includes someone's own house in which he lives, or one which he rents, or has free of charge, or even one where he is a guest.

(Just. *Inst.* 4.4.7.8, tr. Birks and Grant)

Such misbehaviour was also covered by earlier edicts of praetors (*D* 47.2.21.7, 47.10.23). *Iniuria* in general had occurred in the fifth-century BC *Twelve Tables* (Gaius *Inst.* 3.223, Just. *Inst.* 4.4.7). It might also be insult if someone broke down your door (*D* 47.2.54 pr., Paul *xxxix on the Praetor's Edict*). A would-be surreptitious burglar might be charged with contempt if he had not got as far as stealing anything. Lawyers also envisage culprits who got together a band of supporters to break into a house (*D* 47.10.7.5, Ulp. *lvii on the Praetor's Edict*). Lesser offences, which fell short of entering, might also be taken seriously: for instance a woman who sealed up the house of a debtor in his absence might be prosecuted for 'insult' (*D* 47.10.20, Mod.). Iavolenus held (against Labeo) that it might be insult to throw things down into a neighbour's house or to allow smoke to rise into it (*D* 47.10.44, Iav. *ix ex post. Lab.*).

Breaking and entering

Burglary similarly trespasses against the rights of the householder. Victims nowadays commonly say that they feel it as an attack on them personally. Housebreaking, for the Romans, was worse if committed at night: the fifth-century BC *Twelve Tables* (the codification of customary law) exonerated the killer of a nocturnal thief (sc. in the house) or of one caught in daylight with a weapon (*XII Tab.*, M. Crawford 1996b: ii 609–11). That this is still topical is demonstrated by the trial of a British householder for murder (Tony Martin, in 2000) for shooting a nocturnal intruder who subsequently died of his wounds.

Cicero makes it plain that the law means burglars caught in the house:

> Surely the slaves of M. Tullius . . . did not come to rob the house of P. Fabius at night? I think not. Surely they did not come to rob in daylight and defend themselves with a weapon? We cannot say they did. . . . The *Twelve Tables* forbid a thief, that is a robber and bandit, to be killed in daylight; though you catch a definite enemy inside your walls, unless he defends himself with a weapon, they say, even if he has come with a weapon, unless he uses that weapon and fights back, you shall not kill him; but if he fights back, *ENDOPLORATO*, that is, shout aloud that some people may hear and come together. What more could be added to this mercifulness, which does not even allow a man in his own house to defend his own life with the sword without witnesses and arbitrators?
>
> (*Speech for Tullius* 48, 50, 71 BC; cf. Lintott 1999/1968: 13)

Cicero is making an argument in a court case about endemic violence in the Italian countryside, but the focus on the house must be right. Schoolboys of his time learned the *Tables* by heart, so his glosses must not contradict other people's memories.

Burglary was not so bad if no-one was in the house (*D* 47.2.53, Ulp. *xxxviii on the Praetor's Edict*). The Romans were conscious of the suffering and possible terror of the victim as well as of the loss of property.

In Rome an alleged thief's own house benefited from the general inviolability: there were ancient rituals to be observed if a person who alleged he had been robbed were to search it, against the will of the occupant. (*XII Tab.*, M. Crawford 1996b: ii 615–7; Gaius *Inst.* 3.192, cf. 188; Daube 1937; Crifò 1961: 115; Kelly 1966: 143, 161–2). This method lapsed and the custom was not fully understood by later, rationalising lawyers. In later, praetorian law, refusal to allow a search could be met by a legal action (*actio prohibiti*). If, on the other hand, the occupant consented, an informal search with witnesses could be performed, as in the amusing but probably late story told about a sow 'liberated' by the slaves of Tremellius (subsequently called 'the Sow') (Macrobius *Saturnalia* 1.6.30; Daube 1937: 53–60). Daube draws on Hebrew, Greek and Roman literature to show that 'intruding into another's house is regarded as a serious offence all over the world' (Daube 1937: 48–9) and discusses how custom dealt with the problem of discovering stolen goods in the house of a thief, an accomplice or an innocent party.

EXCURSUS: EARLY MODERN COMMON LAW

Here we may look up the great common-law authority to whom Nisbet alludes, Sir William Blackstone (1723–80):

> Burglary, or nocturnal housebreaking, *burgi latrocinium*, . . . has always been looked upon as a very heinous offence: not only because of the abundant terror that it naturally carries with it, but also as it is a forcible invasion and disturbance of that right of habitation; which every individual might acquire even in a state of nature; an invasion which in such a state would be sure to be punished with death unless the assailant were the stronger. . . . And the law of England has so particular and tender a regard to the immunity of a man's house, that it stiles it his castle, and will never suffer it to be violated with impunity: agreeing herein with the sentiments of antient Rome, as expressed in the words of Tully; '*quid enim (enim* inserted by Blackstone) *est sanctius, quid omni religione munitius quam domus unius cuiusque civium?*' ('[For] what is holier and more strongly fortified by all religious awe than the house of each and every

citizen?') For this reason, no doors can in general be broken open to execute any civil process; though in criminal causes, the public safety supersedes the private.

> (Blackstone 1765–9: iv 223; spelling
> his, my translation added)

Blackstone's doctrine is based on Coke's (1797: 62–5), but the excursus on English and Roman attitudes is not in the model. Note that there are two areas of concern: the violation of the house by a burglar and the need for duly constituted authorities sometimes to gain access to a person's house, where force is allowed in a criminal case, but not in a civil suit.

Both legal authorities take a line on domicile comparable with that of the Romans. The house covered by the law on house-breaking must, they say, be a 'mansion-house', which includes rooms in a college/inn of court (cf. Ulpian on students) or room/lodging in any private house).

> . . . no distant barn, warehouse or the like, are under the same privileges, nor looked upon as a man's castle of defence: nor is a breaking open of houses where no man resides, and which therefore for the time being are not mansion-houses, attended with the same circumstances of midnight terror.
>
> (Blackstone 1765–9: iv 224; cf. *stabula* etc.)

Elsewhere, Sir Edward Coke (1552–1634) has an interesting excursus:

> . . . any may assemble his friends and neighbours to keep his house against those that come to rob, or kill him, or to offer him violence in it, and is by construction excepted out of this act: and the sherif, etc., ought not to deal with him upon this act: for a man's house is his castle, *et domus sua cuique est tutissimum refugium* (and each man's house is his safest refuge); for where shall a man be safe, if it be not in his house? and in this sense it is truly said, *Armaque in armatos sumere jura sinunt* (The laws allow us to take up arms against armed men).
>
> (1797: 162; spelling his, bracketed translations mine)

A thief commits an extreme infringement of an individual's rights.

Summons: in ius vocatio

So much for entry by intruders with criminal intent. But how could you get someone out of his house for perfectly legal reasons? Both private citizens and the public authorities might need to do this. The *Twelve Tables* began with rules for summoning people to court. The emphasis here and in later sources is on face-to-face contact in a public place:

> If he (i.e. anyone) summons to a pre-trial, ?he (the defendant) is to go;? if he does not go, he (the plaintiff) is to call to witness; then he is to take him.
> If he (the defendant) delays or drags feet, he (the plaintiff) is to lay a hand on.
>
> (tr. M. Crawford 1996b: ii 579, with 584–6;
> cf. e.g. Horace *Satires* 1.9.74–8;
> Kaser 1966: 47–9; Kelly 1966: 6–12)

In the later juristic passage referred to by Nisbet (which turns out to be the key text for English lawyers), we find:

> Most authorities have held that it is not allowed that anyone should be summoned to court from his house, because the house is the safest refuge and shelter for everyone (*quia domus tutissimum cuique refugium atque receptaculum sit*) and a person who summons him thence appears to use force.
>
> (*D* 2.4.18, Gaius *i on the Twelve Tables*;
> cf. Berger 1953 *sv. Domus*; Polak 1946: 27–8;
> Crifò 1961: 114, adding Quintilian *Inst.* 7.8.6)

That Gaius mentions this rule in a commentary on the *Tables* may suggest he thought the prohibition went back to that time. But it does not occur in the extant fragments. Polak's view that the taboo was so strong that it was taken for granted in the fifth century and not explicitly stated is persuasive (Polak 1946: 253).

This is confirmed:

> If a person were to enter someone else's house against the will of
> the owner, although he is issuing a summons, Ofilius (A. Ofilius,
> late republican authority on the Edict) says an action for con-
> tempt lies against him.
>
> (*D* 47.10.23 Paul *iv on the Praetor's Edict*)

A person could be summoned from his doorway (*D* 2.4.20, if the text
is right), as he could from a bath or theatre (communal spaces), clearly
because there he was not exactly inside but in a '*liminal*' position.
The religious nature of the prohibition is supported by other rules that
a priest could not be issued with a summons while he was sacrificing,
nor anyone when he was in a place from which he could not move
because of its *religio*, taboo (*D* 2.4.2, Ulp. *v on the Praetor's Edict*).

There had to be exceptions. Paul allows a summons sometimes
to be issued to a person in his own house, but adds 'No-one ought to
be dragged out of his own house' (*de domo sua extrahi*) (*D* 2.4.21
and 50.17.103, *i on the Praetor's Edict*). Dragging implies an unwilling
party: we shall see this word repeatedly. A person could allow entry
to his house so that the summons could be issued. If he deliberately
stayed at home to avoid being summoned, the praetor might grant his
adversary the right to seize his goods (*D* 2.4.19, Paul i *on the Praetor's
Edict*). A decree of M. Aurelius in the second century AD on violence
or force, *vis*, (*D* 48.7.7, cf. 4.2.13), which does not specifically mention
the house (but only entering on property), lays down that if creditors
resorted to self-help against debtors, not going through the courts, they
might make themselves liable to the law against 'force'.

Clearly, the proper authorities might also need to summon people
from their houses into court. If the praetor himself needed to call
someone to court, he must ensure that his agent delivered the notice
politely (*verecunde*) and that the person was not dragged from his
house (*extrahi de domo sua*) (*D* 39.2.4.5, Ulp. *i on the Praetor's Edict*;
Polak 1946: 267). This continued to be a live issue: the emperor
Constantine threatened with dire penalties any imperial officer who
dragged a respectable married woman from her dwelling to a public
place (*CTh* 1.22.1, 11 Jan. 316).

The praetor forebade people to lie low (*latitare*) with the deliberate intent of escaping legal action (defrauding creditors or failing to carry out a duty to free a slave (*D* 40.5.1) etc.) on pain of having their goods adjudicated to the plaintiff (Berger 1953: 537; Kelly 1966: 10–11; the *Vocabularium* has a long list of passages). *Latitare* was distinguished from being absent from home for good reason. Usually someone would 'avoid making himself available' by skulking in his house: it was, however, possible to go out in public and still avoid the person who wanted to sue you, by dodging behind columns (*D* 42.4.6.13, 42.5.36 Ulp.)! All these passages take it for granted that a person could successfully lie concealed at home and that strong measures would be needed to deter him. Although Cicero might regard it as shameful to stay at home when political duties beckoned, Ulpian concedes that there might be many good reasons to hide: the cruelty of a tyrant, violence from foreign foes, rebellion. It was only bad from a legal point of view when you did it to defraud some specific person (*D* 42.4.6.13; Treggiari 1999: 42). Even then, it might be a good idea for a daughter to make herself unavailable to a father who could not be trusted with her dowry (*D* 24.3.22.6: note that the householder here is female). Such people were sometimes in practice dragged out of their houses, as Cicero claims Oppianicus was by an unscrupulous official, when an alleged accomplice confessed to a murder charge (*Clu.* 39; Alexander 1990: 138).

For magistrates to have the right to arrest criminals in their homes might seem unsurprising: we may compare what Blackstone says about this being necessary. Apuleius in his novel gives a vivid description of his hero being arrested (by the local officials, not the Roman governor), in a house where he is a guest, in a provincial town in Greece. The charge is triple murder. Lucius thinks he has killed three men when he was drunk the night before, but the whole thing is an elaborate practical joke. The description suggests how frightening it would be to fall foul of authority:

> Meanwhile the double doors were being shaken and repeated shouts rang through the portals. There was no delay: the house was opened up as a crowd broke in and the whole place was filled with the magistrates, their officers and a miscellaneous mob.

Immediately two lictors, at the orders of the magistrates, began to lay hand upon me and drag me, though I did not offer resistance.

(Metamorphoses 3.1; cf. Millar 1981b:
70–2, Gleason 1999: 295–7)

But the delicacy with which the Romans approached such matters may be illustrated by what happened to the Catilinarians condemned as conspirators by the Senate in 63: they were kept under house arrest by reputable men, the most eminent, the patrician and praetor P. Cornelius Lentulus Sura, being entrusted to his kinsman, P. Cornelius Lentulus Spinther (who was aedile). The consul Cicero himself went to escort Sura to the place of execution, while praetors dealt with the others (Sallust *Cat.* 47.3–4, 55.2).

Respect for the house continued well into the Principate: in AD 16 Piso tried to bring a friend of the emperor's mother Julia Augusta into court over an unpaid debt. Urgulania contemptuously removed herself to the emperor's house on the Palatine and ignored his efforts to summon her. The Augusta, according to Tacitus, claimed that Piso was 'violating and diminishing her (the Augusta)' and Tacitus himself approves Piso's daring in trying to 'drag her (Urgulania) to court' *(Annals* 2.34, 4.21; Garnsey 1970: 187–94). It is unclear how far Piso went, but he did not succeed. (The matter was settled by the Augusta out of court.) To my mind, the text shows Tacitus expecting the Augusta to exploit ancient ideas, now expressed in terms of the householder's honour rather than of the sanctity of the dwelling of household gods, and the defendant expecting to be covered by law, as a guest in the palace, and by the influence of the emperor's mother, more effectively than by law alone in her own house *(pace* Goodyear (1981) in his commentary).

It is already clear that all sorts of dwellings and all sorts of householders (daughters-in-power, suspected receivers of stolen goods) were protected by law in various contexts. Polak posed the question, 'Was only the Roman *domus* protected, or the *insula* as well?' (Polak 1946: 266) and decided that Ulpian's ruling *(D* 47.10.5.2, above p. 83) was wide enough to cover the apartment-block *(insula)* as well as the detached house. 'One thing is certain: the protection of the dwelling was never coupled with the right of possession.'[6]

EXCURSUS: EARLY MODERN COMMON LAW

The English lawyers harked back to the words of Gaius (quoting them in a slightly altered form). The idea that a man's house is his castle is invoked in the context of burglary or threatened violence, or when someone wishes to sue him, or when the authorities want to arrest him, summon him to court or search the premises.

Although (in spite of what Pitt said), the king's officials could force an entry if need arose, even their rights were restricted by proper procedures, and the householder was protected against a fellow-subject.

> ... his house is his castle, *et (c) domus sua est unicuique tutissimum refugium* (and each and every man's house is his safest refuge: the Gaius passage). 2. (d) The house of a man has privilege to protect him against arrest by virtue of process of law at the suit of a subject, *vide* (see) Semaine's case ... a man's house is his castle and his defence. ...
>
> > (Coke 1826: vi 155 (Bowles' case, in the thirteenth year of James I), bracketed translation and comment mine)

or:

> That the house of every one is to him as his (a) castle and fortress, as well for his defence against injury and violence, as for his repose ... and the reason of all this is, because *domus sua cuique est tutissimum refugium* (and each man's house is his safest refuge: the Gaius passage).
>
> > (Coke 1826: iii 186, (Semayne's case, in the second year of James I; bracketed translation and comment mine))

Although cases buttressed the argument, it seems to rely chiefly not on common law, but on Gaius' *dictum* and on a widespread sentiment. Max Radin suggests that in the seventeenth century the inviolability of the house was thought of as a right common to all mankind, and that it may have been Pitt who inspired the common phrase, 'The

Englishman's house is his castle'. Freedom from arbitrary search and arrest was (with trial by jury) essential to the freedoms demanded by the parliamentarians of the Civil War (Radin 1937a: 419, 423–7).

Similarly, the American colonists inveighed against searches imposed by the British government:

> Thus our Houses, and even our Bedchambers are exposed to be ransacked, our Boxes, Trunks and Chests broke open, ravaged and plundered. . . .
>
> *(Votes* 1773: 12)

> common law . . . ever regarded a man's house as his castle, or a place of perfect security.
>
> *(Letters* 1768: ix 75)

The right of domestic security was enshrined in the Fourth Amendment:

> The right of the people to be secure in their persons, houses, papers and effects, against unreasonable searches and seizures, shall not be violated, and no Warrants shall issue, but upon probable cause, supported by Oath or affirmation, and particularly describing the place to be searched, and the persons or things to be seized.
>
> *(Constitutions* 1982)

Radin concludes that eighteenth-century views had their roots in Roman law rather than common law, and that Pitt's rhetorical sentence is not an accurate statement of English law.

What it is, I suggest, is an appeal to an emotional belief which resonated for the English, for American colonists and for Romans. Discussions in English evoke the Middle Ages and suggest ancient traditions (including the Roman with which every educated man was acquainted) just as Roman speakers of the first century BC evoke the *Twelve Tables*. What is missing in English is the idea of religious sanctity. Rather, we find a stress on the rights of the individual.

Exsilium

Exile began as a privilege in archaic times and later became a penalty. You may remember that Cicero *Against Vatinius* alluded to (virtual) exile in one's house. He seems to be thinking that a man might renounce the rights and be exempt from the duties and liabilities of a citizen, but take refuge in his own house instead of fleeing abroad. The *OCD* under 'Exile' leads one to Crifò's book, which has an invaluable chapter on exile, house and asylum (Crifò 1961: 109–24) and in turn refers us to Polak. Some of their findings have been incorporated above. Both authors trace the inviolability of the house to the earliest times, when the ancestors of Rome switched from nomadism to a settled life, and the city eventually arose (as the Romans themselves held) from a clustering of houses. The family was self-governing, with its own domestic cult and discipline; the individual had the right to change domicile to another city if he wished (e.g. to escape a blood-feud if he had killed someone): exile was a privilege. Themes of home and country, home and exile, are intertwined in the literary sources, sometimes one contrasted with the other, sometimes made equivalent (Quintilian *Inst.* 3.6.25).

Crifò shows that a house often was a 'castle'. (We could look at Cic. *Mil.* 18, where Pompey 'protected himself, not by right of laws and lawcourts, but by the door and walls of his house'; Cic. *Vat.* 22.) Examples could be multiplied from the disturbances of the late Republic (e.g. Cicero's matter-of-fact instructions to his wife to put the house in a defensible state: *F* 144/14.18.2). People threatened with violence commonly take refuge in a nearby house (Sallust *Hist.* fr. 2. 42 Maurenbrecher, 45 Reynolds; McGushin 1994: 50 (tr.), 209 (comm.)).

Crifò argues, however, that lesser men than Pompey or Bibulus or a Caecilia Metella might not be able to take advantage of their legal privilege (Cic. *Rosc. Am.* 27). But Roscius took refuge with Metella only after he had lost his own house. Livy envisages the informer Aebutius finding adequate protection in the house of a client of the consul, clearly less prestigious accomodation than that arranged for his lover, the prostitute Hispala, who was put up in an apartment attached to the house of the consul's mother-in-law (with its usual direct access to the outside world being closed off for safety)

(Livy 39.14.2–3). Such people (like Urgulania) no doubt expected that the well-built and well-staffed house of a prestigious patron would afford the best protection, but we cannot deduce that the poorer house would give none. The practicalities might simply be different. What would happen if an upper-class Roman, in person or through his staff, wanted to take legal action against the fuller who had lost his toga in the wash? Could he force his way into the rented attic in a slum street in the Subura with impunity? Or would he be met with a shout for help and a shower of stones and abuse from indignant neighbours?

Folk-justice: Convicium, occentare, flagitare / flagitatio, paraclausithyron

Like the *Twelve Tables'* rules on delivering a summons, folk custom seems to presuppose that no-one could enter a house without an invitation. When a Roman of the upper classes was ready to receive his (or her) clients, the great double-doors were ceremonially opened, a tacit invitation into the reception rooms. Access was controlled by slaves.

The doorway becomes a focal point for those not admitted. Someone seeking redress could stand outside it all day (Plautus *Mostell.* 767–8). If a person considered himself unjustly treated, he could dress in mourning, wait outside the offender's house and then dog his footsteps through all the public areas of the city (Lintott 1999/1968: 16–17; see, e.g. Elder Seneca *Controversies* 10.1). Abuse of this custom (because it ruined the reputation of the person followed) could be contempt or insult (Elder Seneca *Controversies* 10.1, D 47.10.15.27). An obscurer but similar custom, *obvagulare* ('to bawl, raise a hullabaloo'), involved a person on whose behalf someone failed to give evidence, going to the latter's house and shouting every other day (Festus *Glossaria Latina* 262 Lindsay, *XII Tab.*, M. Crawford 1996b: ii 621; cf. Radin 1937b).

Convicium, reviling an opponent with the worst possible insults (often reciprocal), took place even in the Senate as well as on the speakers' platform outside: Veyne perceptively remarks that this is the senatorial version of a popular *genre* of abuse (Veyne 1983: 10).

95

It might be done face-to-face or not. (There are splendid examples in Cicero, for instance an abusive dialogue between Clodius and Cicero in *A* 1.16/16.9–10; see too Plut. *Caes*. 8.5) A person's house was an obvious place to deliver a tirade if he was unobtainable, just as you would send a legal notice there if you could not have it delivered personally (*D* 39.2.4.5 etc.). 'Rough music' or 'charivari' in Rome as in later societies (cf. e.g. N.Z. Davis 1975) includes chanting and noise outside the house. Scholars who have explored these fascinating forms of self-help (Usener 1901; Fraenkel 1961: 49–50; Kelly 1966: 21–3; Lintott 1999/1968: ch. 1; Veyne 1983) show how a man might be followed silently (Elder Seneca *Controversies* 10.1.1, 6, (Quintilian) *Decl. Min.* 316) or with insults and hissing (Cic. *A* 2.18/38.1); or stopped in the street, surrounded and subjected to rhythmic chants by protesters. (Plautus *Pseud.* 357–70 parodies this, with the victim, the pimp Ballio, accepting each insulting epithet or allegation.) If he shut himself up in his house, the chanting (*occentare*, 'to sing against someone') or repetitive demand (*flagitatio* – the verb *flagitare* is more commonly used in the sources than the abstract noun by which moderns describe the custom) might take place outside his door. In one comedy by Plautus, the usurer, an unsympathetic character, chants, 'Give me the interest, give back the interest'. (*Mostell.* 603–5, 768, cf. *Curc.* 145–55; Plut. *Caes.* 11.1; Veyne 1983: 21).

Conviciari was often done at night (when the householder would be at home and wanting to sleep) and might be performed solo ((Quintilian) *Decl. Min.* 364), though the expectation was that neighbours would rally from surrounding streets. It was usually the instrument of the oppressed against the powerful, who would lose face when the racket came to public attention. To be publicly exposed as having (allegedly) wronged someone was shaming in a society where honour, the reputation of being a good man and the community's acceptance of the claim, was important, both to elected politicians and to private citizens.

The crowd might back up their verbal harrying by piling charcoal against the doors and setting fire to them (Plautus *Persa* 569, *Merc.* 405–11). We have examples in the late Republic (all described from the point of view of the householder) of groups of men (allegedly led or inspired by *popularis* politicians) 'besieging' the houses of their political opponents or sometimes 'attacking' them, throwing stones or firebrands from outside (Lintott 1999/1968: 8; e.g. Cic. *A* 75/4.3.2–3; cf. Lintott 1967 on Cic. *QF* 15/2.11.1, 5). (Stone-throwing is often mentioned without full description of the circumstances, but sometimes clearly means pelting people in the open: e.g. Cic. *Sulla* 15, *Sest.* 2, 27, 34, 53, 77.) Bombardment of doors – to the point when they let in the light – is attested by a wax-tablet from Herculaneum, where the wealthy L. Cominius Primus, owner of the House of the Bicentenary, claims that his house has been stoned by several named slaves of Caria Longina and others. The document is formally witnessed and was obviously intended to be produced in court in a private suit (Arangio-Ruiz 1948/1974).

These violent demonstrations seem to be in the tradition of popular justice: *flagitatio* is connected with words for burning. In later ages, demonstrators would naturally make their feelings felt by throwing stones and breaking windows, which make a satisfactory noise. But the great Roman houses seem to have presented a blank wall to the street: the doors were the only vulnerable part, and both battering and fire (reverberating noise and stench) would have an effect on those within.

We should try to visualise the great Roman town house, but the surviving archaeological evidence is disappointing. Our understanding of the houses of people of local importance and comparative wealth in Pompeii and Herculaneum is relatively full, and it is clear that there only doorways and shop-fronts broke the façade at ground-floor level. But it is inadvisable to equate the residences of the great men in Rome itself with these. The senatorial houses on the slopes of the Palatine in Rome are documented only by basements, so that we do not know what they looked like to someone who approached them. Pleasure villas in the country or at the seaside are in a different category. What is clear from the literary sources is how people focused on the door as an imposing feature which marked the transition from the public street to private property.

Cicero describes the wronged citizens of Lampsacus (on the Hellespont) attacking the lodging of the legate Verres, after his companion Rubrius had provoked a violent disturbance in the house of his provincial host by asking for the daughter of the house to join the drinking party. He gives a vivid account of how they battered the doors with stones and iron tools, put timber and brushwood around them and set fire to them (*Verr.* 2.1.69). This demonstration by non-Romans (which Cicero claims was led by leading townsmen who thought that Rome would not object to an attack on an official in defence of the chastity of their children!) is described along the same lines as similar actions by Romans.

Cicero in the next paragraph in fact recalls a certain C. Fabius Hadrianus, whose avarice and cruelty as governor allegedly made him so unpopular with Roman citizens at Utica (in Africa) that they burned his house down with him in it (82 BC) – and everyone thought it served him right, so no action was taken against the perpetrators (*Verr.* 2.1.70; other sources in *MRR* ii 69). According to Cicero's deft narrative, the incidents at Utica and Lampsacus gave Verres a preview of what might have happened when he bungled a campaign against pirates when governor of Sicily (*Verr.* 2.5.92–5). While the news of a defeat came to Syracuse and the general slept on, a crowd gathered in the streets (*curritur, concursabat . . . multitudo, concursus atque impetus*) and then made a row outside his house. When he made a formal appearance in public at daybreak, in military dress and with the usual escort, the crowd shouted taunts about his drinking orgies and beach parties, calling his girl-friends by name and inquiring why he had not shown his face for so long. (See Nisbet 1992 for analysis of the rhetoric of this section of the speech.) This imaginative reconstruction again shows how Cicero thought *occentare* by Roman citizens worked, whether in public or at the victim's house.

Sometimes a crowd was asking a politician to take action, sometimes stigmatising what he had done. Plautus highlights the use of popular methods of obtaining justice or penalising the offender in private life. The alleged vices which provoked such demonstrations include sexual offences (violation of the reputation of respectable people, flaunting one's orgies with a whole bunch of disreputable women before the eyes of shocked citizens), financial oppression (Fabius, the man who failed to pay Plautus' usurer); lack of attention to duty; dishonesty (Catullus 42); cruelty. Both private and public wrongs could be dealt with in this way.

Cicero himself was the object of *flagitatio* on his return from exile in 57 BC, when a grain shortage led to demonstrations (including stone-throwing) as the Senate met. Then there was a gathering of people during the night, *operarum illa concursatio nocturna* (clearly at Cicero's house) which, at Clodius' instigation, demanded grain from him (Cic. *Dom.* 11–16).

There are many descriptions of the damage done in 58 BC to Cicero's Palatine house (after he went into exile) by supporters of Clodius, with the consuls allegedly conniving (e.g. Cic. *Dom.* 113; cf. 60–62, *Har. resp.* 15, *Mil.* 87). One gets the idea sometimes that the crowd looted, fired (not accidentally, says Cicero) and destroyed it, not so much because incited by Cicero's senatorial enemies (as he wants us to believe), but because the crowd wanted to demonstrate its own disapproval of what he had done in 63 BC. When Cicero, as consul, presided over the execution without trial of Catilinarians whom he proved to the Senate were guilty of treasonous conspiracy, he had over-ridden citizens' rights to due process and appeal. Those who put the sovereignty of the People above the authority of the Senate were naturally outraged. He could be seen as having trampled on the civil liberties of citizens. This was the charge on which Clodius drove him into exile in 58 BC.

It was in Cicero's interest on his return from exile the next year to blame a few individuals and to suggest that the Roman People (apart from a few hired thugs) were on his side throughout. Cicero is often concerned to distinguish between the followers of Clodius, who are gangs of marginal desperadoes and 'the whole Roman people', who supported him, Cicero (see e.g. Cic. *Dom.* 15.) This is a grotesque over-simplification. Clodius was tapping into sections of the urban plebs who had grievances and an agenda of their own. The destruction of Cicero's house in 58 BC could have been a much more 'grass-roots' demonstration than he allows. In Cic. *Dom.* 12 he visualises three possibilities: the *plebs* acting of its own volition, or incited by Clodius, or both at once. As has often been pointed out, the house of a politician rejected for tyrannical behaviour becomes a surrogate for the human enemy. To destroy a house deliberately was an extreme measure, a deprivation of identity and prestige for the victim, an oblit-eration of his memory for his fellow-citizens, a release of indignation and hatred. Paradoxically, this shows the symbolic and emotional importance of houses, which were normally to be respected.

A great deal of fire-imagery is associated with Clodius from the time of the scandal of the Good Goddess (late 62 BC, e.g. *Har. resp.* 4) down to his (according to Cicero) botched cremation by his supporters in 52 BC (*Mil.* 12–13, 33, 90–91; cf. Treggiari 1999: 39). Clodius is portrayed as fired by violent emotions (e.g. *Dom.* 107); he is called a flame or a firebrand. It would be appropriate if such imagery was associated with *popularis* reformers because fire was the tool which came to hand when popular protest passed from verbal taunts to displays of violence (cf. Verg. *Aeneid* 1.150). Sometimes, the fire would get out of control; often it was intended only to smoke a man out so that he would answer for his perceived misdeeds.

Often, despite Cicero's insistence that harm to people and destruction of buildings was the object, it seems likely that the crowd intended to frighten, compel or persuade. Various reactions were possible: to sit tight (fortifications were useful here, e.g. Cic. *Cat.* 1.10, *F* 144/14.18.2; we expect to hear about water for fire-fighting but do not), to try to disperse the crowd (by sending out counter-attacks (Cic. *A* 75/4.3.3)), or to come out and reason with them (like Verres at Syracuse).

The people in the house might bombard the attackers from the roof with stones or even arrows (Asc. *Mil.* 33C), with the advantage of gravity. Even a prostitute could defend her house with a hail of stones when there was an attempted break-in. Aulus Gellius, author of a literary and historical miscellany 'published' *c.* AD 180, (4.14) gives an example from a trustworthy source (the jurist C. Ateius Capito, *cos* AD 5). An aedile (A. Hostilius Mancinus, in, perhaps, 151 BC), the worse for wine, tried to get into the courtesan's house at a time when she found it inconvenient to entertain him. He was hit by a stone and complained to the authorities, but the tribunes exculpated her.

In all this, the closed door plays a key role. The crowd is on the outside, on communal ground, the object of their attentions inside his or her domicile. The householder, staff and family will find it embarrassing, difficult or even impossible to leave the house and go about business as usual. If the crowd is noisy or violent they will be harassed even if safe inside. Occasionally a 'siege' went further. When the crowd actually broke down the doors and invaded the atrium of the patrician *interrex* in 52 BC, this was shocking (Cic. *Mil.* 13, Asc.

33, 36, 43C). A taboo had been breached. Asconius emphasises the violation of the seat of a family: the mob cast down the ancestral portraits, broke the (ceremonial) bed which stood for the married status of the master and the chastity of the mistress of the house and destroyed the looms which represented her industry and frugality (and again, by implication, her virtue). Although he does not mention *Lares* here, religion is implicit.

'Friendly' demonstrations, intended to bring pressure on a householder, also took place outside his door. Supporters rallied to a politician's house. Asconius describes crowds at the beginning of 52 BC, when there was no consul, taking the consular insignia to the houses of two possible candidates, and then going off to the suburban 'park' of Pompey to shout for him as consul or dictator (Asc. 33C).

Demonstrations continued in this tradition under the Principate, when the emperor in times of upheaval might be subjected to visits which did not stop at the door (Tacitus *Histories* 1.35, 82). During the mutiny of AD 14, the emperor's adoptive son and general, Germanicus, was the victim of what Tacitus describes as a *flagitatio* which went too far. Some of the soldiers, at a time when most people were in bed, decided they wanted a standard which was kept in Germanicus' house. So they began to demand it, and, gathering at his door (*concursu*), broke it down, dragged the general out of his bed and forced him (for fear of death) to hand the standard over (*Ann.* 1.39.4).

Shut-out lovers trying to gain admission to the mistress's house serenaded the door rather than, as in more modern romantic convention about Italian or Spanish houses, the balcony. This would be an insult to any woman who was not a professional courtesan and would damage her reputation. Apuleius (*Apol.* 75), trying to show that an upper-class enemy ran what amounted to a brothel in his house, has a lurid description of young men fooling around insultingly outside day and night, pounding the door with kicks and singing songs to the windows. The literary expression of this is 'beside the closed door', *paraclausithyron* (e.g. Horace *Odes* 3.10, Ovid *Amores* 1.6, with McKeown 1989: 120–3). As Ovid neatly puts it, you could address either blandishments (*blanditiae*) or invective (*convicia*) to the door post (*Remedies for Love* 507).

If Seneca is to be believed, the sea-front at Baiae was made hideous to the philosopher by adulteresses in boats and by nocturnal sung *convicia* (*Epistles* 51.12). John Yardley (1978) has elucidated what is specifically Roman in the elegiac poets' exploitation of this theme: that the lover addresses the door (not the woman) with prayers or curses (Ovid, in a further twist, talks to the slave-doorkeeper), and that the lover is an illicit one. I would add that the incantatory mode used is reminiscent of the *flagitatio* as well as of the religious language of prayer which Yardley recognises. The well-behaved lover observes the limit set by a closed door; rowdy groups of young drunks might break it down (Cicero 1904: x.3). This is literary commonplace in Greek and Roman society, but it seems to have happened in real life too (*D* 47.2.39 pr.). Horace, in a humorous poem where he takes his leave of love, dumps a wide range of tools which could be used against doors, including torches and crowbars (*Odes* 3.26.6–8). A rhetorical exercise (Elder Seneca *Controversies* 4.3) mentions a ravisher bursting into the house of an exile in order to abduct his daughter. This was to insult him by acting as if he was helpless because he was in exile. The house symbolises the father's rights, even though he had been banished and was not living there. In real life, door-breaking came under the law on damages (*D* 9.2.27.31).

Religion

Finally, we come to the religious associations of the house. Exactly what is sacred, to use Saller's term? It is hard for many of us to realise how much regular religious observance took place in the domestic setting, where every householder was his own priest and where every family member, slave or free, would take part. It helps, perhaps, to think of modern Judaic custom of religious ceremonies at home. We may broadly contrast the Christian focus on separate churches (which replaced early house-churches) and a separate priesthood, though we must not forget that family-prayers and grace before meals have been customary in Christian homes too. Romans had their temples and official priests, but homes and temples were a natural pair.

When a city came into being, it was theoretically a good idea to prescribe legal marriage, legitimate children, holy (*sanctae*) dwellings for the store-room gods (*Penates*) and the protective *Lares* (Cic. *Republic* 5.7). In reality, all these institutions in Rome arose from prehistoric custom, not a law-giver. It is the last item that we shall examine here, the places connected with divinities.

Wachsmuth 1980 has considered the sacred quality of a dwelling from the Stone Age on. He is especially helpful on definitions. He shows that in Roman legal terms the home of a Roman was not a *locus sacer* ('sacred place', declared to be holy by the People or other authority) or *religiosus* ('religious', 'taboo', especially dedicated to the dead, like a tomb) or even in itself holy, *sanctus*, (as were city-walls and gates, *D* 1.8.1, Gaius). Things in these three categories were under divine law and could not be privately owned (*D* 1.8.6.2). But a house, of course, is privately owned. It was the holy things in it which gave it protection. Wachsmuth quotes the telling passage *D* 1.8.8 pr., Marcian.: 'A thing is holy, *sanctus*, which is defended and protected against injury by people.' (Cf. 1.8.8.1 on the alleged derivation of the word *sanctus*, which emphasises protection from violation.)

> The difference between the sacred (*sacrum*) and the holy (*sanctum*) and the taboo (*religiosum*) is splendidly expressed by Aelius Gallus (a late republican jurist): he says it is agreed that a building consecrated to a god is *sacrum*, a wall around a city is *sanctum*, a tomb with a dead person buried in it is *religiosum*.
> (Festus p. 278M)

Various things, then, (laws, city-walls etc.) fitted into the category of holy, *sancta*. This comes between the sacred (*sacra*) and the non-sacred or secular (*profana*, *D* 1.8.8, 9.3).

> Sacred places are those which are publicly dedicated ... Note that a sacred place is not the same as a *sacrarium* (shrine). A sacred place is a consecrated place, a *sacrarium* is a place in which sacred things are put. This can be even in a private building. ... We use *sancta*, correctly, of those things which are neither sacred (*sacra*) nor non-sacred (*profana*), but are secured by some sanction, for example laws ...
> (*D* 1.8.9.1–3, Ulp. *lxviii on the Praetor's Edict*)

In non-legal usage, the distinction is obscured. A look at Merguet's concordance to Cicero's speeches will show that Cicero uses *sanctus*, not only of deities, temples, city-walls, sacrosanct tribunes and so on, but of virtuous people, virtues like good faith, good things like friendship or law. Bold and wicked men violate what is *sanctum* when they murder a parent or a brother's unborn child (*Rosc. Am.* 70, *Clu.* 31) The context here is duty to family. Holy discipline, *sanctissima disciplina*, (*Phil.* 2.69) can characterise the running of a house.

The *Oxford Latin Dictionary* shows that *sanctus* is widely used, for things such as laws and obligations secured by religious sanctions (oaths, faith, duties, statutes etc.), people who hold a particular office (e.g. tribunes or ambassadors, who were inviolable); places (e.g. cities), things associated with the gods or under divine protection (mountains, rivers; shrines, tombs; festivals etc.). It can describe a god, a parent, the Senate, a state, or any virtuous person or action. The adjective derives from the verb *sancio*, 'to ratify solemnly, sanction'.

Houses may originally have been used for burial of ancestors, which in historic times took place outside the city. They certainly contained, for centuries, the food-store (*penus*) protected by the *Penates* and the *Lares* (whether represented in a shrine or not), guardians of the home, and the hearth (essential for heat and cooking) where offerings were made (e.g. Bayet 1969: 63), until at least Theodosius' prohibition in 391. Our document on this imperial ruling (*CTh* 16.10.12) is actually our most vivid listing of the details of cult: the worshipper, great or humble is not to venerate the *Lar, Genius* or *Penates* with perfume, light lamps, burn incense or hang up garlands, on pain of confiscation of the house. These divine beings are, in origin, exclusively Latin.

The *Genius*, the 'male spirit of a *gens* (lineage) existing during his lifetime in the head of the family' (*OCD*) might be associated with the marital bed and portrayed on the bed-head (Juvenal 6.22). The female equivalent of the *genius*, the *Iuno* of the *materfamilias*, was also worshipped by the staff. But here let us concentrate on the other deities.

The *Lares* were supposed to guard the house (Ennius *Annals* 620). Ovid imagines thieves being chased away by a watchful *Lar* and the household dogs (*Fasti* 5.141–2). Fraser 1929 comments on this passage:

The notion that the rights of property are protected against thieves by supernatural powers, whether magical or divine, is widespread in the world, and has no doubt done much to establish the institution of private property.

(Fraser 1929)

Cicero claims that, by divinely-inspired custom, the priests had state and homes equally under their supervision: 'the whole dignity of the commonwealth, the safety of all citizens, their life, liberty, altars, hearths, store-room gods, goods, fortunes, domiciles . . .' (*On his house* 1). Cicero appeals often to the idea of the household gods, for instance, the Galatian Deiotarus could not have planned to murder Caesar in the sight of his (Deiotarus') *Penates* (*Deiot.* 15). To attack a man in front of his own *Lares* was equally shocking (Cic. *Quinct.* 85).

Representations of the *Lares* occur often in rooms through which people would frequently pass in the relatively well-preserved houses of Pompeii. Ordinary daily cult of small offerings would be paid by slaves and members of the family. Cicero assumes that any house contained divinities who witnessed what went on and who protected the residents.

The emotional content of *Lares* continues strong in a variety of literary genres throughout our period, as *TLL* demonstrates (e.g. Cic. *Verr.* 2.3.27; *Sest.* 30; *F* 20/1.9.20; Sallust *Cat.* 20.11; Horace *Epistles* 1.7.58, 2.2.50–1; Livy 1.29.4). *Penates* also struck a sentimental chord in Roman hearts (e.g. Plautus *Merc.* 834; Cic. *Phil.* 2.68; Horace *Odes* 3.14.3).

For our purposes, it is particularly relevant to note how often this idea that the holiness of a home is epitomised by the Lares is attached to humbler houses. Martial uses it of a small estate and villa, with a dirty (i.e. smoke-begrimed) Lar (12.57.2). Horace writes of the dinners of the poor eaten under the little Lar (Odes 3.29.14–15, cf. 1.12.43–4), Silus of little Lares in a low-built house (7.173). 'Small' Lares are commonplace (Prop. 4.1.128; Seneca Phoen. 594; Apul. Metamorphoses 1.23). Lucan (5.527–8) praises the safe life of the poor and their straitened Lares. Adjectives get transposed between house, gods and family: so a North African on his epitaph (?3rd century) may claim to be 'sprung from a poor Lar and little parent' who did not own a house (CLE 1238 = Musa Lapidaria 109.3–4, cf. 18–19). Penates too might be poor and hungry and so on (Valerius Maximus 4.4.9; Seneca Phaedra 209).

The Romans hallowed the alleged hut of their founder Romulus on the Palatine. They were compelled, therefore, to write of the cottages of the poor as havens of antique virtue. It was a little thatched cottage which played host to Jupiter and Mercury in disguise, when the big houses locked their doors (Ovid *Metamorphoses* 8.628–30, 699). The shack (*tugurium*) or cottage (*casa*) gets a good press (e.g. Varro *Rust*. 3.1.3; Vergil *Eclogues* 1.68, 2.29; Valerius Maximus 7.1.2). Moderation in choice of house is praised (Persius 5.109). The *domus* in imaginative literature is often characterised as humble, small or poor (Vergil *Aeneid* 12.519; Ovid *Tristia* 4.8.9; Seneca *Phaedra* 1138–9, Mart. 9.97.8, 10.20 (19) 10). It is unsurprising, therefore, that the Romans should regard the humblest house as a refuge, 'the safest possible shelter', *tutissimum receptaculum*, as Donatus says in explaining a proverb about a *casa* (on Terence *Phormio* 768, a phrase picked up by English lawyers nurtured on Roman comedy (Radin 1937a: 425–6)).

The household gods were worshipped by slave members of the household as well as the free. It was natural that Latin writers (about whose own devoutness or lack of it in the performance of domestic cults it would be dangerous to generalise) should imply that at least the poor and simple were particularly attached to their *Lares* and *Penates*.

The hearth, an open fireplace, was centrally placed, not against a wall, and chimneyless. Its fire was symbolised by the goddess Vesta in public cult, but was associated with the *Lar* in the private house. Offerings might be thrown into the flames (Plautus *Aul*. 386) and garlands hung above the hearth (Cato *Agr*. 143). The hearth symbolised the home (e.g. Cic. *A* 7.11.134/3).

Antiquarians in the Christian period might teach that under good King Janus all homes were protected by holiness and religious awe, which is why he was deified and all entrances and exits were consecrated to him (Macrobius *Saturnalia* 1.9.2). Superstition notoriously attached to the threshold: it was a bad omen to trip as you went in or out, and so brides had to be lifted over by their attendants (*TLL* under *limen*). The lintel might be hung with charms, as Pliny says some people hung a toad over a barn-door at harvest-time (*Natural History*

18.303). A phallus was the usual way of repelling the evil eye and the malice of outsiders (cf. Frend 1952: 102–3). The door-posts (*postes*) were anointed (ideally with wolf-fat!) and bound with woollen fillets by the bride when she came to her husband's house. They, or the door itself, were decorated with bay-trees or garlands for a wedding (Juvenal 6.51–2, with Courtney 1980, 79, 227–8) or the birth of a baby (Juvenal 9.85) and other family celebrations, or hung with polished military equipment (Ovid *Tristia* 3.1.33–4).

The door (*ianua*) or double-doors (*fores*) faced both ways, like the two-faced god Janus, to the sanctuary of the house and to the outside world. Janus might be needed to protect the actions of opening and shutting. People (as now) were sensitive to rude knocks on their doors (Plautus *Rudens* 414, Apul. *Metamorphoses* 1.22). Marks of honour granted to those who had served their country well were necessarily attached to the visible side of the house which fronted on the public street. A sixth-century decree allowed the two Poplicolae to make their doors open outwards as a particular mark of distinction (Pliny *Natural History* 36.112; Plutarch *Popl.* 20.2). Caesar Augustus had his oak crown and laurels (*Res Gestae* 34.2; Ovid *Tristia* 3.1.36, 39) and later an inscription attesting his title of 'Father of the fatherland' (*Res Gestae* 35.1).

If a house is 'holy', it is implied that attacks on it or wicked behaviour in it would do more than mere physical damage. This is borne out by some of the Romans' vocabulary: a house may be violated (Cic. *Har. resp.* 15, Florus 3.5.7), contaminated (Livy 29.18.8, Valerius Maximus 6.1.2) or polluted (Horace *Odes* 4.5.21).

In an improving tale about the moral impact Scipio Africanus had on all who came in contact with him, Valerius Maximus (2.10.2, under 'majesty') tells how a bunch of brigands went to see him in his villa to pay their respects: when he ordered them to be admitted they venerated the door-posts, kissed his hand and left gifts before the fore-court. The 'sacred aura' of that house was intertwined with the aura of Scipio.

Conclusion

We have learned that the word in common use for what Saller calls 'sacred' in relation to the house would be *sanctus*, which we should perhaps translate as 'holy' (though the *Oxford Latin Dictionary* also allows 'sacred', a translation I have reserved for *sacer*). If we want to say where the holy was located in Roman ideas about the house, we could point to the paintings or mosaics of the *Lares* placed in the little shrines, images of gods which were *sacra*. We would mention that these divinities were thought to protect the house and guard it against interlopers. We would indicate the hearth, door, threshold and lintel, which were under divine protection. We could say that these religious beliefs were backed up by the strong loyalty to a familiar building and its objects. The data we gathered on folk-custom suggest that the door and threshold marked an important dividing-line between private and public property, between the dwelling of an individual owner and the family and staff who lived there and the street where friendly or hostile crowds could gather and no private citizen prevent them, between the area into which you needed an invitation, explicit or tacit, to penetrate and the communal ground where anyone might go.

The evidence collected more than justifies Saller's opinion: the Roman's house was a holy place, however often that holiness might be violated and however hard it is to pin down the emotions, rules and compromises which surrounded it. In theory, the 'sacred aura', the religious feelings, the legal protection and the social taboos covered all dwellings, not only the shacks and cottages of the virtuous poor, the middling houses of Pompeii with their little shrines to the household gods, and the palaces of the élite who paraded their wealth and power, but even the rented flat, the prostitute's house and the student's digs. Dependent status or sex made no difference to these.

This conclusion brings us to the end of the search. No two scholars would have proceeded in the same way, set out the same texts nor weighed the evidence similarly. There is plenty of room for other nuances and shades of interpretation.

This study, though it has taken us into obscure byways of classical texts, turns out to have some ordinary human interest and also to relate to areas of concern even in a modern age, such as the rights of an individual to privacy and security and the interests of a community in protecting citizens from crime or oppression and in policing morals.

Chapter 6

How to get further into the subject

One man is as good as another until he has written a book.
(Benjamin Jowett, *Oxford Dictionary of Quotations* (1979): 285)

Whom can you talk to?

The Romans learned much of what they knew from live human beings, a resource which should not be neglected. We often tend to forget that someone with knowledge and interests in the field we are exploring may be near us, in a school or university or college of further education, or outside such institutions.

Individuals

Your first resource, if you are a registered student, is whoever is responsible for this or related subjects in your institution. Probably procedures allow for plenty of consultation when you decide on choices in the syllabus. If specialists are formally teaching you at the present time, you will know the procedure for consulting them. All I can advise is that you should approach them in whatever is the customary manner and that you should not be afraid to do so. Reference librarians may also be consulted about library resources.

Once you embark on a topic and find out who is writing in that area, you will be able to locate specialists, through printed or electronic lists of university staff and through membership lists of learned societies. If you are a student and the people whose work interests you are in your own institution, go and knock on doors – though it would be considerate to telephone or write to announce yourself first. Scholars are interested in talking about their field and the busiest are often the most generous with their time and energy. The more precise your questions, the better. If they do not have an immediate answer, they may be able to suggest approaches and further reading. If your topic is right in their field, they may even be willing to read your work. If people are at a distance, a letter or email may initiate an exchange of question, answer and comment. (Authors of journal-articles sometimes give their email address as well as institutional affiliation.) It is not a good idea to email scholars, give the bare topic of your essay or thesis and expect them to expound 'their theories on the subject'. Questioners of this sort often have topics which demand book-length treatment.

Learned societies

It is an excellent idea to join local and national learned societies. Most have special subscription-rates for registered students. The list which follows does not pretend to be exhaustive. The Classical Association (of England: Hon. Treas. Richard Wallace, Classics, University of Keele, Keele, Newcastle-under-Lyme, Staffs, ST5 5BG; cla02@cc. keele.ac.uk) through its branches, has a lively programme of events at the local level, which would enable you to meet people with similar interests. There are allied associations in the rest of the UK and in Commonwealth countries. The Society for the Promotion of Roman Studies is the major association for Roman historians in the English-speaking world (Senate House, Malet Street, London WC1E 7HU; romansoc@sas.ac.uk): membership confers the privilege of using the library of the Institute of Classical Studies in London and of receiving the *The Journal of Roman Studies* and/or *Britannia* (concerned primarily with the archaeology and history of the province), and there is an annual programme of meetings (chiefly in London, but including local lectures in conjunction with local branches of the Classical Association). Students, who need to be sponsored by a tutor or supervisor, pay at a special rate, which makes this a real bargain. For British-based Roman historians, the Joint Association of Classical Teachers (Senate House, Malet Street, London WC1E 7HU), though primarily concerned with how classical subjects should be taught, provides reviews and sources in translation which may be helpful to the student.

In North America, the major general classical association is the American Philological Association. There are numerous classical associations covering broad areas, e.g. the Classical Association of the Middle West and South. The Societé Canadienne des études Classiques/Classical Association of Canada is the big Canadian organisation. Some US states and Canadian provinces (e.g. Quebec and Ontario) and smaller areas (e.g. Vancouver Island) also have their own associations. Many cities (including Canadian ones) have chapters of the Archaeological Institute of America. Though the APA includes a specialised group called the Friends of Ancient History, and ancient history is within the purview of the American Historical Association, there is only one society exclusively devoted to ancient history, the Association of Ancient Historians, to which all US and Canadian students interested in this field should belong. The annual meetings are friendly and relatively small (about 100–120 participants) and take place in May on interesting campuses. The student subscription is a bargain and the publications are useful, even if you cannot get to meetings. There are also associations for subdisciplines such as epigraphy and papyrology.

In the other Commonwealth countries, the Classical Association will normally be the first resource.

Most universities also have student classical societies. All these groups offer you the chance to meet people and discuss topics of interest. Many of them, from time to time, publish a membership list. What do you do if you want to find out who is interested in a particular field? There is a very useful *Directory of Ancient Historians in the United States*, updated by K.H. Kinzl on the Web (http://ivory.trentu.ca/www/cl/aahdir.html) and other directories accessible through his site of resources (http://ivory.trentu.ca/www/cl/resources/html). The *Directory of Classicists* published from time to time by the *Classical World* also lists research interests.

There is a limit to what you can learn from informal contacts. These may be stimulating, but what matters most at the outset is to obtain formal, thorough training from a practitioner. Summer schools and workshops (run by universities and societies, e.g. one on Greek and Latin epigraphy in Oxford in 2001) provide opportunities. And nothing substitutes for books.

What can you read?

How do you find relevant printed material among the million or so items on Classics published by twentieth-century scholars (W. Scheidel 1997: 288)? People can give you useful bibliographical tips. A subject may be tracked by entering a key-word into the subject (or title) listing of a computerised library catalogue. This, of course, does not guarantee quality.

Encyclopaedias

Standard reference-books like *OCD* or *Neue Pauly* (in progress) will provide up-to-date and fundamental bibliography, chosen as reliable. *Paulys Real-Encyclopädie der classischen Altertumswissenschaft* (*RE*), the multi-volume and very comprehensive encyclopaedia, provides older bibliography. Use the index to avoid missing articles which appeared in the supplementary volumes. *RE* (though inevitably becoming dated) is invaluable for full and authoritative discussion of many topics and for citation of ancient sources. The *Reallexikon für Antike und Christentum* (on the relation of the classical world and Christianity, Stuttgart: Hiersemann, 1950– in progress) is often very useful for social history. Volume i would give you 'Adoption', 'Altar', 'Antisemitism', 'Baths' etc. Topics relevant to epigraphy are usefully covered by *Dizionario epigrafico di antichità romana* (Rome: Pasqualucci, 1895– in progress), intended to link epigraphy and antiquities, which cites sources. Again, you could find adoption, altars (both *altaria* and *arae*), baths (though under their Latin names). If you do not read German or Italian, such reference books are still usable as a way into the English bibliography and sources. For law, I would not want to be without Berger's *Encyclopedic Dictionary of Roman Law*, where you can look up institutions, statutes, jurists or legal terms. How else would I find out that, if you promise to give someone a 'hippocentaur' (half-man, half-horse), you cannot be held to it?

Bibliographies and reviews of the current state of scholarship

There are books of bibliography. For Roman history in general, Wells 1995, a critical bibliography compiled for the American Historical Association, is discriminating and wide-ranging. There are very stimulating articles on directions of research since the 1980s in the Association of Ancient Historians' booklet (Burstein *et al.* 1997), by A.M. Ward and R. MacMullen. There are also volumes listing bibliography on specific areas, such as slavery or the family, but these date quickly (e.g. Vogt 1971, Krause 1992, 1998). Electronic search tools will supersede them.

L'Année philologique (Paris: Les belles lettres, annual, from 1924, growing steadily fatter in recent years) is the (almost exhaustive: in particular it excludes school texts) listing of recent publications (books and articles) in Classics. Each item receives a summary description (in English, French, German or Italian). Items are categorised under names of classical authors or under subject areas. The editors, who are now converting to computers, are making a determined effort to record items missed in previous years. They have also (for 1996, published 1999) revised and increased the subdivisions for history (now general history, institutions, economy and society, regional history and historical geography, mentalities and daily life, religions, intellectual and artistic life, each with a subdivision for 'Roman'). The social historian will need also to consult the sections on law or technology, among others. Some items appear in more than one section, which decreases the risk of missing relevant material. Including cross-references, there are 14,290 records for 1996. This alarming figure underlines the need to find ways of selecting: do not waste your time on modern work which the experts agree is sub-standard. *APh* offers the opportunity to find out where reviews have appeared for any book in which you are interested. Dee Clayman has edited a *Database of classical bibliography* (*DCB*) on CD-ROM, with interface in English, which makes the material of *APh* for 1976–89 searchable by key-word. There are more retrospective data to come, and the current *APh* should eventually appear on CD-ROM (Lisa Carson 1998).

The periodical *Gnomon* publishes lists of recent publications in Classics four times a year – a resource while the new *APh* is in preparation. Roman law journals are useful for information on new publications in Roman history: *Labeo* (Naples: Iovene, three times a year) categorises current publications under very specific headings in its *Schedario. Index. International Survey of Roman Law* (Naples: Iovene, annually) categorises under broad headings and gives multilingual summaries. *Classical World* occasionally devotes a whole issue to a critical and comprehensive survey of bibliography on an author or topic (e.g. Jane DeRose Evans, 1998). *Greece and Rome*'s very readable and stimulating booklets, *New Surveys in the Classics*, have a more selective approach: the series has recently included P.D.A. Garnsey and Richard Saller, *The Early Principate* (1982), T.E.J. Wiedemann, *Slavery* (1987), G. Clark, *Women in the ancient world* (1989), besides studies of authors.

The periodical *Lustrum. Internationale Forschungsberichte aus dem Bereich des klassischen Altertums* (Göttingen: Vanderhoek and Ruprecht) deals with scholarship of specific topics. O. Hiltbrunner, *Bibliographie zur lateinischen Wortforschung* (Bern and Munich: Francke, 1981–, in progress) is useful for the study of 'mentalities', since it lists articles on a selection of individual Latin words: you will find there rich collections on terms such as *amicitia* (151 items), *amo* etc. (97), *amor* (126) and *collegium* (93). K. Christ, *Römische Geschichte. Einfuhrung, Quellenkunde, Bibliographie* (Darmstadt: Wissenschaftliche Gesellschaft, 1980) is an introduction to the whole subject of Roman history: the bibliographic listings under topics (inevitably dated) are convenient even if you do not read German, and include a good selection of work in English. Another German manual, by Gullath and Heidtmann 1992, may also help.

Aufstieg und Niedergang der römischen Welt (*ANRW*, 1970–, in progress) aims to describe the state of play in international scholarship, with weighty bibliographies. It is arranged in theoretical volumes and sub-volumes. What you hold in your two hands is one of the latter, a tome of considerable weight made up of articles of considerable length, in various languages. The early four sub-volumes (*'Band* I') belong to Part I, on the Republic. Part II, on the Principate, is subdivided into Political History, provinces, art, law, religion, language and literature, philosophy and medicine. With some volumes or sub-volumes not yet published, the work has reached volume 37, at the time of writing. Part III, on late antiquity, has not yet appeared. To find your way in this labyrinth, you need Stephen Schwerdtfeger and Ute Ilchmann eds, *Inhaltsverzeichnis mit Autorenregister* (Berlin and New York: De Gruyter, 1997), which gives an index down to 1996. A searchable website may, at the time of writing, be found at www.uky.edu/Arts Sciences/Classics/biblio/anrw.html. The purpose of this monumental work (it was originally an exceptionally ambitious tribute to J. Vogt) seems to grow as it progresses, so there is a serious imbalance between the earlier and later period: there are four articles on Cicero (only one on the speeches, dealing with the *Defence of Caelius*); thirteen on Ovid; eight on Seneca's tragedies; forty-six on Tacitus. Many of the articles are authoritative and helpful: the difficulty is to remember to check for them.

Books in your area will often provide the most valuable modern bibliography. The volumes of the second edition of the *Cambridge Ancient History* (vii.2 (1989), viii (1989), ix (1994), x (1996), xiii (1998)) have rich classified bibliography which makes a good starting-point. At the introductory level, Grant and Kitzinger 1988, which has useful essays on topics such as crafts and craftsmen (A. Burford), farming and animal husbandry (K.D. White) or sacrifice and ritual (J. North) provides classified bibliography.

Nothing dates faster than bibliography. Usually the best way into a subject is through a recent book or article by a reputable author. Follow up some of the citations which look promising and start creating a working list of works to consult. It is no longer possible to read everything published on even quite a small topic and in English, so every scholar must select what to read. Skim tables of contents and reviews in learned journals and pay attention to the citations of specialists as you build up a working bibliography of things you think you will need to read.

Reviews and review articles

Journals are particularly helpful. *Greece and Rome* (twice a year) gives a review of recent books (mainly in English), arranged in fields such as 'Roman history' and 'archaeology' and the catch-all 'General', which is particularly useful on social history. The *Journal of Roman Studies*, as well as giving serious scholarly reviews to a good selection of works on Roman history and Latin literature, includes an annual list of 'Publications received', which provides the reader with an excellent overview of what is going on in the subject. The *Journal of Roman Archaeology* does a similar job for Roman history and archaeology, with many substantial review articles.

I find the following other journals particularly useful for reviews: *American Journal of Philology*; *Bryn Mawr Classical Review* (also on the Web); *Classical Journal*; *Classical Philology*; *Classical Review*; *Classical Views/Echos du monde classique*; *Gnomon*; *Joint Association of Classical Teachers Bulletin*; *Phoenix*. Many other classical periodicals publish reviews. Ancient history is also reviewed in *English Historical Review* and *American Historical Review* and *Times Literary Supplement*. Critical reviews in learned journals provide one of the best ways of getting an idea of what will be worth your time reading among recent books. Since scholars may disagree, one should read more than one such review before making a tentative decision to read or not read a new book. So much is now published that it is no longer physically possible to read everything that appears even in an apparently restricted field like Roman social history. The same is now true of sub-fields, such as the family or slavery. Most of us will attempt to dip into new books which seem relevant to our current interests and to keep an eye open for others which may turn out to be relevant. This is why tips from other people or from publications are so vital.

Survey articles

The *Journal of Roman Studies* publishes a survey of recent work in epigraphy every five years. For archaeology, note the surveys of recent progress in the City of Rome and central and southern Italy in the same journal by Patterson 1992 and E. Curti and others 1996. For papyrology, see, e.g. Cotton *et al.* 1995. The *Greece and Rome New Surveys in the Classics* and surveys in *ANRW* have been mentioned.

Other lists

Publishers' catalogues too: besides showcasing their books in print, they quote (selectively) what other scholars wrote about the books. Booksellers' catalogues (e.g. L'Erma di Bretschneider) give insights into what is available from foreign publishers. Specialised second-hand dealers have attractive catalogues: beware, however, of outdated editions or books. It is important to acquire for yourself the books which you will use constantly, especially texts and commentaries, but also monographs. Secondhand bookshops are indispensable.

Theses, completed or in progress, are listed in *Bulletin of the Institute of Classical Studies* (London: ICS) (Britain), *American Philological Association Newsletter* (North America) etc. and, increasingly, on the Web. If you are going to write a thesis yourself, you should try to avoid (too much) overlap with another scholar.

Help from other reference tools

TLL (in progress) lists and categorises word-usage (following chronological order of author). It is therefore useful for tracking down concepts and getting a sense of changes over time. There are often concordances (word-lists) for individual authors and selective indices on vocabulary in commentaries. The *Dizionario epigrafico* lists some words used in inscriptions.

For the inscriptions of Rome published in *CIL* vi, E.J. Jory's printed computer indices enable you to look up any word or name which interests you and see all its occurrences. (You will have to be careful to look up all possible inflections, and if the inscription was mis-spelled this will be reflected in the index!) Similar indices are gradually being published to accompany volumes on other areas of the Empire.

For the biographies of eminent individuals, *RE* is the standard authority for the republican period (in German) and *Prosopographia imperii romani saeculi I, II, III* for the Principate (in Latin). You can use these for their full citations of the sources without being able to read the articles themselves.

The *Princeton Encyclopedia of classical sites* (ed. Richard Stillwell 1976) and Talbert's *Atlas* are authoritative on the setting and nature of the towns and other features of the Roman world. *The Oxford Companion to Archaeology* (ed. Brian M. Fagan, New York and Oxford: Oxford University Press, 1996) is a useful guide for archaeological methods and aims, but, being a general work, brief on classical archaeology, with incomplete coverage of sites.

Computers

Classical Latin literary texts are accessible on CD-ROM (Packard Humanities Institute, PHI). You may trace a word in an individual text or author or through the whole of Latin literature – a useful procedure for a rare word. The problem will often be that your search will yield too much. Thus, if you are interested in *domus*, a house, you would want to find the word in all its cases. That would mean: (1) looking for *dom* (beginning of word only), which would mean you would collect forms of *domo* (I subdue), *dominus* (master) and a lot of other words as well as what you want. Or (2) you would have to do a number of separate searches for the forms of *domus* (nominative singular and plural, genitive singular, sometimes accusative plural), *domum* (accusative sg.), *domi* (locative – this would also get you *domibus*, dative and ablative plural) and so on. It is less stressful to use *TLL* (where it exists) for such words of frequent occurrence. Suppose, however, that you want to trace the *Penates*: looking up *Penat* would give you a list of relatively manageable size, with everything relevant to your topic.

Thesaurus linguae graecae (*TLG*, nearly complete; http://www.tlg.uci.edu/~tlg) similarly allows Greek texts to be searched on line.

Internet and Web

Resources are constantly expanding and changing, so only the most general guidance can be given here. The 'whirl-wind introductory tour' for historians given by Hellstern, Scott and Garrison (1998: 145–53) may help.

The interchange facilitated by the meetings of learned societies and by conferences is now supplemented by electronic discussion. You may join an email group for discussion or consult material put up on a web-site. The possibilities are endlessly changing, so I can only point you in the general direction. A 'limited area search of the ancient and medieval internet' may be performed on Argos (http://argos. evansville.edu). Konrad Kinzl of Trent University, Ontario, has an excellent site offering resources of various kinds in ancient history: (http://ivory.trentu.ca/www/cl/resources.html). Some other classical sites are particularly good as gateways to more specialised sites. Try, for instance, the Classics Departments of the Universities of Reading (http://www.rdg.ac.uk/Roman/Studies/gate.html), Oxford (http://www. classics.ox.ac.uk) and Michigan (http://classics.lsa.umich.edu). There is a user-friendly German site called Kirke: (http://www.phil.uni-erlangen.de/~pzlatein/kirke/kirkerah.html).

Learned societies also have websites: e.g. the Roman Society (http://www.sas.ac.uk/icls/roman). So do publishers, e.g. Routledge: (www.routledge.com). Journals are increasingly putting tables of contents and even whole articles on the Web, e.g. *Ancient History Bulletin* (http://ivory.trentu.ca/www/cl/ahb). The British Broadcasting Corporation has its history material (www.bbc.co.uk/education/ history). The Perseus home-page (rich in Greek material) includes Greek cities in the Roman period (http://www.Perseus.tufts.edu/); the Roman Perseus is in its early stages (http://www.Perseus.tufts.edu/ neh.ann.html). Roman buildings can be viewed on the virtual reality site of the University of California at Los Angeles, humnet.ucla. edu/cvrlab/. There is useful material such as maps and stemmata on the Roman Emperors site (http://www.roman-emperors.org).

Journals

It is a good idea to develop the habit of scanning the contents list of journals as they come out. Most university libraries will keep the current issues in a convenient place for browsing. Specialist libraries which put all the Classics and ancient history together will let you get a quick overview.

Much of the most exciting work comes out in the form of articles. An article lends itself to very detailed consideration of a restricted topic. Since journals appear annually or more often, publication may be relatively rapid: an author is able to present a viewpoint and hope for a reaction from peers – even a counter-argument – presented in the next issue. Or a journal may find that it has attracted a series of contributions on related topics. An ongoing debate takes place. This can be very productive.

Journals come in different flavours. Their characteristics are determined by tradition and by the input of editors, editorial boards and sometimes learned societies. In addition to those cited above for their reviews, you will find interesting material in *American Journal of Ancient History*, *Papers of the British School at Rome* and many foreign-language journals. Although there is little on the ancient world in most general historical journals, there are striking exceptions: I pick out *Past and Present* as a distinguished example. (Full list of journals, with the standard abbreviations, in *APh*.)

Journals have been mentioned earlier as the source of critical reviews.

Tracking down sources

Unless you are exploiting a limited range of sources, as in Chapter Four, it is often difficult to collect a list of the sources to be exploited. The resources discussed above will often help.

Older introductory books on social history are often a good way into the sources (though their modern bibliography will be dated). There is, for instance, a mass of information in Friedländer 1939, Balsdon 1969.

Once you find data, you have to collect, store, sort and analyse them, Some researchers find card indices work for them: they write down the sources (or merely the citations and relevant points) on cards, which can then be categorised. Or they use a computer database, to the same effect. Others find running notes or even scraps of paper are enough for them. A lap-top computer is probably taking over as the tool most people choose. In any case, we must collect and categorise evidence before we can deploy it.

Warnings

There is always a risk of picking up a book which is unreliable or dated: the only way to avoid mistakes is to consult reviews (see what the experts say – but assess their expertise) and develop your own critical sense. You should evaluate the logic of the argument, see how effectively the writer cites evidence, check for bias. But this will only take you so far: if you are unacquainted with the primary evidence, you cannot tell for sure if the author knows it well, has thought about it and deploys it adequately.

Beware getting bogged down in moderns hashing and rehashing the same, limited or non-existent data. Certain questions are unanswerable. As M. H. Crawford says of a vexed problem in archaic law, 'The bibliography is enormous and there is no evidence' (1996: ii 639). There is no point in involving yourself in such topics.

Horace (*Ars P.* 269) told Latin writers to study Greek texts night and day: the historian must be in constant dialogue with the primary sources. This chapter has been about short-cuts, ways of getting at the sources and ways of seeing how others have used and assessed them. I come back to the theme of Chapter 1. Your most important job is to familiarise yourself with the evidence which is the basis for your topic. This means soaking yourself in texts, using all the tools you need to achieve a full understanding – commentaries, dictionaries, reference works. As you do this, you may go to and fro to modern work on the historical context from which the text emerged (reading monographs and articles on the author or his times). Ideally, you will be able to see where you disagree with the moderns and why. Similar considerations apply with artefacts or sites: exploit the facts which the moderns should provide, but interpret the data by your own lights. Scholarship progresses by constant re-thinking, by taking nothing for granted, by being prepared to dissent from 'authorities'. The tools I have listed here are as reliable as people could make them, but not infallible. Make up your own mind.

Doing the writing

Once you have done the research, you are faced with the job of writing. Most people find it hard to shape their material and their own thoughts for others to read. The search for perfection is inhibiting. In my experience (in guiding students and in flailing around until I settle down to my own writing) it helps if you don't set your sights too high. Aim at getting something down on paper. It does not matter whether you use a pen, a pencil or a PC. You can amend, reshape and improve.

Define what you are trying to do. Thesis proposals, grant proposals, a finished thesis, a book or an article all begin with a statement of aims and intents, what you are attempting to prove. It is very helpful to lay this out as clearly and in as much detail as possible, even if the eventual polished preface to thesis or book turns out to be very different from the original proposal.

Perhaps begin with a section of your essay or thesis with which you feel particularly familiar and confident. Try to break the matter down into short sections and get something written every day. If you need to write a thesis of 150 pages, the thought can be daunting, but if you can write two pages a day and ten pages a week (allowing time for continuing research and correction of drafts), you could theoretically have a complete draft in fifteen weeks. 'All those . . . who have lived as literary men . . . will agree with me that three hours a day will produce as much as a man ought to write.' (Trollope 1950: 271). Anthony Trollope spoke as a novelist and journalist in middle age, who had a full-time job, energetic recreations and a full social life. Yet by getting to his desk at 5.30 am he could produce ten pages of a novel in a day. Who could emulate him in scholarly writing? Yet that kind of application and involvement is something to aim at.

You need time to ponder on what you have written or are going to write. Often the best ideas come when you are not sitting at your desk. You must be as rigorous as possible in putting questions, assessing evidence and arriving at conclusions or hypotheses, but you should also let your imagination play on your subject. As long as you are actively engaged in it, your mind will throw up ideas when you are not deliberately thinking.

A good deal of the work is hard grind. But unless your subject excites you, the labour is pointless. For this reason, you need to fall in love with the topic on which you are going to spend so much time and effort: this initial enthusiasm will help carry you through the fatigue and possible disillusion or depression which affect most writers during the process.

In practice, composition of 150 pages will take longer than fifteen weeks. Then you must budget ample time for re-drafting (especially to take account of your supervisor's criticisms), editing (style, accuracy, coherence, clarity, consistency) and checking references. It also helps to have friends reading your draft for content and style. You should budget adequate time for this phase. Much the same applies to shorter research papers.

The same rules apply to this field as to other work in history or Classics. There are useful tips (aimed especially at US undergraduates) in Cargill 1997; Hellstern, Scott and Garrison 1998. Every historian owes it to the reader to write correctly and clearly and as elegantly as possible, in an individual style. The harder the writer has worked on expression, the easier it is for the reader to follow the argument. Our subject is interesting and we should not make it difficult for the reader to enjoy it. Successful attempts at writing social history will follow the rules which have been developed for all fields of history. So we have come full circle.

Appendix 1

Sources on Tullia

Shackleton Bailey's citations from the speeches of Cicero

In Verrem/Against Verres 2.1.112 (70 BC)

In Catilinam/Against Catiline 4.3 (5 Dec. 63 BC)

Post Reditum in Senatu/On his return, in the Senate 1, 27 (5 Sept. 57 BC)

Post Reditum ad Quirites/On his return, to the citizens 2, 5, 8 (a few days after 5 Sept. 57 BC)

De Domo/On his house 59, 96 (29 Sept. 57 BC)

Pro Sestio/In defence of Sestius 49, 54, 131, 144–5 (trial Feb.–March 14 56 BC; Cicero spoke last)

De Haruspicum responso/On the reply of the haruspices 16 (?late May 56 BC)

In Pisonem/Against Piso fr. xiii Nisbet (late summer 55 BC)

Pro Plancio/In defence of Plancius 69, 73 (late Aug. or early Sept. 54 BC)

Pro Milone/In defence of Milo 87, 100 (trial 4–8 April 52 BC)

Shackleton Bailey's citations from the letters of Cicero

(Bailey's number follows the slash.) The fourth number is that of the
paragraph and does not appear in all translations.

A 1.5/1.8, to Atticus, Rome, November 68

A 1.8/4.3, to Atticus, Rome, after 13 February 67
A 1.10/6.6, to Atticus, Tusculum, *c.* May 67
A 1.3/8.3, to Atticus, Rome, end of 67

A 1.18/18.1, to Atticus, Rome, 20 January 60

A 2.8/28.2, to Atticus, Antium, 16 (?) April 59

F 14.4/6.3, to his family, Brundisium, 29 April 58
F 14.4/6.6, to his family, Brundisium, 29 April 58
QF 1.3/3.3, to his brother, Thessalonica, 13 June 58
QF 1.3/3.10, to his brother, Thessalonica, 13 June 58
A 3.10/55.2, to Atticus, Thessalonica, 17 June 58
A 3.15/60.4, to Atticus, Thessalonica, 17 August 58
A 3.19/64.2(f), to Atticus, Thessalonica, 15 September 58
F 14.2/7.1, to his family, Thessalonica, 5 October 58
F 14.1/8.1, to Terentia, Dispatched from Dyrrhachium,
        25 November 58
F 14.1/8.6, to Terentia, Dispatched from Dyrrhachium,
        25 November 58

A 4.1/73.4, to Atticus, Rome, about 10 September 57
A 4.2/74.7, to Atticus, Rome, beginning of October 57

QF 2.4/8.2, to his brother, Rome, mid March 56
QF 2.6/10.1, to his brother, en route to Anagnia, 9 April 56
        A 4.4a/78.2 , to Atticus, Antium, *c.* June (?), *c.* 20 June (Loeb) 56
F 1.7/18.11, to Lentulus Spinther, late June or July 56

A 4.16/89.4, to Atticus, Rome, about 1 July 54
A 4.15/90.4, to Atticus, Rome, 27 July 54

F 16.16/44.1, Q. Cicero to Cicero, Transalpine Gaul, May (end) or
    June (beginning) 53

A 5.4/97.1, to Atticus, Beneventum, 12 May 51
A 5.13/106.3, to Atticus, Ephesus, 26 July 51
A 5.14/107.3, to Atticus, Tralles (?), 27 July 51
A 5.17/110.4, to Atticus, en route, 15 August (?) 51

A 5.21/114.14, to Atticus, Laodicea, 13 February 50
A 6.1/115.10, to Atticus, Laodicea, 20 February 50
F 8.13/94.1, Caelius Rufus to Cicero, Rome, early June 50
A 6.4/118.2, to Atticus, en route, mid (?) June 50
A 6.6/121.1, to Atticus, Side, *c.* 3 August 50
F 2.15/96.2, to Caelius Rufus, Side, 3 or 4 August 50
F 3.12/75.2, to Ap. Claudius Pulcher, Side, 3 or 4 August 50
A 6.8/122.1, to Atticus, Ephesus, 1 October 50
A 6.9/123.5, to Atticus, Athens, 15 October 50
F 14.5/119.1, to Terentia, Athens, 16 October 50
F 14.5/119.1f., to Terentia, Athens, 16 October 50
A 7.3/126.12, to Atticus, near Trebula, 9 December 50

A 7.12/135.6, to Atticus, Formiae, 22 January 49
F 14.18/144, to Terentia and Tullia, Formiae, 22 January 49
    (added item)
A 7.13/136.3, to Atticus, Minturnae, 23 January 49
F 14.14/145, to Terentia and Tullia, Minturnae, 23 January 49
    (added item)
A 7.13a/137.3, to Atticus, Minturnae, 24 January 49
A 7.14/138.3, to Atticus, Cales, 25 January 49
F 16.12/146.6, to Tiro, Capua, 27 January 49
A 7.16/140.3, to Atticus, Cales, 28 January 49
A 7.17/141.5, to Atticus, Formiae, 2 February 49
A 7.18/142.1, to Atticus, Formiae, 3 February 49
A 7.20/144.2, to Atticus, Capua, 5 February 49
A 7.23/147.2, to Atticus, Formiae, 10 February 49
A 8.2/152.4, to Atticus, Formiae, 17 February 49
A 9.6/172.4, Formiae, 11 March 49

A 10.1a/191, to Atticus, Laterium, 4 April 49

A 10.2/192.2, to Atticus, Laterium or Arcanum, Arcanum (Loeb),
    5 or 6 April 49

A 10.8/199.1, 9f. to Atticus, Cumae, 2 May 49

A 10.8A/199A.1, Antonius tribune, propraetor to Cicero *imperator*,
    place uncertain, 1 May (?) 49

A 10.9A/200A.1, Caelius to Cicero, Liguria (?), *c.* 16 April 49

F 2.16/154.5, to Caelius Rufus, Cumae, 2 or 3 May 49

A 10.13/205.1, to Atticus, Cumae, 7 May 49

A 10.18/210.1, to Atticus, Cumae, 19 May 49

F 14.7/155.1f., to Terentia, aboard ship, Caieta, 7 June 49

A 11.2/212.2, to Atticus, Epirus, middle of March (?) 48

F 9.9/157.1, Dolabella to Cicero, Caesar's camp near Dyrrhachium,
    May 48

A 11.3/213.1, to Atticus, Pompey's camp at Dyrrhachium, 13 June 48

F 14.19/160, to Terentia, Brundisium, 27 November 48

A 11.6/217.4, to Atticus, Brundisium, 27 November 48

A 11.7/218.6, to Atticus, Brundisium, 17 December 48

F 14.9/161, to Terentia, Brundisium, 17 (?) December 48

F 14.17/162, to Terentia, Brundisium, 23 (?) December 48

A 11.9/220.3, to Atticus, Brundisium, 3 January 47

A 11.17/228, to Atticus, Brundisium, 12 or 13 June 47

A 11.17a/229.1, to Atticus, Brundisium 14 June 47

F 14.11/166, to Terentia, Brundisium, 14 June 47

F 14.15/167, to Terentia, Brundisium, 19 June 47

A 11.25/231.3, to Atticus, Brundisium, 5 July 47

A 11.23/232.3, to Atticus, Brundisium, 9 July 47

A 11.24/234.1 (f.), to Atticus, Brundisium, 6 August 47

A 11.21/236.2, to Atticus, Brundisium, 25 August 47

A 12.5c/241, to Atticus, Tusculum, 12 June (?) 46

A 12.1/248.1, to Atticus, Arpinum, 27 November (by the sun) 46

F 7.23/209.4, to M. Fabius Gallus, Rome, December 46

F 6.18/218.5, to Q. Lepta, Rome, January 45

F 4.5/248.1, Servius Sulpicius Rufus to Cicero, Athens, mid-March 45

F 4.5/248.2–6, Servius Sulpicius Rufus to Cicero, Athens, mid March 45

(*A* 12.23/262.1, to Atticus, Tusculum, 19 March 45)

(*F* 4.6/249.1f.), to Servius Sulpicius, Atticus' villa near Nomentum, mid April 45

A 12.3/239.2, to Atticus, Tusculum, May or June 46 (??), now redated to 30 May 45 (Bailey 1999: 300–1), which involves removing the reference to Tullia

Select list of
translations

L = Loeb Classical Library (Cambridge, MA: Harvard University Press)
O = Oxford: Oxford University Press, World's Classics
P = London: Penguin

Select sources

Braund, David (1985) *Augustus to Nero. A sourcebook on Roman history, 31 BC–AD 68*, London: Croom Helm

Gardner, Jane and Thomas Wiedemann (1991) *The Roman Household. A Sourcebook*, London: Routledge

Humphrey, John W. and John P. Oleson (1997) *Greek and Roman Technology. A Sourcebook*, London: Routledge

Levick, Barbara (1985) *The Government of the Roman Empire. A Sourcebook,* London: Routledge

Lewis, N. and M. Reinhold (1990) *Roman Civilisation*, 2 vols., New York: Columbia University Press, 3rd edn

Lomas, Kathryn (1996) *Roman Italy 338 BC–AD 200. A Sourcebook*, London: Routledge

Wiedemann, Thomas (1981) *Greek and Roman Slavery*, London: Croom Helm (Routledge 1997)

Collections

Reardon, Bryan P. (1989) (ed.) *Collected Ancient Greek Novels,* Berkeley & Los Angeles: University of California Press

Stephens, Susan A. and John J. Winkler (1995) *Ancient Greek Novels. The Fragments: Introduction, Text, Translation and Commentary*, Princeton: Princeton University Press

Appian *The Civil Wars* P: J. Carter, 1996

Apuleius O: *Metamorphoses. 'The Golden Ass'* L: J. Arthur Hanson, 1989; P: E.J. Kenney, 1998; O: P.G. Walsh, 1994

—— *Rhetorical works* tr. and comm. Stephen Harrison, John Hilton and Vincent Hunink, Oxford University Press, 2001

Artemidorus *The Interpretation of Dreams* Robert J. White, Park Ridge, New Jersey: Noyes Press, 1975

Augustus *Res Gestae divi Augusti. The Achievements of the Divine Augustus*, P.A. Brunt and J.M. Moore, Oxford: Oxford University Press, 1967

M. Aurelius *Meditations and a Selection of the Letters of Marcus and Fronto* O: A.S.C. Farquharson, R.B. Rutherford, 1989

Caesar *The Gallic War* O: C. Hammond, 1996

—— *The Conquest of Gaul* P: S.A. Handford, J.F. Gardner, 1982

—— *The Civil War* P: S.A. Handford, J.F. Gardner, 1982; O: J. Carter, 1996

Cassius Dio *The Roman History. The Reign of Augustus* P: I. Scott-Kilvert, J. Carter, 1987

Catullus O: G. Lee, 1990

Cicero *Selected political speeches* P: M. Grant, 1969

—— *Letters to Atticus* L: D.R. Shackleton Bailey, 1999, 4 vols

—— *Letters to his friends* D.R. Shackleton Bailey, Atlanta, Georgia: Scholars Press, 1988

—— *The Republic and the Laws* O: N. Rudd, 1998

Digest Watson *et al*, 1985, Philadelphia: Pennsylvania University Press, 4 vols; revd. pb. without Latin text, 1998, 2 vols

Documents

Inscriptions of Roman Britain Lactor 4 Valerie A. Maxfield and Brian Dobson, 3rd edn. (1995)

Lewis, Naphtali (1974) *Greek historical documents: The Roman Principate 27 BC–285 AD* Toronto: Hakkert

Oliver, James H. (1989) *Greek Constitutions of Early Roman Emperors from Inscriptions and Papyri*, (text, tr. and comm.) Philadelphia: American

Philosophical Society Memoirs of the American Philosophical Society 178

Sherk, Robert K. (1988) *Translated documents of Greece and Rome* vi: *The Roman Empire: Augustus to Hadrian*, Cambridge: Cambridge University Press

Gaius *Institutiones* = *The Institutes of Gaius*: W.M. Gordon and O.F. Robinson 1988, London: Duckworth/Ithaca: Cornell University Press

Horace *Satires and Epistles*, Persius *Satires* P: N. Rudd, 1979
—— *The complete Odes and Epodes* P: W.G. Shepherd, B. Radice, 1983
—— *The complete Odes and Epode*s O: D. West, 1997

Justinian *The Digest of Justinian*: Alan Watson, Philadelphia: The University of Pennsylvania Press, 1985, 4 vols.; revd. pb. without Latin text, 1998, 2 vols
—— *Institutes*: Peter Birks and Grant McLeod 1987, London: Duckworth/ Ithaca: Cornell University Press

Juvenal *The Sixteen Satires* P: P. Green, 1998
—— *The Satires* O: N. Rudd, W. Barr, 1992

Laudatio Turiae see Wistrand

Livy *The Rise of Rome*, O: T.J. Luce, 1998

Lucretius *On the Nature of the Universe* O: R. Melville, D. & P. Fowler, 1999

Martial *Epigrams* (selected) P: J. Michie, 1978

Musa lapidaria. A Selection of Latin Verse Inscriptions E. Courtney (ed.) 1995, Atlanta: Scholars Press, American Classical Studies 36.

Musonius see Lutz

Nepos: *Cato, Atticus*: tr. and comm. N. Horsfall, Oxford: Clarendon Press, 1989, Clarendon Ancient History

Nicolaus of Damascus *Life of Augustus*: tr. and comm. Jane Bellemore 1984, Bristol Classical Press

Ovid *The Erotic Poems* P: P. Green, 1982
—— *The Love Poems* O: A.D. Melville, 1990
—— *Sorrows of an Exile* O: A.D. Melville, E.J. Kenney, 1995

Petronius *Satyrica* B. Branham, D. Kinney, London: Everyman, 1998

Pliny *The Letters of the Younger Pliny* P: B. Radice, 1969

Plutarch The Fall of the Roman Republic P: R. Warner, R. Seager, 1972
—— *Roman Lives: a Selection of Eight Lives* O: R. Waterfield 1999
—— *Essays* P: I. Kidd, R. Waterfield, 1992
—— *Select Essays and Dialogues* D.A. Russell 1993, Oxford: Clarendon Press

Sallust *The Jugurthine War*, the Conspiracy of Catiline P: S.A. Handford, 1963

—— *Histories* see McGushin

Seneca *Letters from a Stoic* (selected) R. Campbell, 1969

Soranus Temkin, Owsei (1991) *Soranus' Gynecology*, Baltimore and London: Softshell Books

Suetonius *The Twelve Caesars* P: Robert Graves

—— *The lives of the Caesars. The Lives of Illustrious Men* L: J.C. Rolfe, Donna W. Hurley, G.P. Goold, revd. edn 1998, 1997, 2 vols

—— *On Teachers of Grammar and Rhetoric* Kaster, Robert A. ed., tr. and comm. (1995) *Suetonius de grammaticis et rhetoribus* Oxford: Clarendon Press

Tacitus *Agricola and Germany* O: A. Birley, 1999

—— *Germany*: tr. and comm. J.B. Rives, Oxford: Clarendon Press, 1999, Clarendon Ancient History

—— *Annals of Imperial Rome* P: M. Grant, 1996

—— *The Histories* O: W.H. Fyfe, D.S. Levene, 1997

Valerius Maximus *Memorable doings and sayings* L: D.R. Shackleton Bailey, 2000, 2 vols. Routledge: P.J. Smith, 2001

Vitruvius Pollio, *Ten books on architecture*: tr. and comm. Thomas N. Howe, Ingrid D. Rowland, Michael J. Dewar, Cambridge: Cambridge University Press, 1999

Virgil *Eclogues and Georgics*, O: C. Day Lewis, R.O.A.M. Lyne, 1983

—— *The Georgics* P: L.P. Wilkinson, 1982

—— *Aeneid* P: W.F.J. Knight, 1958; O: C. Day Lewis, J. Griffin, 1998

Glossary

Amicitia	friendship
Amo	I love
Amor	love
Collegium	club, society
Convicium	noisy importuning; abuse, mockery
Cos	consul, one of the pair of annual chief executives of the Roman state
Cos. suff.	replacement consul
Di(i)	gods
Domicilium	residence, domicile
Dominus	owner, master
Domus	house, household, family
Eques, pl. *equites*	member(s) of second order in the state, below Senate
Exsilium	exile
Fides	good faith, trust
Filiafamilias	daughter of a household, daughter in paternal power
Flagitatio	importunate request
Flagito	beset a person with demands, importune, clamour for a thing
Genius	the divine 'double' of a Roman man
Gens, pl. *gentes*	tribe, nation, clan

133

Habitatio	dwelling
Horti	'vegetable gardens', the name the rich gave to their suburban villas on the outskirts of Rome
Ides	the 13th or (in March, May, July, Oct.) the 15th day of the month
Imperium	military command; empire.
Iniuria	contempt, insult, injury
Insula	apartment block
Interrex	senior patrician, usually ex-consul, who held power temporarily when no consul had been elected
Lar, pl. *Lares*	protective divinity of the home (also of crossroads etc.)
Lex	law, a statute
Materfamilias	mother of a household, wife of a *paterfamilias*
Occento	I sing at
Ordo	order, rank
Paterfamilias, pl. *patresfamiliarum*	father of a household
Patronus/a, pl. *patroni/ae*	patron of client/freed slave
Penates	divinities of the stores
Perfugium	refuge
Pietas	dutiful affection (including self-sacrifice)
Plebs	the non-patricians as a body
Populares (plural)	those who try to please the people (*popularis* singular) noun and adjective.
Populus (Romanus)	The (Roman) people
Princeps pl. *Principes*	leading man, men
Prudentia	good sense, prudence
Pudor	modesty and self-respect, sense of propriety
Res gestae	deeds
Societas	partnership
Socius	ally, partner
Urbs, pl. *urbes*	city
Vis	violence, force

Notes

1 Introduction

1   Momigliano puts it well: 'historicism is the recognition that each of us sees past events from a point of view determined or at least in part conditioned by our own individual changing situation in history' (1977: 366). For a lively recent book on 'key debates in the theory and practice of history in relation to the practice of ancient history' see Morley 1999, who refers to some of the immense bibliography on the philosophy of history. Burke 1991 (essays by practitioners) surveys new developments in various fields and gives a vivid picture of what is going on in the discipline as a whole. Burke 1992 is an indispensable overview of what we need to know about the cross-fertilisation of history and the social sciences, clearly illustrated by examples from recent historiography.

2 Evidence

1   R. MacMullen 1997: 79–80.
2   As Balsdon pointed out in his splendidly readable article 1958 'that is the only evidence which, for any reconstruction whatever, cannot possibly be disregarded' (81). Unfortunately, he does not discuss the murder itself. For the run-up to the murder, see Nicholas Horsfall 1974, who says 'On the Ides more varied and abundant information survives,

I believe, than on any other day in Roman or Greek history.' He does not describe the actual stabbing. Holmes 1923 lists the sources (iii: 339–44).

3 *A* 14.4/358.2, 10 April; 14.6/360.1, 12 April; 14.9/363.2, 17 April; 14.11/365.1, 21 April; 14.12/366.1–2, 22 April; 14.13/367.2, 26 April; 14.14/368.2–3, 28/9 April; 14.18/373.4, 9 May; 14.21/375.3, 11 May; 14.22/376.2, 14 May; 15.4/381.2, 24 May. Cf. *F* 12.1/327.2, to Cassius, 3 May. SB's number follows the slash.

4 *Periochae* 116. The conspirators named by Livy are Brutus, Cassius, D. Brutus and Trebonius. Velleius, in his very compact history, published in AD 30, has the same list, but tells us nothing but the fact of the murder (2.56.3). He is more interested in soothsayers and dreams (2.57).

5 4.5.6. He was also interested in the dream of Calpurnia (1.7.2) and in the soothsayer (8.11.2).

6 Vergil *Aeneid* 6.834–5 has one direct appeal to Caesar not to incur the guilt of civil war. Vergil *Eclogues* 9.47 and Horace *Odes* 1.12.47 refer to the star which represented apotheosis. In Verg. *Georgics* 1.466 the sun foresees and pities the disasters which will befall Rome because of Caesar's death. The absence of Julius Caesar from the Shield of Aeneas in *Aen.* 8.625–731 is especially notable. See Syme 1939: 317–18.

7 Plutarch *Caes.* 66, Suetonius *Julius* 81.4–82.3; cf. App. *BC* 2.117, Cass. Dio 44.19. There are also the minor compilers: Florus (2nd c. AD?) 2.13.95, Eutropius (4th c.) 6.25, Obsequens (4th/early 5th c. AD) 67, Orosius (5th c.) 6.17.1, Ps.-Aurelius Victor *de viris illustribus* 78.10, all highly derivative.

8 Among those in English attention may be drawn here, for example, to the very full Cambridge Classical Texts and Commentaries on Cicero by Berry 1996 and Shackleton Bailey 1965–70, 1977, 1980 and on Tacitus by Goodyear 1972, 1981, Woodman and Martin 1989, 1996; to the Oxford editions of Ciceronian speeches by R.G. Nisbet 1939 and R.G.M. Nisbet 1961, of Vergil *Georgics* by Mynors 1990 and of Horace *Odes* i 1970 and ii 1978 by R.G.M. Nisbet and M. Hubbard. Smaller and older 'school' editions are not to be despised. All these can be used selectively by the reader who does not understand the Latin. The *Clarendon Ancient History* series offers translations and commentary on the English text and is therefore completely accessible to the Latin-less user.

9 The standard histories of literature give the essential overview and bibliographies on individual authors: *CHGL*, *CHLL*, Lesky 1966,

Conte 1994, Dihle 1994. See also *OCD* under 'Latin literature', gen-res and individuals. For the historian's point of view see Wells 1992: Ch. 2, Potter 1999. Fantham 1996 puts authors and audiences in their social context and, in working 'toward a social history of Latin litera-ture', makes a contribution to social history and to the historian's understanding of the literary sources.

10 See Select List of Translations (p. 129). The existence of a Loeb for individual authors may be assumed unless I note otherwise.

11 The tradition goes back to Ennius (239–169 BC), who went to Ambracia with M. Fulvius Nobilior (189–7). The work of the 'tame poets' in Greek and Latin for leading Romans such as Marius or Pompey does not survive. 'Themselves': e.g. Cicero *de consulatu suo*.

12 Up-to-date guidebooks are essential. Note, e.g. (beyond the indis-pensable comprehensive *Blue Guides* published by A. & C. Black of London/ W.W. Norton of New York) for Italy the *Guide archeologiche Laterza* (in Italian) directed by F. Coarelli (Rome-Bari: Laterza); *Oxford Archaeological Guides* edited by B. Cunliffe (Oxford: Oxford University Press), e.g. Claridge 1998, Collins 1998; Bromwich 1993. Also introductory surveys to read before a visit: e.g. Keay 1988, T.W. Potter 1987, Potter and Johns 1992. For the City of Rome, Richardson 1992, *LTUR* (multilingual).

13 (When asked by a lady why he defined 'pastern' as the 'knee' of a horse in his Dictionary) 'Ignorance, madam, pure ignorance.' (*Oxford Dictionary of Quotations*).

14 This criticism, often heard at conferences, derives from a comment by Dr Johnson: 'Your manuscript is both good and original; but the part that is good is not original, and the part that is original is not good.' I am grateful to Stephen Harrison for the attribution.

5 Case study II: How holy was the house?

1 There is something wrong with the text: at the least, it has been 'tele-scoped', but that does not affect the part in which we are interested. *Lar* occurs perhaps in one other *Digest* text (conjectural): 6.1.38 Celsus *iii dig.*, where a man of modest landed property (*pauper*) risks losing his *Lares*. We may certainly compare a later legal text, a rescript of the emperors Diocletian and Maximian, *CJ* 10.40 (39).7.1: '... where someone sets up his *Lar* ('ubi quis larem ... constituit') and the total-ity of his property and fortunes'. With our *Digest* text's 'larem collo-care' we may compare Ovid *Metamorphoses* 1.173–4: 'In this quarter

the powerful and famous inhabitants of heaven have set their *Penates*' ('hac parte potentes / caelicolae clarique suos *posuere Penates*'), deftly translated by Wiseman 1981/94: 109 as 'have made their homes'.

2   E.g. *Dizionario epigraphico* iv 1.13 (1946) on *Lares*, Orr 1978, Bayet 1969: 63–6.

3   Neither David A. Sills 1972 nor A. and J. Kuper 1985 has anything relevant. In an interdisciplinary and theoretical volume, Kent 1990a, Kent 1990b surveys theories on the interaction of human beings with their environment and domestic buildings; Jameson 1990 has a balanced and critical account of the symbolism of the Greek house, especially the hearth; Sanders 1990 gives a useful account of theories of personal space, territoriality, distancing and boundaries at 47–9.

4   The Excise Bill was a Bill which imposed duty on cider and perry 'subjecting the makers of those liquors to the laws of excise. He (the Elder Pitt) opposed this Bill very strongly, upon the dangerous precedent of admitting the officers of excise into private houses. Every man's house was his castle, he said. If this tax is endured, he said, it will necessarily lead to introducing the laws of excise into the domestic concerns of every private family.' (*Anecdotes* 1810: 368). This seems a suitable context for the words Nisbet quotes. But Brougham, still the authority, 1845: 53–4 does not specify the speech or occasion. (In pre-Hansard days, accounts of debates came from newspaper reports. The Elder Pitt's's oratory is as poorly known as that of Julius Caesar (Brougham 1845: 39–40).) He quotes the passage as follows:

> Perhaps the finest of them all is his allusion to the maxim of English law, that every man's house is his castle. 'The poorest man may in his cottage bid defiance to all the forces of the crown. It may be frail – its roof may shake – the wind may blow through it – the storm may enter – the rain may enter – but the King of England cannot enter! – all his force dares not cross the threshold of the ruined tenement!'

5   The *Vocabularium* gives references in the form of a number in large type, followed by a number in small type, with or without a bar on top. The former refers to the column in Mommsen's two-volume edition of *D*, the latter to the line. The bar indicates vol. ii. Later editions, including Watson's translation, indicate the columns and lines in the margin.

6   The tenant had rights against the landlord (*D* 43.32).

Bibliography

This list does not include translations or everything mentioned in Chapter 6.

Alcock, Susan (1993) *Graecia capta. The landscapes of Roman Greece*, Cambridge: Cambridge University Press.

Alexander, Michael C. (1990) *Trials in the Late Roman Republic, 149 BC to 50 BC* Toronto: University of Toronto Press.

Anecdotes of the life of the Rt. Hon. William Pitt, Earl of Chatham, and of the principal events of his time, with his speeches in Parliament from the year 1736 to the year 1778, 7th edn 1810, London: Longman, Hurst, Rees and Orme.

Arafat, K(arim) W. (1996) *Pausanias' Greece. Ancient artist and Roman ruler*, Cambridge: Cambridge University Press.

Arangio-Ruiz, Vincenzo (1948, 1974) 'Les tablettes d'Herculanum', *Revue internationale des droits de l'Antiquité* 1 (1948) 9–25 = *Studi epigrafici e papyrologici*, L. Bove (ed.) (Naples: Giannini) 295–308.

Arjava, Antti (1996) *Women and Law in Late Antiquity*, Oxford: Clarendon Press.

Bagnall, Roger (1995) *Reading Papyri, Writing Ancient History*, London and New York: Routledge.

—— and Bruce W. Frier (1994) *The Demography of Roman Egypt*, Cambridge: Cambridge University Press, Cambridge Studies in Population, Economy and Society in Past Times, 23.

Bailey, D.R.S. (1965–70) *Cicero's letters to Atticus*, Cambridge: Cambridge University Press, 7 vols.

—— (1977) *Cicero Epistulae ad Familiares*, Cambridge: Cambridge University Press, 2 vols.

—— (1980) *Cicero Epistulae ad Quintum Fratrem et M. Brutum*, Cambridge: Cambridge University Press.

—— (1988) *Cicero's Letters to his Friends*, Atlanta, Georgia: Scholars Press.

—— (1992) *Onomasticon to Cicero's Speeches*, Stuttgart and Leipzig: Teubner.

—— (1995) *Onomasticon to Cicero's Letters,* Stuttgart and Leipzig: Teubner.

—— (1996) *Onomasticon to Cicero's Treatises*, Stuttgart and Leipzig: Teubner.

—— (1999) *Cicero Letters to Atticus*, Cambridge, Mass., and London: Harvard University Press (Loeb), 4 vols.

Balsdon, J.P.V.D.(1958) 'The Ides of March', *Historia* 7: 80–94.

—— (1962, rev. 1974) *Roman Women. Their History and Habits*, London: Bodley Head.

—— (1969) *Life and Leisure in Ancient Rome*, London: Bodley Head.

—— (1979) *Romans and Aliens*, London: Duckworth.

Bannon, Cynthia J. (1997) *The brothers of Romulus. Fraternal Pietas in Roman Law, Literature and Society*, Princeton: Princeton University Press.

Barnes, Timothy D. (1971, rev. 1985) *Tertullian. A Historical and Literary Study*, Oxford: Clarendon Press.

Bayet, Jean (1969) *Histoire politique et psychologique de la religion romaine,* Paris: Payot, 2nd edn.

Beard, Mary, John North and Simon Price (1998) *Religions of Rome,* i *A History,* ii *A Sourcebook*, Cambridge: Cambridge University Press.

Berger, Adolf (1953, repr. 1980) *Encyclopedic Dictionary of Roman Law*, Philadelphia: the American Philosophical Society, Transactions 43.2.

Berry, D. H. (1996) *Cicero pro P. Sulla oratio*, Cambridge: Cambridge University Press.

Blackstone, William (1765–9) *Commentaries on the Laws of England*, Oxford: Clarendon Press, repr. Chicago and London: University of Chicago Press 1979, 4 vols.

Bodel, John (ed.) (2001) *Epigraphic Evidence,* London: Routledge.

Boulay, Juliet du (1974) *Portrait of a Greek Mountain Village*, Oxford: Clarendon Press.

Bowman, Alan K. and David Thomas (1994) *The Vindolanda Writing-Tablets (Tabulae Vindolandenses)* ii with contributions by J.N. Adams (ed., trans. and comm.), London: British Museum.

Bradley, Keith R. (1984, 1987) *Slaves and Masters in the Roman Empire. A Study in Social Control*, Brussels: Latomus, Collection Latomus 185 = New York: Oxford University Press.

—— (1986) 'Wet-nursing at Rome: a Study in Social Relations' in B. Rawson (1986) 201–29.

—— (1991) *Discovering the Roman Family. Studies in Roman Social History*, New York and Oxford: Oxford University Press.

—— (1993) 'Writing the History of the Roman Family', *CP* 88 237–50.

—— (1994) *Slavery and Society at Rome*, Cambridge: Cambridge University Press.

—— (1997) 'Law, magic and culture in the *Apologia* of Apuleius', *Phoenix* 51: 203–23.

—— (1998) 'The sentimental education of the Roman child: the role of pet-keeping', *Latomus* 57: 523–57.

Bromwich, James (1993) *The Roman Remains of Southern France. A Guidebook*, London: Routledge.

Brougham, Henry, Lord (1845) *Historical Sketches of Statesmen who Flourished in the Time of George III, to which are added Remarks on Party and an Appendix* First series i, London: Charles Knight.

Bruns, Karl G. (1909–12) *Fontes iuris Romani antiqui* (7th edn, revised by O. Gradenwitz) Tübingen: Möhr, 3 vols; republished 1969 Aalen: Scientia Verlag, 2 vols in 1.

Brunt, P.A. (1971a) *Italian Manpower 225 BC–AD 14*, Oxford: Clarendon Press.

—— (1971b) *Social Conflicts in the Roman Republic*, London: Chatto and Windus.

—— (1973) 'Aspects of the social thought of Dio Chrysostom and of the Stoics', *Proceedings of the Cambridge Philological Society* 19: 9–34.

—— (1988a) *The Fall of the Roman Republic and Related Essays*, Oxford: Clarendon Press.

—— (1988b) '*Amicitia*', in 1988a: 351–81.

—— (1988c) '*Clientela*', in 1988a: 382–442.

—— and J.M. Moore (1967) *Res Gestae divi Augusti. The Achievements of the Divine Augustus*, Oxford: Oxford University Press.

Burke, Peter, (ed.) (1991) *New perspectives on Historical Writing*, Cambridge: Polity Press.

—— (1992) *History and social theory*, Cambridge: Polity Press.

Burstein, Stanley, Ramsay MacMullen, Kurt A. Raaflaub, Allen M. Ward (1997) *Ancient History. Recent Work and New Directions*, Claremont, California: Regina Books and AAH, Publications of the Association of Ancient Historians 5.

Cambridge Ancient History 1970– (2nd edn), Cambridge: Cambridge University Press.

Carcopino, J. (1956) *Daily Life in Ancient Rome. The people and the City at the Height of the Empire*, Harmondsworth: Penguin, tr. H.T. Rowell.

Cargill, Jack (1997) *Handbook for Ancient History Classes*, Claremont, California: The Paige Press.

Carson, Lisa (1998) 'CD-ROM technology and *L'Année Philologique*', *Classical World* 91: 553–64.

Cartledge, Paul (1996) 'Class struggle' in *OCD* 335–6.

Cèbe, Jean-Pierre (ed.) (1972–) *Varron. Satires Menippées*, Rome: Ecole française de Rome, Collection de l'Ecole française de Rome 9.

Champlin, Edward (1980) *Fronto and Antonine Rome,* Cambridge, Mass.: Harvard University Press.

—— (1991) *Final Judgments. Duty and Emotion in Roman Wills 200 BC–AD 250*, Berkeley: University of California Press.

Cherry, David (1998) *Frontier and Society in Roman North Africa*, Oxford: Clarendon Press.

Chilver, G.E.F. (1979) *A Historical Commentary on Tacitus' Histories i and ii*, Oxford: Clarendon Press.

—— and G.B. Townend (1985) *A Historical Commentary on Tacitus' Histories iv and v*, Oxford: Clarendon Press.

Cicero (1904) *M. Tulli Ciceronis scripta quae manserunt omnia* (ed.) C.F.W. Mueller iv, 3 Leipzig: Teubner. (Contains philosophic fragments.)

Claridge, Amanda (1998) *Rome*, Oxford: Oxford University Press, Oxford Archaeological Guides.

Clark, Patricia A. (1991) 'Tullia and Crassipes', *Phoenix* 45: 28–38.

Clarke, Katherine (1999) *Between Geography and History. Hellenistic Constructions of the Roman World*, Oxford: Clarendon Press, Oxford Classical Monographs.

Clarke, M. L. (1965) 'Non hominis nomen, sed eloquentiae' in T.A. Dorey (ed.) *Cicero*, London: Routledge and Kegan Paul: 81–107.

Clayman, Dee (ed.) *Database of Classical Bibliography (DCB)* on CD-ROM, Atlanta, GA: Scholars Press.

Coke, Sir Edward (1797) *The Third Part of the Institutes of the Laws of England*, London: E. and R. Brooke.

—— (1826) *The Reports*, London: Butterworth, 6 vols.

Collingwood, R.G. and R.P. Wright (eds) (1967) *The Roman Inscriptions of Britain,* i: *Inscriptions on Stone*, Oxford: Clarendon Press.

Collins, Roger (1998) *Spain. An Oxford Archaeological Guide*, Oxford: Oxford University Press.

Constitutions of the United States, National and State (1982) i, Dobbs Ferry, NY: Oceana.

Conte, Gian Biagio (1994) *Latin Literature. A history*, tr. J. Solodow, Baltimore and London: Johns Hopkins University Press.

Cotton, H.M., W.E.H. Cockle, F.G.B. Millar (1995) 'The papyrology of the Roman Near East: a survey', *JRS* 85: 214–35.

Courtney, Edward (1980) *A Commentary on the Satires of Juvenal*, London: Athlone Press.

Crawford, Jane W. (1984) *M. Tullius Cicero. The lost and unpublished orations*, Göttingen: Vandenhoek and Ruprecht, Hypomnemata 80.

—— (1994) (ed. with comm.) *Cicero. The Fragmentary Speeches,* Atlanta: Scholars Press.

Crawford Michael H. (1983) (ed.) *Sources for Ancient History*, Cambridge: Cambridge University Press, The Sources of History. Studies in the Uses of Historical Evidence (ed. G.R. Elton).

—— (1996a) 'Citizenship, Roman' in *OCD*: 334–5.

—— (ed.) (1996b) *Roman Statutes*, London: Institute of Classical Studies, 2 vols.

Crifò, Giuliano (1961) *Ricerche sull 'exilium' nel periodo repubblicano* i, Milan: Giuffrè.

Crook, John A. (1967) *Law and Life of Rome*, London: Thames and Hudson.

Curti, E., E. Dench and John R. Patterson (1996) 'The archaeology of central and southern Roman Italy: recent trends and approaches', *JRS* 86: 170–89.

Damon, Cynthia and Takács, Sarolta (eds) (1999), *The Senatus consultum de Cn. Pisone patre. Text, translation and discussion, AJP* 120.1.

D'Arms, John H. (1970) *Romans on the Bay of Naples. A Social and Cultural Study of the Villas and Their Owners*, Cambridge, MA: Harvard University Press, Loeb Classical Monographs.

—— (1981) *Commerce and Social Standing in Ancient Rome*, Cambridge, Mass.: Harvard University Press.

Daube, David (1937) 'Some comparative law – *furtum conceptum*', *TvR* 15: 48–77.

Davis, David Brion (1970) *The Problem of Slavery in Western Culture*, Harmondsworth: Penguin.

Davis, Natalie Zemon (1975) 'The reasons of misrule' in *ead. Society and Culture in Early Modern France*, London: Duckworth: 97–123, 296–309.

Dickens, Charles (1986) *The Pickwick Papers*, Oxford: Clarendon Press (originally published in volume form 1847).

Dihle, A. (1994) *Greek and Latin literature of the Roman Empire from Augustus to Justinian* tr. M. Malzhan from *Die griechischen und lateinischen Literatur der Kaiserzeit von Augustus bis Justinian* (1989), London: Routledge.

Dixon, Suzanne (1984) 'Family finances: Tullia and Terentia', *Antichthon* 18: 78–107.

—— (1986) 'Family finances: Terentia and Tullia' in Rawson 1986: 93–120.

—— (1988) *The Roman Mother*, London and Sydney: Routledge.

—— (1992) *The Roman Family*, Baltimore: Johns Hopkins University Press.

Drumann, Wilhelm Karl August and P. Groebe (1899–1929) *Geschichte Roms in seinem Übergange von der republikanischen zur monarchischen Verfassung oder Pompeius, Caesar, Cicero und ihre Zeitgenossen*, Leipzig: Borntraeger, 6 vols., 2nd edn.

Dunbabin, Katherine M.D. (1999) *Mosaics of the Greek and Roman world*, Cambridge: Cambridge University Press.

Duncan-Jones, Richard (1974) 'The finances of a senator' in *id.* (1982) *The Economy of the Roman Empire. Quantitative Studies*, Cambridge: Cambridge University Press, 2nd edn: 17–32.

Dyson, Stephen L. (1992) *Community and Society in Roman Italy*, Baltimore and London: Johns Hopkins University Press.

Evans, Jane DeRose (1998) 'Recent research in Roman Crafts 1985–1995', *Classical World* 91, 4: 235–72.

Evans, J.K. (1991) *War, Women and Children in Ancient Rome*, London and New York: Routledge.

Evans Grubbs, Judith (1995) *Law and Family in Late Antiquity. The Emperor Constantine's Marriage Legislation*, Oxford: Clarendon Press.

Fantham, R. Elaine (1996) *Roman Literary Culture from Cicero to Apuleius*, Baltimore and London: Johns Hopkins University Press.

——, H.P. Foley, N.B. Kampen, S.B. Pomeroy and H. A. Shapiro (1994) *Women in the Classical World. Image and Text*, New York: Oxford University Press.

Fischler, David Hackett (1970) *Historians' Fallacies. Toward a Logic of Historical Thought*, New York: Harper.

Flower, Harriet (1996) *Ancestor Masks and Aristocratic Power in Roman Culture*, Oxford: Clarendon Press.

Fraenkel, Eduard (1961) 'Two poems of Catullus', *JRS* 51: 46–53.

Fraser, James G. (1929) *P. Ovidii Nasonis fastorum libri sex. The Fasti of Ovid* iv, London: Macmillan.

Frend, W.H.C. (1952), *The Donatist Church. A movement of protest in Roman North Africa*, Oxford: Clarendon Press.

Frere, S.S. and R.S.O. Tomlin (eds) (1990–94) *The Roman inscriptions of Britain* ii: *Instrumentum domesticum*, Oxford: Clarendon Press.

Friedländer, Ludwig (1939) *Roman Life and Manners under the Early Empire* tr. J.H. Freese and L.A. Magnus, London: Routledge, 3 vols.

Frier, Bruce W. (1996) 'Status, legal and social, Roman', *OCD* 1441–2.

Gardner, Jane F. (1986) *Women in Roman law and society*, London: Croom Helm.

—— (1993) *Being a Roman Citizen*, London: Routledge.

—— (1998) *Family and Familia in Roman Law and Life*, Oxford: Clarendon Press.

Garnsey, Peter D.A. (1970) *Social Status and Legal Privilege in the Roman Empire*, Oxford: Clarendon Press.

—— and Richard P. Saller (1987) *The Roman Empire. Economy, Society and Culture*, Berkeley: University of California Press.

Girouard, Mark (1978) *Life in the English Country House*, New Haven: Yale University Press.

Gleason, Maud (1999) 'Truth contests and talking corpses' in James I. Porter (ed.) *Constructions of the Classical Body*, Ann Arbor: University of Michigan Press: 287–309.

Golden, Mark (1992) 'The uses of cross-cultural comparison in ancient social history', *CV/EMC* 36 ns 11: 309–31.

Goodman, Martin (1997) *The Roman World 44 BC–AD 180*, London: Routledge.

Goodyear (1972) *Tacitus Annals* i, Cambridge: Cambridge University Press.

—— (1981) *Tacitus Annals* ii, Cambridge: Cambridge University Press.

Gowing, Alain M. (1992) *The Triumviral Narratives of Appian and Cassius Dio*, Ann Arbor: University of Michigan Press.

Grant, Michael and Rachel Kitzinger (eds) (1988) *Civilization of the Ancient Mediterranean. Greece and Rome*, New York: Scribner, 3 vols.

Griffin, Jasper (1985) *Latin Poets and Roman life,* London: Duckworth.

Griffin, Miriam (1976) *Seneca. A Philosopher in Politics*, Oxford: Clarendon Press.

—— (1997) 'The Senate's story', *JRS* 87: 249–63.

Gullath, Brigitte and Frank Heidtmann (1992) *Wie findich ich wissen-schaftlicher Literatur Klassische Philologie, Mittel- und Neulatein, Byzantinistik, Alte Geschichte und Klassische Archäologie*, Berlin: Arno Spitz.

Habicht, Christian (1998) *Pausanias' guide to ancient Greece*, Berkeley: University of California Press, Sather Lectures, revd. pb. edn.

Harl, Kenneth W. (1996) *Coinage in the Roman Economy 300 BC to AD 700*, Baltimore: Johns Hopkins University Press.

Harris, W.V. (1993) 'Between archaic and modern: some current problems in the history of the Roman economy' in Harris (ed.), *The Inscribed Economy. Production and Distribution in the Roman Empire in the Light of Instrumentum Domesticum*, Ann Arbor: University of Michigan Press.

Harrison, Stephen (ed.) (1999) *Oxford Readings in the Roman Novel*, Oxford: Clarendon Press.

Hart-Davis, Rupert (1978) *The Lyttelton Hart-Davis Letters. Correspondence of George Lyttelton and Rupert Hart-Davis 1955–56*, London: Murray.

Hayes, John W. (1997) *Handbook of Mediterranean Pottery*, London: British Museum.

Hellstern, Mark, Gregory M. Scott, Stephen M. Garrison, (1998) *The History Student Writer's Manual*, Upper Saddle River, New Jersey: Prentice Hall.

Hexter, J. H. (1971) *Doing History*, Bloomington and London: George Allen and Unwin.

Holmes, T. Rice S. (1923) *The Roman Republic and the Founder of the Empire*, Oxford: Clarendon Press.

Hopkins, M. Keith (1983) *Death and Renewal. Sociological Studies in Roman History* ii, Cambridge: Cambridge University Press.

Horsfall, Nicholas (1974) 'The Ides of March: some new problems', *Greece and Rome* 21: 191–9.

—— (1989) *Nepos: Cato, Atticus*, Oxford: Clarendon Press.

—— (1996) *La cultura della plebs romana*, Barcelona: PPU.

Howgego, Christopher (1995) *Ancient History from Coins*, London: Routledge.

Hutchinson, G.O. (1998) *Cicero's Correspondence. A Literary Study*, Oxford: Clarendon Press.

Innes, Michael (1970) *Death at the Chase*, London: Gollancz (Penguin 1971).

Jameson, Michael H. (1990) 'Space in the Greek city state' in Kent 1990a 92–113.

Jones, Christopher P. (1971) *Plutarch and Rome*, Oxford: Clarendon Press.

—— (1978) *The Roman World of Dio Chrysostom*, Cambridge, MA: Harvard University Press.

—— (1986) *Culture and Society in Lucian*, Cambridge, MA: Harvard University Press.

Kaser, M. (1966) *Das römische Zivilprozessrecht* (Handbuch der Altertumswissenschaft) Munich: Beck.

Kaster, Robert A. (ed.) and tr. (1995) *Suetonius de grammaticis et rhetoribus*, Oxford: Clarendon Press.

Keay, S. J. (1988) *Roman Spain*, London: British Museum, Exploring the Roman world.

Kehoe, D.P. (1997) *Investment, Profit, and Tenancy. The Jurists and the Roman Agrarian Economy*, Ann Arbor: University of Michigan Press.

Kelly, J.M. (1966) *Roman Litigation*, Oxford: Clarendon Press.

Kent, Susan (1990a) *Domestic Architecture and the Use of Space. an Interdisciplinary Cross-cultural Study*, Cambridge: Cambridge University Press.

—— 1990b, 'Activity areas and architecture: an interdisciplinary view of the relationship between use of space and domestic built environments' in 1990 a: 1–8.

Keppie, Lawrence (1991) *Understanding Roman Inscriptions*, Baltimore and London: Johns Hopkins University Press.

Kertzer, David I. and Richard P. Saller (eds) (1991) *The Family in Italy from Antiquity to the Present*, New Haven and London: Yale University Press.

Kleine Pauly, Der Lexikon der Antike, Stuttgart: Druckenmüller, 1964–75.

Krause, Jens-Uwe (ed.) (1992) *Die Familie und weitere anthropologische Grundlagen*, Stuttgart: Steiner, Heidelberger Althistorische Beiträge und Epigraphische Studien 11. Bibliographie zur römischen Sozialgeschichte 1.

—— *et al.* (eds) (1998) *Bibliographie zur römischen Sozialgeschichte 2: Schichten, Konflikte, religiöse Gruppen, materielle Kultur*, Stuttgart: Steiner, Heidelberger Althistorische Beiträge und Epigraphische Studien 26

Kuper, Adam and Jessica (1985) *The Social Science Encyclopedia*, London: Routledge and Kegan Paul.

Lendon, J.E. (1997) *Empire of Honour. The Art of Government in the Roman World*, Oxford: Clarendon Press.

Lesky, Albin (1966) *A History of Greek Literature*, tr. James Willis and Cornelius de Heer, London: Methuen.

Letters from a farmer in Pennsylvania to the inhabitants of the British colonies regarding the right of taxation and several other important points. To which are added the speeches of Lord Chatham and Lord Camden, the one upon the Stamp Act, the other on the Declaratory Bill (1768) Dublin: Sheppard (Bodleian G. Pamphl. 338 (10)).

Ling, Roger (1990) *Roman Painting,* Cambridge: Cambridge University Press.

Lintott, A.W. (1967) 'Popular justice in a letter of Cicero to Quintus', *RhM* 110: 65–9.

—— (1999, 1st edn 1968) *Violence in Republican Rome*, Oxford: Clarendon Press.

Lutz, Cora (1947) 'Musonius Rufus: the Roman Socrates', *Yale Classical Studies* 10: 3–147.

McDonnell, Myles (1983) 'Divorce initiated by women in Rome: the evidence of Plautus', *American Journal of Ancient History* 8: 54–80.

McGinn, Thomas A.J. (1998) *Prostitution, Sexuality and the Law in Ancient Rome*, New York and Oxford: Oxford University Press.

McGushin, Patrick (1992) *Sallust The Histories* i, tr. with introduction and commentary, Oxford: Clarendon, Clarendon Ancient History.

—— (1994) *Sallust The Histories* ii, tr. with introduction and commentary, Oxford: Clarendon Press, Clarendon Ancient History.

McKeown, J.C. (1989) *Ovid Amores. Text, Prolegomena and Commentary* ii, Leeds: F. Cairns, ARCA 22.

MacMullen, Ramsay (1982) 'The epigraphic habit in the Roman Empire', *AJP* 103: 233–46.

—— (1990) *Changes in the Roman Empire. Essays in the Ordinary*, Princeton: Princeton University Press.

—— (1997) 'The Roman Empire' in Burstein 1997: 79–102.

Malcovati, Enrica (ed.) (1930) *Oratorum Romanorum Fragmenta liberae reipublicae* , Turin: Paravia, 3 vols., reissued 1976–9, 2 vols.

Mellor, Ronald (1995) *Tacitus. The Classical Heritage*, New York and London: Garland.

Merguet, H. (1964) *Handlexikon zu Cicero*, Hildesheim: Olms.

Millar, Fergus (1964) *A study of Cassius Dio*, Oxford: Clarendon Press.

—— (1981a, 1st edn 1967) *The Roman Empire and its Neighbours*, London: Duckworth.

—— (1981b) 'The world of the *Golden Ass*', *JRS* 71: 63–75.

—— (1983) 'Epigraphy' in Crawford, Michael H. 1983: 80–136.

—— (1998) *The Crowd in Rome in the Late Republic*, Ann Arbor: University of Michigan Press.

Momigliano, Arnaldo (1977) 'Historicism revisited' in *id. Essays in Ancient and Modern Historiography*, Oxford: Blackwell, 365–73.

—— (1984) 'The rhetoric of history and the history of rhetoric: on Hayden White's tropes' in *id. Settimo contributo alla storia degli studi classici e del mondo antico*, Rome: Edizioni di storia e letteratura: 49–59.

Morley, Neville (1999) *Writing Ancient History*, London: Duckworth and Ithaca, N.Y.: Cornell University Press.

Mynors, Sir Roger (1990) *Virgil Georgics*, Oxford: Clarendon Press.

Neue Pauly, Der Enzyklopädie der Antike, Stuttgart: Metzler, 1996.

Nicolet, C. (1994) 'Economy and society 133–43 BC' in *CAH* ix: 599–643.

Nisbet, R.G. (1939) *M. Tulli Ciceronis de domo sua ad pontifices oratio*, Oxford: Clarendon Press.

Nisbet, R.G.M. (1961) *Cicero in L. Calpurnium Pisonem*, Oxford: Clarendon Press.

—— (1992, 1995) 'The orator and the reader: manipulation and response in Cicero's *Fifth Verrine*', in A.J. Woodman and J.G.P. Powell (eds) *Author and Audience in Latin Literature,* Cambridge: Cambridge University Press: 1–17, 218–8 = *Collected Papers on Latin literature*, Oxford: Clarendon Press: 362–80.

—— and Margaret Hubbard (1970) *A Commentary on Horace Odes Book I*, Oxford: Clarendon Press.

—— (1978) *A Commentary on Horace Odes Book ii*, Oxford: Clarendon Press.

Orr, David G. (1978) 'Roman domestic religion: the evidence of the household shrines' in *ANRW* 16.2: 1575–91.

Parkin, Tim (1992) *Demography and Roman Society*, Baltimore: Johns Hopkins University Press.

—— (1997) 'Out of sight, out of mind: elderly members of the Roman family' in B. Rawson and Weaver (eds) 1997: 123–48.

Patterson, John R. (1992) 'The city of Rome from Republic to Empire', *JRS* 82: 186–215.

Patterson, Orlando (1982) *Slavery and Social Death. A Comparative Study*, Harvard: Harvard University Press.

Peacock, D.P.S. (1982) *Pottery in the Roman World*, London and New York: Longman, Longman Archaeological Series.

—— and D.F. Williams (1986) *Amphorae and the Roman Economy. An Introductory Guide*, London and New York: Longman, Longman Archaeological Series.

Peter, Hermann (1914–16, 2nd edn, 1st edn 1883) *Historicorum Romanorum Reliquiae*, Leipzig: Teubner, 2 vols.

Pocock, Lewis G. (1967, repr. of 1926 edn) *A Commentary on Cicero in Vatinium*, Amsterdam: Hakkert.

Polak, J.M. (1946) 'The Roman conception of the inviolability of the house' in *Symbolae ad ius et historiam antiquitatis pertinentes Julio Christiano van Oven dedicatae* eds. M. David, B.A. van Groningen, E.M. Meijers, Leiden: Brill: 251–68.

Potter, David (1999) *Literary Texts and the Roman Historian*, London: Routledge.

Potter, T.W. (1987) *Roman Italy*, London: British Museum, Berkeley and Los Angeles: University of California Press.

—— and Catherine Johns (1992) *Roman Britain*, London: British Museum/ Berkeley and Los Angeles: University of California Press.

Price, Simon R.F. (1986) 'The future of dreams: from Freud to Artemidorus', *Past and Present* 113: 3–37.

Prosopographia imperii romani saeculi I, II, III (1933–, 2nd edn, E. Groag), Berlin: De Gruyter.

Purcell, Nicholas (1994) 'The city of Rome and the *plebs urbana* in the late Republic', *CAH* ix: 644–88.

—— (1996) 'House, Italian' in *OCD* 731–2.

Radin, Max (1937a) 'The rivalry of common-law and civil law ideas in the American colonies' in Alison Reppy (ed.) *Law. A Century of Progress*, New York: New York University Press/London: H. Milford, Oxford University Press ii: 404–31.

—— (1937b) '*Obvagulatio*' in *RE* xvii.2 1747–50.

Rawson, Beryl (1986) (ed.) *The Family in Ancient Rome. New Perspectives*, London and Sydney: Croom Helm.

—— (1991) (ed.) *Marriage, Divorce and Children in Ancient Rome*, Oxford: Clarendon Press.

—— (1997) 'The iconography of Roman childhood', in Rawson and Weaver 1997: 233–8.

—— and Paul Weaver (1997) (eds) *The Roman Family in Italy. Status, Sentiment, Space*, Canberra: Humanities Research Centre and Oxford: Clarendon Press.

Reardon, B.P. (1991) *The form of Greek romance*, Princeton: Princeton University Press.

Reinhold, Meyer (1988) *From Republic to Principate. An Historical Commentary on Cassius Dio's Roman History Books 49–52 (36–29 BC)*, Atlanta: Scholars Press, American Philological Association Monograph Series.

Reynolds, L.D. (1983) (ed.) *Texts and Transmission. A Survey of the Latin Classics*, Oxford: Clarendon Press.

—— and N.G. Wilson (1991, 1st edn 1968) *Scribes and Scholars. A Guide to the Transmission of Greek and Latin Literature*, Oxford: Clarendon Press.

Richardson, Lawrence (1992) *A New Topographical Dictionary of Ancient Rome*, Baltimore: Johns Hopkins University Press.

Riposati, Benedetto (1939) *M. Terenti Varronis De Vita Populi Romani*, Milan: Soc. editr. Vita e Pensiero, Pubblicazioni dell' Università Cattolica del Sacro Cuore.

Rives, James B. (1995) *Religion and Authority in Roman Carthage from Augustus to Constantine*, Oxford: Clarendon Press.

Robinson, Olivia F. (1997) *The Sources of Roman Law. Problems and Methods for Ancient Historians*, London: Routledge.

Russell, D.A. (1972) *Plutarch*, London: Duckworth.

Sacks, Kenneth S. (1990) *Diodorus Siculus and the First Century*, Princeton: Princeton University Press.

Saller, Richard P. (1980) 'Anecdotes as historical evidence for the Principate', *Greece and Rome* 27: 69–83.

—— (1982) *Personal Patronage under the Early Empire*, Cambridge: Cambridge University Press.

—— (1987) 'Men's age at marriage and its consequences in the Roman family', *CP* 82: 21–34.

—— (1989) 'Patronage and friendship in early imperial Rome' in Wallace-Hadrill 1989a: 49–62.

—— (1994) *Patriarchy, property and death in the Roman family,*, Cambridge: Cambridge University Press.

Sanders, Donald (1990) 'Behavioral conventions and archaeology: methods for the analysis of ancient architecture' in Kent 1990a 43–72.

Scheidel, Walter (1995–6) 'The most silent women of Greece and Rome: rural labour and women's life in the ancient world i, ii', *G&R* 42: 202–17, 43: 1–10.

—— (1994) 'Libitina's bitter gains: seasonal mortality and endemic disease in the ancient City of Rome', *Ancient Society* (Louvain) 25: 151–75.

—— (1997) 'Continuity and change in classical scholarship: a quantitative survey 1924–1992', *Ancient Society* 28: 265–89.

Schulz, F. (1936) *Principles of Roman Law*, Oxford: Clarendon Press.

—— (1951) *Classical Roman Law* , Oxford: Clarendon Press.

Scobie, A. (1986) 'Slums, sanitation and mortality in the Roman world', *Klio* 68: 399–433.

Shaw, B. D. (1987) 'The age of Roman girls at marriage: some reconsiderations', *JRS* 77: 30–46.

Sherwin-White, A.N. (1966) *The Letters of Pliny. A Historical and Social Commentary*, Oxford: Clarendon Press.

—— (1972) 'The Roman citizenship: a survey of its development into a world franchise', *ANRW* I.2: 23–58.

Sills, David L. (1972) *International Encyclopedia of the Social Sciences*, London: Macmillan.

Spurr, M.S. (1986) *Arable Cultivation in Roman Italy c. 200 BC – c. AD 100*, London: Society for the Promotion of Roman Studies, Journal of Roman Studies Monographs 3.

Steinby, Eva Margareta (ed.) (1993–) *Lexicon topographicum urbis Romae*, Rome: Edizioni Quasar.

Stillwell, Richard (ed.) (1976) *The Princeton Encyclopedia of Classical Sites*, Princeton: Princeton University Press.

Stone, Lawrence and Jeanne C. Fawtier Stone (1986) *An Open Elite? England 1540–1880*, Oxford: Oxford University Press, abridged edn.

Sumner, G.V. (1971) 'The Lex annalis under Caesar', *Phoenix* 25 246–71 and 357–71.

Syme, Sir Ronald (1939) *The Roman Revolution*, Oxford: Clarendon Press.

—— (1958) *Tacitus,* Oxford: Clarendon Press, 2 vols.

—— (1979–91) *Roman papers*, Oxford: Clarendon Press, 7 vols.

Talbert, Richard J.A. (ed.) (2000) *Barrington Atlas of the Greek and Roman World*, Princeton: Princeton University Press.

Treggiari, Susan (1975a) 'Roman social history: recent interpretations' *Social History/Histoire sociale* 8: 149–64.

—— (1975b) 'Jobs in the household of Livia', *Papers of the British School at Rome* 43: 48–77.

—— (1980) 'Urban labour in Rome: *mercennarii* and *tabernarii*', in Peter Garnsey (ed.) *Non-slave labour in the Greco-Roman World,* Cambridge: Cambridge Philological Society: 48–64.

—— (1991) *Roman Marriage. Iusti coniuges from the time of Cicero to the time of Ulpian*, Oxford: Clarendon Press.

—— (1996) 'Social status and social legislation' in *CAH* x: 873–904.

—— (1998) 'Home and forum: Cicero between "public" and "private"', *TAPA* 128: 1–23.

—— (1999) 'The walls are witnesses': the upper-class house as symbol and focus of emotion in Cicero, *JRA* 12: 61–84.

Usener, H. (1901) 'Italische Volksjustiz', *RhM* 56: 1–28 = *Kleine Schriften* iv, Leipzig: Teubner, 1913: 356–82.

Veyne, Paul (1983) 'Le folklore à Rome et les droits de la conscience politique sur la conduite individuelle', *Latomus* 42 3–30.

Vogt, J. (1971) *Bibliographie zur antiken Sklaverei,* Bochum: Brockmeyer.

Votes (1773) *The Votes and Proceedings of the freeholders and other inhabitants of the Town of Boston in town meeting assembled according to law*, Dublin: Faulkner (Bodleian G. Pamphl. 338 (11)).

Wachsmuth, D. (1980) 'Aspekte des antiken mediterranen Hauskults', *Numen* 27: 34–75.

Wallace-Hadrill, Andrew (ed.) (1989a) *Patronage in Ancient Society,* London: Routledge, Leicester-Nottingham Studies in ancient society vol. 1.

—— (1989b) 'Patronage in Roman society' in Wallace-Hadrill 1989a: 63–87.

—— (1994) 'The social structure of the Roman house', *PBSR* 56 (1988): 43–97, as revised in *id. Houses and Society in Pompeii and Herculaneum* (Princeton) Part 1.

—— (1996) 'Patronage, power and government', *CAH* x 296–306 in *id.* 'The imperial court', *CAH* x: 283–308.

Ward, A.M. (1997) 'The Roman Republic' in Burstein 1997: 55–78.

Watson, Alan (1967) *The Law of Persons in the Later Roman Republic*, Oxford: Clarendon Press.

—— (1968) *The Law of Property in the Later Roman Republic*, Oxford: Clarendon Press.

Weaver, P.R.C. (1972) *Familia Caesaris. A Social Study of the Emperor's Freedmen and Slaves*, Cambridge: Cambridge University Press.

Wellesley, Kenneth (1972) *Cornelius Tacitus The Histories Book iii*, Sydney: Sydney University Press.

Wells, Colin M. (1972) *The German Policy of Augustus. An Examination of the Archaeological Evidence,* Oxford: Clarendon Press.

—— (1992) *The Roman Empire*, London: Fontana, 2nd edn.

—— and others (1995) 'Early Western Europe, pre-Roman North Africa, and Rome', Section 7 in *The American Historical Association's Guide to Historical Literature* 3rd edn, New York and Oxford: Oxford University Press: 192–230.

West, David (1995) *Horace Odes i. Carpe diem*, Oxford: Clarendon Press.

—— (1998) *Horace Odes ii. Vatis amici*, Oxford: Clarendon Press.

White, K.D. (1970) *Roman Farming*, London: Thames and Hudson.

Whittaker, C.R. (1994) *Frontiers of the Roman empire. A social and economic study*, Baltimore: Johns Hopkins.

Wilkinson Beryl M. (= Beryl Rawson) (1966) 'Family life among the lower classes in Rome in the first two centuries of the Empire', *CP* 61: 71–83.

Winterbottom, Michael (ed.) (1984) *The Minor Declamations Ascribed to Quintilian*, Berlin and New York: de Gruyter.

Wiseman, T. Peter (1971) *New Men in the Roman Senate 139BC–AD 14*, Oxford: Clarendon Press.

—— (1981, 1994) '*Conspicui postes tectaque digna deo*: the public image of aristocratic and imperial houses in the Late Republic and Early Empire' in *L'Urbs. Espace urbain et histoire (Ier siècle av. J.-C. – IIIe siècle ap. J.-C.),* Rome: Ecole française: 393–413 = *Historiography and imagination* (Exeter, Exeter University Press, 1994): 98–115, 154–61.

—— (1994a) 'Caesar, Pompey and Rome', in *CAH* ix 368–423.

—— (1998) *Roman Drama and Roman History*, Exeter, Exeter University Press.

Wistrand, Erik (1976) *The so-called Laudatio Turiae*, Göteborg: Universitas Gothoburgensis, Studia Graeca et Latina Gothoburgensia 34.

Woodman, A.J. and R.H. Martin (eds) (1989) *The Annals of Tacitus Book iv*, Cambridge: Cambridge University Press, Cambridge Classical Texts and Commentaries.

—— (eds) (1996) *The Annals of Tacitus Book iii*, Cambridge: Cambridge University Press, Cambridge Classical Texts and Commentaries.

Woolf, Greg (1998) *Becoming Roman. The Origins of Provincial Civilization in Gaul*, Cambridge: Cambridge University Press.

Yardley, J.C. (1978) 'The elegiac paraclausithyron', *Eranos* 76: 19–34.

Zanker, Paul (1988) *The Power of Images in the Age of Augustus*, Ann Arbor: University of Michigan Press, Jerome Lectures. (*Augustus und der Macht der Bilder*, Munich: Beck, 1987).

Index

Individuals are listed by the name by which they are best known, often the *cognomen* (e.g. Cicero), sometimes the *praenomen* (e.g. the emperor Tiberius). Page references may cover more than one mention on the same page. Reference to modern authors cited in parenthetical notes and endnotes has not been included.

WRITER-FILES

General Editor: Simon Trussler

Associate Editor: Malcolm Page

File on
PINTER

Compiled by Malcolm Page

Methuen Drama

A Methuen Drama Book
First published in 1993 as a paperback original
by Methuen Drama, Michelin House,
81 Fulham Road, London SW3 6RB,
and distributed by HEB Inc., 361 Hanover Street,
Portsmouth, New Hampshire 03801-3959, USA

Copyright in the compilation
©1993 by Malcolm Page
Copyright in the series format
©1993 by Methuen Drama
Copyright in the editorial presentation
©1993 by Simon Trussler

Typeset in 9/10 Times by
L. Anderson Typesetting,
Woodchurch, Kent TN26 3TB

Printed in Great Britain
by Cox & Wyman Ltd.,
Cardiff Road, Reading

ISBN 413 53620 3

British Library Cataloguing in Publication Data
is available from the British Library

Front cover photo by Nigel Parry

This paperback edition is sold subject to the
condition that it shall not, by way of trade or
otherwise, be lent, resold, hired out, or otherwise
circulated without the publisher's prior consent in
any form of binding or cover other than that in
which it is published and without a similar condition
including this condition being imposed on the
subsequent purchaser.

Contents

CONCORDIA UNIVERSITY LIBRARY
PORTLAND, OR 97211

The theatre is, by its nature, an ephemeral art: yet it is a daunting task to track down the newspaper reviews, or contemporary statements from the writer or his director, which are often all that remain to help us recreate some sense of what a particular production was like. This series is therefore intended to make readily available a selection of the comments that the critics made about the plays of leading modern dramatists at the time of their production — and to trace, too, the course of each writer's own views about his work and his world.

In addition to combining a uniquely convenient source of such elusive *documentation*, the 'Writer-Files' series also assembles the *information* necessary for readers to pursue further their interest in a particular writer or work. Variations in quantity between one writer's output and another's, differences in temperament which make some readier than others to talk about their work, and the variety of critical response, all mean that the presentation and balance of material shifts between one volume and another: but we have tried to arrive at a format for the series which will nevertheless enable users of one volume readily to find their way around any other.

Section 1, 'A Brief Chronology', provides a quick conspective overview of each playwright's life and career. *Section 2* deals with the plays themselves, arranged chronologically in the order of their composition: information on first performances, major revivals, and publication is followed by a brief synopsis (for quick reference set in slightly larger, italic type), then by a representative selection of the critical response, and of the dramatist's own comments on the play and its theme.

Section 3 offers concise guidance to each writer's work in non-dramatic forms, while *Section 4*, 'The Writer on His Work', brings together comments from the playwright himself on more general matters of construction, opinion, and artistic development. Finally, *Section 5* provides a bibliographical guide to other primary and secondary sources of further reading, among which full details will be found of works cited elsewhere under short titles, and of collected editions of the plays — but not of individual titles, particulars of which will be found with the other factual data in Section 2.

The 'Writer-Files' hope by striking this kind of balance between information and a wide range of opinion to offer 'companions' to the study of major playwrights in the modern repertoire — not in that dangerous pre-digested fashion which

can too readily quench the desire to read the plays themselves, nor so prescriptively as to allow any single line of approach to predominate, but rather to encourage readers to form their own judgements of the plays in a wide-ranging context.

Harold Pinter emerges from this volume a much less enigmatic writer than he was first made out. Partly this is due to the gradual acceptance of what once seemed startlingly new conventions in his work — conventions which actors were quicker than critics to recognize, drawing as they did upon subtextual energies which they were glad of the opportunity to exercise. Texts famously replete with all those apparently confining 'pauses' and 'silences' have turned out to be highly adaptable — as responsive to Peter Hall's modulated, almost musical variations of mood and tempo as to the brisk, no-nonsense manner of a Kevin Billington. And plays which were once variously perceived as either ultra-realistic or as 'absurdist' combinations of vague menace and non-communication are now more readily accepted, unlabelled, as being about three or four people in a room. Indeed, 'meanings' have ironically come to matter less as the concerns of criticism have shifted from interpretation to structure.

At first (and sometimes aggressively) non-political, Pinter now acknowledges the importance of the social forces which control our lives — though these forces were never absent from his plays, whether overtly, as in the presence of Goldberg and McCann in *The Birthday Party*, or covertly, as in *The Caretaker*, where the loss of social security papers is no less significant than the trauma of 'therapy' in a state institution. It is surely no coincidence that a recurrent political concern in his recent plays has been with that very right to communicate freely with which his earlier characters were said to have such difficulties. Perhaps if there is a 'line' in which we may helpfully see his work, it is one which stretches back to Georg Büchner and *Woyzeck*, and forward to his own close contemporary, Arnold Wesker — both of whom in very different ways are concerned with the importance of articulacy to personal freedom.

As Pinter himself has ascended the social ladder, so have his characters come to cover up their conversational inanities with the smooth veneer of middle-class self-assurance. Yet the dialogue in *Party Time* conceals and reveals the same gulf between words and their import as one felt during poor Stanley's birthday party all those decades ago. As quoted here (p. 105), Pinter feels that he was then 'sleepwalking' in an 'ivory tower': yet he has also recently and rightly claimed (p. 13) that Petey's line to Stanley, 'Stan, don't let them tell you what to do!' is one of the most important he has ever written. Again, it was Arnold Wesker who remarked that one of the functions of art was to serve as a warning, and in that sense Pinter's art has never been confined to an ivory tower.

Simon Trussler

1930   10 October, born in Hackney, East London, only child of a Jewish tailor.

1939   Evacuated on outbreak of war to Cornwall, later nearer London.

1942   September, to July 1948, attended Hackney Downs Grammar School: played Macbeth and Romeo; active in cricket, running, and football.

1948–49   Attended Royal Academy of Dramatic Art irregularly for two terms. Registered as conscientious objector to military service; turned down by local and appellate tribunals. Prosecuted for failure to respond to conscription, and twice fined (unusually: in this situation a prison sentence was normal).

1951   Actor training at Central School of Speech and Drama. September, touring in Ireland with Anew McMaster Company for a year, acting in eleven plays, seven of them by Shakespeare.

1953   Played small parts in eight plays in Donald Wolfit's company, King's Theatre, Hammersmith.

1954–59   Acting in repertory companies at Whitby, Eastbourne, Huddersfield, Colchester, Bournemouth, Torquay, Birmingham, Palmers Green, Worthing, and elsewhere: a full list is in David T. Thompson, *Pinter: the Player's Playwright* (Macmillan, 1985).

1956   Married the actress Vivien Merchant.

1957   Wrote first play, *The Room*, at request of Henry Woolf for Bristol University Drama Department.

1958   April-May, *The Birthday Party* staged: short tour and one week at Lyric Theatre, Hammersmith. His son Daniel born. Wrote *The Hothouse*.

1959   February, *The Dumb Waiter* staged in Germany. July, *A Slight Ache* on radio.

1960   January, *The Room* (directed by Pinter) and *The Dumb Waiter* staged at Hampstead Theatre Club. March, *A Night Out*

on radio, and on TV in April, with Pinter playing Seeley in both. April, *The Caretaker* a success at Arts Theatre. July, *Night School* televised. December, *The Dwarfs* on radio.

1961   January, *A Slight Ache* staged in a triple-bill at Arts Theatre. February–March, Pinter played Mick in *The Caretaker* for four weeks. May, *The Collection* televised. September, *A Night Out* staged in triple-bill at Comedy Theatre.

1962   February, co-directed *The Collection* with Peter Hall, for Royal Shakespeare Company at Aldwych Theatre.

1963   March, *The Lover* televised. September, directed *The Lover* and *The Dwarfs*, Arts Theatre. *The Caretaker* filmed. Wrote film script of *The Servant*.

1964   June, directed *The Birthday Party*, Aldwych Theatre. Wrote film script of *The Pumpkin Eater*.

1965   March, *Tea Party* televised. June, *The Homecoming* staged, Aldwych Theatre. November, played Garcia in Sartre's *Huis Clos*, BBC TV.

1966   Received CBE. Wrote film script of *The Quiller Memorandum*.

1967   February, *The Basement* televised, with Pinter playing Stott. July, directed *The Man in the Glass Booth*, by Robert Shaw, St. Martin's Theatre, and later in New York. Wrote film script of *Accident*. Co-edited *PEN Anthology of New Poems*.

1968   April, *Landscape* on radio. *Poems* published.

1969   February, played Lenny in *The Homecoming*, Palace Theatre, Watford. April, *Night* staged in *Mixed Doubles*, bill of eight plays at Comedy Theatre. July, *Landscape* and *Silence* staged, Aldwych Theatre. Wrote film script of *The Go-Between*.

1970   September, *Tea Party* and *The Basement* staged, Duchess Theatre. November, directed *Exiles*, by James Joyce, Mermaid Theatre.

1971   June, *Old Times* staged, Aldwych Theatre. July, directed *Butley*, by Simon Gray, Criterion Theatre (and directed film of the play, 1973).

1972   Wrote *The Proust Screenplay* (published 1978, but the film was not made).

1973   *Monologue* televised, and staged later in the year in a double bill with *Night*, Orange Tree Theatre, Richmond. Appointed Associate Director, National Theatre (served until 1983). Anger at American role in overthrow of Allende in Chile leads to his gradually becoming more active in politics.

1974   May, directed *Next of Kin*, by John Hopkins, National Theatre.

1975   April, *No Man's Land* staged, National Theatre. July, directed *Otherwise Engaged*, by Simon Gray, Queen's Theatre. Wrote film script of *The Last Tycoon*.

1976   June, directed *Blithe Spirit*, by Noël Coward, National Theatre. October, directed *The Innocents*, by William Archibald, Morosco Theatre, New York.

1978   February, directed *The Rear Column*, by Simon Gray, Globe Theatre (later also directed the play for television). November, *Betrayal* staged, National Theatre. *Poems and Prose, 1949–1977* published. Wrote script of *Langrishe, Go Down* for television.

1979   May, directed *Close of Play*, by Simon Gray, National Theatre.

1980   April, directed *The Hothouse*, Hampstead Theatre. Divorced Vivien Merchant, and married Lady Antonia Fraser.

1981   January, *Family Voices* on radio, and in February at National Theatre. July, directed *Quartermaine's Terms*, by Simon Gray, Queen's Theatre. Directed *Incident at Tulse Hill*, Hampstead Theatre. Wrote film script of *The French Lieutenant's Woman*.

1982   October, *Family Voices* staged with *A Kind of Alaska* and *Victoria Station*, National Theatre. Directed *The Hothouse* for BBC TV. Wrote film script of *Victory* (film not made).

1983   Directed *The Trojan War Will Not Take Place*, by Jean Giraudoux, National Theatre.

1984   March, directed *One for the Road* and *Victoria Station*, Lyric Theatre, Hammersmith. June, directed *The Common Pursuit*, by Simon Gray, Lyric Theatre, Hammersmith.

1985   Directed *Sweet Bird of Youth*, by Tennessee Williams, Haymarket Theatre. Wrote film script of *Turtle Diary*. Autumn, acted in his *Old*

Times in St. Louis and Los Angeles. Visited Turkey with Arthur Miller for International PEN to investigate human rights abuses.

1986   June, directed *Circe and Bravo*, by Donald Freed, Haymarket Theatre. Co-edited *100 Poems by 100 Poets* for Methuen.

1988   October, directed *Mountain Language*, National Theatre. Involved in an informal group of left-wing artists, the 20 June Group, meeting at his home, with Margaret Drabble, Michael Holroyd, John Mortimer, and others.

1989   Wrote script of *The Heat of the Day* for television. Wrote film scripts of *The Handmaid's Tale*, *Reunion*, and *The Comfort of Strangers*.

1990   May, directed *Vanilla*, by Jane Stanton Hitchcock, Lyric Theatre. October, played Robert in *Betrayal*, BBC Radio. Wrote film script of *The Remains of the Day*, by Kazuo Ishiguro.

1991   June, directed revival of *The Caretaker*, Comedy Theatre. July, directed his short piece *The New World Order*, Royal Court Theatre Upstairs. October, directed *Party Time* and *Mountain Language*, Almeida Theatre.

a: Full-Length Stage Plays

The Birthday Party

Play in three acts.

First London production: Lyric Th., Hammersmith, 19 May
1958, preceded by provincial tour, starting in Cambridge
(dir. Peter Wood; with Willoughby Gray as Petey, Beatrix
Lehmann as Meg, Richard Pearson as Stanley, Wendy
Hutchinson as Lulu, John Slater as Goldberg, and John
Stratton as McCann).

Revived: Royal Shakespeare Co. at Aldwych Th., 18 June
1964 (dir. Pinter; with Newton Blick as Petey, Doris Hare
as Meg, Bryan Pringle as Stanley, Janet Suzman as Lulu,
Brewster Mason as Goldberg, and Patrick Magee as
McCann); Shaw Th., 8 Jan. 1975 (dir. Kevin Billington;
with John Alderton as Stanley); Shared Experience at The
Place, 21 Nov. 1990, preceded by provincial tour (dir.
Nancy Meckler; with John Halstead as Petey, Sandra Voe
as Meg, Michael Packer as Stanley, Cecilia Noble as Lulu,
Peter Whitman as Goldberg, and Paul Higgins as McCann).

First New York production: Booth Th., 3 Oct. 1967 (dir. Alan
Schneider). *Revived:* Forum Th., Lincoln Centre, 5 Feb.
1971 (dir. Jules Irving); Classic Stage Co. Repertory Th.,
12 Apr. 1988 (dir. Carey Perloff).

Film: released 1970 (dir. William Friedkin; with Moultrie
Kensall as Petey, Dandy Nichols as Meg, Robert Shaw as
Stanley, Helen Fraser as Lulu, Sydney Tafler as Goldberg,
and Patrick Magee as McCann).

Television: A-R TV, 22 Mar. 1960 (dir. Joan Kemp-Welch;
with Richard Pearson as Stanley); 'Theatre Night', BBC-2,
21 June 1987 (dir. Kenneth Ives; with Robert Lang as
Petey, Joan Plowright as Meg, Kenneth Cranham as
Stanley, Julie Walters as Lulu, Pinter as Goldberg, and
Colin Blakely as McCann).

Published: Methuen, 1960; revised ed., 1965; Methuen
Student Edition, with commentary by Patricia Hern, notes
by Glenda Leeming, 1981; in *Plays: One*, Methuen, 1976.

---

*Stanley — perhaps a former pianist — is the only lodger
at a rundown seaside boarding house, run by Meg and*

her weak, evasive husband Petey. Two mysterious strangers,
Goldberg and McCann, arrive, and the first act ends with Stanley
beating frantically on a drum. The intruders terrorize Stanley in
a questioning ritual. They call for a party, also attended by Lulu,
the pretty girl-next-door. At the party, Stanley's glasses are
broken, he treads on the drum, the lights go out. Next morning,
with Meg out, the men take Stanley away, ignoring Petey's feeble
protests. Stanley is now respectably dressed and unable to speak.

I was on tour with a farce called *A Horse, a Horse* in which I was an
ASM. I had to go behind the window with a big horse, and pull the
horse's ears. It was a most miserable week, because it was at Eastbourne, and apart from the fact that it was raining all the time and
I couldn't get on with this horse at all, I found digs in which a man had
to share a room with a man in a kind of attic, sleeping on a bed which
had a sofa above it. The sofa was upside down, almost against the ceil-
ing, and I was under the sofa, and he was in the other bed. There was a
terrible landlady, and it was all quite incredibly dirty. And at the end of
the week I said to this fellow, who turned out to have been a concert
pianist on the pier: 'Why do you stay here?' And he said: 'There's
nowhere else to go.' I left with that ringing in my ears. Then about a
year later or so I started to write *The Birthday Party*, but it has no relation to that original thing, that situation in Eastbourne, other than that
there were two people who got me onto the first page.

Pinter, interviewed by Joan Bakewell,
The Listener, 6 Nov. 1969, p. 630

The other day a friend of mine gave me a letter I wrote to him in
nineteen-fifty something, Christ knows when it was. This is what it says:
'I have filthy insane digs, a great bulging scrag of a woman with breasts
rolling at her belly, an obscene household, cats, dogs, filth, tea-strainers,
mess, oh bullocks, talk, chat rubbish shit scratch dung poison, infantility,
deficient order in the upper fretwork, fucking roll on. . . .' Now the thing
about this is *that* was *The Birthday Party*.

Pinter, interview in *Theatre at Work*, ed. Charles Marowitz and
Simon Trussler (Methuen, 1967), p. 98, from *Paris Review*, 1966

The play exists now apart from me, you, or anybody. I believe that what
happens on this stage will possess a potent dramatic image and a great
deal of this will be visual. . . . The play in fact merely states that two

men come down to take away another man and do so. Will the audience absorb the implications or will they not? Ask the barber.

Pinter, 'A Letter to Peter Wood', 30 Mar. 1958,
reprinted in Harold Pinter: The Birthday Party,
The Caretaker and The Homecoming,
ed. Michael Scott (Macmillan, 1986), p. 79-82

[In *The Room*] this old woman is living in a room which, she is convinced, is the best in the house, and she refuses to know anything about the basement downstairs. She says it's damp and nasty, and the world outside is cold and icy, and that in her warm and comfortable room her security is complete. But, of course, it isn't; an intruder comes to upset the balance of everything, in other words points to the delusion on which she is basing her life. I think the same thing applies in *The Birthday Party*. Again this man is hidden away in a seaside boarding house . . . then two people arrive out of nowhere, and I don't consider this an unnatural happening. I don't think it is all that surrealistic and curious because surely this thing, of people arriving at the door, has been happening in Europe in the last twenty years. Not only the last twenty years, the last two to three hundred.

Pinter, interviewed by John Sherwood,
BBC European Service, 3 Mar. 1960,
quoted in Martin Esslin, Pinter the Playwright (Methuen, 1984), p. 28

In 1958, *The Birthday Party* was generally found to be incomprehensible. It's now been done throughout the world, and it's clearly *comprehensible*. Some things change. The play hasn't changed. It's exactly the same.

Pinter, quoted by Mel Gussow,
New York Times, 30 Dec. 1979, Sec. II, p. 7

Petey says one of the most important lines I've ever written. As Stanley is taken away, Petey says, 'Stan, don't let them tell you what to do.' I've lived that line all my damn life. Never more than now.

Pinter, quoted by Mel Gussow,
New York Times, 6 Dec. 1988, Sec. III, p. 22

The author never got down to earth long enough to explain what his play was about, so I can't tell you. But I can give you some sort of sketch of

what happens, and to whom. To begi n with there is Meg, who lets lodgings in a seaside town. She is mad. Thwarted maternity is (I think) her trouble and it makes her go soppy over her unsavoury lodger, Stanley. He is mad too. He strangles people. And I think he must have strangled one person too many, because a couple of very sinister (and quite mad) characters arrive bent on — I suppose — vengeance. There is also a mad girl, nymphomania being her fancy. The one sane character is Meg's husband, but sanity does him no good.

W. A. Darlington, *Daily Telegraph*, 20 May 1958

I am willing to risk whatever reputation I have as a judge of plays by saying that *The Birthday Party* is not a Fourth, not even a Second, but a First; and that Mr. Pinter, on the evidence of this work, possesses the most original, disturbing, and arresting talent in theatrical London. . . . *The Birthday Party* is absorbing. It is witty. Its characters . . . are fascinating. The plot, which consists with all kinds of verbal arabesques and echoing explorations of memory and fancy, of the springing of the trap, is first-rate. The whole play has the same atmosphere of delicious, impalpable and hair-raising terror which makes *The Turn of the Screw* one of the best stories in the world. Mr. Pinter has got hold of a primary fact of existence. We live on the verge of disaster.

Harold Hobson, *Sunday Times*, 25 May 1958

[Several of the original reviews, all negative except for Hobson's, are reprinted both in John Elsom, *Post-War British Theatre Criticism* (Routledge and Kegan Paul, 1981), p. 80-6, and in Gareth and Barbara Lloyd Evans, *Plays in Review, 1956–1980* (Batsford, 1985), p. 63-5.]

Authors desperately need a director, particularly when the play has a 'meaning' which can either be brought out or left in. The skeleton of the meaning, every little bone of it, is far too near the surface of the author's own mind and he will impart this self-consciousness to his actors. . . . Apart from the direction of the actors, the main difference in this production is that Pinter has tried to make every detail as ordinary as possible — the seaside boarding-house, its inhabitants, and the two dark-suited thugs who come to take Stanley away. I see his point — the more familiar the context, the more real the menace which develops — and certainly this theory sometimes works (witness the terror that Hitchcock built up in *The Birds* with ordinary seagulls in an ordinary seaside town). The snag is that, as written, Pinter's characters in this play just aren't ordinary. They are a gallery of fascinating grotesques. . . .

Pinter's production probably reveals the play's meaning more clearly than Peter Wood's, though this is not necessarily a gain since the meaning, by itself, is fairly ordinary — in brief, the pressures and guilt brought to bear by ideas of family and success (Goldberg), politics and religion (McCann) on a second-rate artist who has opted out of society and wants just to vegetate — and such details as Stanley's sudden dumbness once he has conformed look rather too bald if underlined. The best plays of this genre (*Waiting for Godot* or *The Birthday Party* well done) are fables which lodge entire in the mind, and only there, after the event, breed their full implications.

Bamber Gascoigne, *The Observer*, 21 June 1964

Kevin Billington's production neatly puts paid to several Pinter preconceptions. Not solemn or too serious, it takes its tone from summer sunshine and a rollicking seaside song creating an almost happy-holiday atmosphere. Setting and treatment of characters is explicitly realistic, not overtly symbolic or 'Pinteresque'. Emphasis is not on pregnant punctuation and pauses, but on colloquial rhythms and repartee. Menace is concrete rather than vague. It is made clear that terrible events are taking place in a real world to real people, some unaware of what's going on, others aware but unable to alter the course of events. Billington's direction probably contradicts every Peter Hall 'Pinter principle' — but it works, as do the 'anti-Pinteresque' portrayals of the characters. John Alderton's Stanley is guilty. He knows it; Goldberg and McCann know that he knows; and we all know that they know that he knows. . . . Above all, Billington's *Birthday Party* was funny — throw-away lines are milked for laughs and laughs they got. . . . The play operates on at least four non-contradictory interpretative levels: that Stanley is the non-conformist whom society (in Goldberg and McCann) claims back and forces to conform (hence his departure in pinstripe and bowler hat); that Stanley's loss of identity is a symbolic, painful process of dying (hence his corpse-like condition at the end); that Stanley is in fact born (hence the title), expelled from the womb and forced to face adult sexuality (hence his attempt to strangle Meg and to rape Lulu); and that the fear and guilt of Stanley's subconscious become concretely dramatized and consume him. Kevin Billington's pleasant production communicates simultaneously the possibilities of the first three dimensions of meaning, but not the last. Never could any of the characters in this production be projections of Stanley's subconscious. It is this ultimate metaphor which is missing, making the production prosaic rather than poetic.

Catherine Itzin, *Plays and Players*,
March 1975, p. 26-7

With the author himself there and dominating the mood [of the TV production] you have to assume that this is the play as Pinter wants it to be: faster, tighter, lighter on that famous menace, and much funnier than you expect. The only trouble here, as with Orton's *What the Butler Saw*, is that this is comedy that only gives full value in the presence of an audience, that needs undistracted listening and collective laughter. At the other extreme, the chilling moments — like Stanley's struggle to break the silence and speak before he is carted away — gain power when a face fills the whole screen.

Hugh Hebert, *The Guardian*, 22 June 1987, p. 23

What is new in Meckler's production is the tone: it is slightly mannered without being artificial; it dramatizes the feeling you sometimes have that everything around you is realistic but unreal, as if being 'performed'. The feeling is rather like a dream you think you may have had between spells of insomnia — which is why people without sleep problems and insecurities will never fully respond to Pinter's plays. The result is theatrically gripping but uneasy: there are parts of the play, such as its ribald humour, which it doesn't reach. Naturalistic productions, by contrast, are wobbly on the symbolism.

John Peter, *Sunday Times*,
25 November 1990, Sec. 8, p. 14

This *Birthday Party* keeps turning into the domestic melodrama of a kind of *Coronation Street* household, presided over by a Meg with the fussy gentility of a Hilda Ogden and passively inhabited by a Petey who looks more like a retired bank manager than a deck-chair attendant. If this production ultimately disappoints, it is because it goes for psychological rather than verbal structures. It concentrates on establishing motivations — which narrow and circumscribe — rather than on the speaking of the text. In the words and in the famous silences it looks for human relationships at the expense of the unspeakable horror and black comedy at the heart of things.

Inga-Stina Ewbank, *Times Literary Supplement*,
12 October 1990, p. 1101

The Film

The Birthday Party, apart from a couple of shots of desolate seaside streets and a row of empty deck-chairs on the front, stays resolutely inside Meg's front parlour. . . . *The Birthday Party* could be said to be a

study in guilt, power, the relationship between victimiser and victim. . .
and that is already enough. Robert Shaw plays Stanley, the victim,
slopping about in a pyjama jacket under a ragged sweater, hunted,
violent, courageous, and finally, as a human being, eliminated. . . .
Dandy Nichols's Meg, a hideous slattern, crowds the screen with a
horrible, silly innocence. . . . Although some of the 1957 Pinter dialogue
may now seem something of a cliché, it is finally fascinating entertain-
ment as well as being a valuable record of one of the most revolutionary
plays of our time.

Penelope Mortimer, The Observer,
15 February 1970, p. 28

The Hothouse

Play in two acts.
Written: Winter 1958, and put aside. ['In 1979 I re-read *The Hothouse*
and decided it was worth presenting on stage' ('Author's Note').]
First London production: Hampstead Th., 24 Apr. 1980, transferred to
Ambassador's Th., 25 June 1980 (dir. Pinter; with Derek Newark as
Roote, James Grant as Gibbs, and Angela Pleasence as Miss Cutts).
First New York production: Trinity Square Repertory Co., Providence,
Rhode Island, 26 Feb. 1982, transferred to Playhouse Th., New York,
30 Apr. 1982 (dir. Adrian Hall).
Television: BBC-2, 27 Mar. 1982 (dir. Pinter; with stage principals).
Published: Methuen, 1980; added to *Plays: One*, 1986.

The Hothouse *is set in an institution whose nature is never
entirely made known to us (the staff refer to 'patients', and use
the terms 'rest home' and 'convalescent home'), but which seems
to be that of a mental hospital. The patients are known by
numbers, not names, and remain offstage; the staff, in their grey
suits and impersonal surroundings, are the only people we see.
Roote, the director (an ex-army man), Gibbs, his immediate
subordinate, Miss Cutts, their mistress, and Lush, a man in his
thirties — these are the four principal characters, and during the
day and evening of the action much of their time is taken up in
investigating two mysteries: the death of patient 6457 and the
birth of a child to patient 6459. Suspicion centres on a fifth
character, Lamb, as innocent-seeming as the name suggests; but*

blame, after a debacle in which all but one of the staff are massacred by the patients, officially falls on Roote, although Gibbs might also be guilty. . . . The hothouse of the title has something to do with questions of power and pressure: Roote is feeling the heat; he also makes life hot for others. So, too, in the interrogation sequence, Gibbs and Miss Cutts give Lamb a grilling. The action takes place on Christmas Day, and there are several references to Easter; a child is born, a man dies, a father is sought; Lamb is accused and tried, Roote speaks of himself as a 'delegate' of some higher power. The Christian references are lightly handled.

Blake Morrison, *Times Literary Supplement,* 9 May 1980

I found it very funny. And the point I want to stress about it is that it was fantasy when I wrote it, but now it has become, I think, far more relevant. Reality has overtaken it.

Pinter, quoted in
'Suddenly — Pinter's Vintage Fantasy Becomes Reality',
Radio Times, 27 Mar.–2 Apr. 1982, p. 5

There are the expected tappings back and forth of banalities, as though in some metaphysical game of ping-pong in which each player has convinced himself that defeat will mean death; the expected *non sequiturs,* down which the characters escape from each other, like so many White Rabbits; the expected mystifications, which make the head of the institution exclaim at one point: 'Something is happening but I don't know what'. (Any member of the cast or of the audience might be hard put to explain it to him). . . . The chief interest of this baffling, not wholly satisfactory work is that it still exhibits traces of all the separate ingredients — Beckett, Ionesco, Kafka, and so forth — that Mr. Pinter was later to synthesize into a manner wholly his own.

Francis King, *Sunday Telegraph,*
4 May 1980, p. 14

Walk warily through the play's chambers, peeping into its corners as you go, and you'll find infantile longings, sadistic urges, lust, misogyny, sudden and unpredictable violence, suspicion, paranoia, dread, and more dread. Anything may happen, from any angle and for no apparent reason. Something *will* happen. Something does happen. Perhaps this makes *The Hothouse* sound disconcertingly grotesque and random.

Certainly, the situation is much quirkier than that of the play which followed it, *The Caretaker*; but the characters are recognizably real and their confrontations have purpose and shape, in essence Pinter's familiar tussle for power and territory. Roote, the boss, blusters and threatens in what's clearly a desperate and losing attempt to maintain some semblance of authority and even of identity. . . . This Pinter is already impressively in command of his distinctive talent: the question asked, repeated, left ominously unanswered; the edgy, loaded argument about, of all things, whether the Christmas turkey was bone-dry or thoroughly swimming in gravy; the lies, the emotional camouflage, the obliquity, the uncertainty, the silence.

Benedict Nightingale,
New Statesman, 9 May 1980

The Hothouse is hardly the best written of Pinter's works or the most exquisitely engineered, but it has a kind of unbuttoned, careering energy I found impossible to resist, and it suggests a road he might have taken had he not chosen to perfect the art of tergiversation. . . .

The play, for all its familiar Pinterian mystery and menace, also possesses a cogent farcical urgency that builds to a remorseless indictment of totalitarian procedures. These qualities have been caught perfectly by Eugene Lee's set at Trinity Square Rep — a cage made out of pipes and doors and grates and grilles, crowned by a clock with only one hand. Adrian Hall's production likewise has identified the appropriate tone — flat, uninflected, punctuated by the slamming of gates and doors — with which to express the deadened nature of this ghastly place. . . . *The Hothouse* shows us a Pinter moved more by a capacity for indignation than by a love of elegance — Pinter as redskin rather than paleface. This is a way of saying that it is animated by a boiling energy he hasn't shown in his work since *The Homecoming*, and a sense of personal engagement he perhaps has never shown.

Robert Brustein, *New Republic*, 7 Apr. 1982, p. 26-7

The play can be viewed as a parable of concealed irrationality versus explicit irrationality, statism versus individualism, with plentiful et ceteras. What the play basically is about is a young theatre animal showing how well he knows his magical habitat. . . . Sheer theatrical wizardry is what marks *The Hothouse* before it's two minutes along: we know we are in the hands of a writer who can set moods and evoke laughs simply by jeweller-like precision, done deadpan.

Stanley Kauffmann, *Theater Criticisms*
(New York: PAJ Publications, 1983), p. 158-9

19

The Caretaker

Play in three acts.

First London production: Arts Th., 27 Apr. 1960, transferred to Duchess
   Th., 30 May (dir. Donald McWhinnie; with Alan Bates as Mick,
   Peter Woodthorpe as Aston, and Donald Pleasence as Davies).

Revivals: Mermaid Th., 2 Mar. 1972 (dir. Christopher Morahan; with
   John Hurt as Mick, Jeremy Kemp as Aston, and Leonard Rossiter as
   Davies); Shaw Th., Apr. 1976 (dir. Kevin Billington; with Simon
   Rouse as Mick, Roger Lloyd Pack as Aston, and Fulton Mackay as
   Davies); Greenwich Th., Oct. 1977 (dir. Paul Joyce; with Anthony
   Higgins as Mick, Peter Guinness as Aston, and Max Wall as Davies);
   National Th. (Lyttelton), 11 Nov. 1980 (dir. Kenneth Ives; with
   Jonathan Pryce as Mick, Kenneth Cranham as Aston, and Warren
   Mitchell as Davies), restaged 26 May 1981 (dir. Ives; with Troy
   Foster as Mick, Oscar James as Aston, and Norman Beaton as
   Davies); Young Vic, 28 May 1983 (dir. Stewart Trotter); Comedy
   Th., 18 June 1991 (dir. Pinter; with Peter Howitt as Mick, Colin Firth
   as Aston, and Donald Pleasence as Davies).

First New York production: Lyceum Th., 4 Oct. 1962 (as London
   production, with Robert Shaw as Aston). *Revivals:* Roundabout Th.,
   21 June 1973 (dir. Gene Feist); Circle in the Square Th., 10 Jan. 1986
   (dir. John Malkovich).

Film: released 1964 (dir. Clive Donner; with Alan Bates as Mick,
   Robert Shaw as Aston, and Donald Pleasence as Davies).

Television: ITV, 1966 (with Ian MacShane as Mick, John Rees as Aston,
   and Roy Dotrice as Davies); BBC-1, 7 June 1981 (as National
   Theatre 1980 production).

Published: Methuen, 1960; Methuen Student Edition; in *Plays: Two.*

---

*A slavish, peevish, vicious old down-and-out named Davies is
offered lodgings in a junk-filled room, part of a network
of apartments waiting to be redecorated. His benefactor, the
would-be decorator, is a listless, dull-witted chap named Aston,
who has collected Davies in much the same impersonal way he
has collected the other useless articles in the place. Aston gives
Davies a bed, money, shoes, clothes, and a caretaking job, which
the derelict, consumed with defences and prejudices, accepts or
rejects with alternating gratitude and grumbles. Though they live
in the same room and share a quality of spiritual paralysis
(Aston wants but is unable to build a toolshed; Davies is desirous*

but incapable of going to Sidcup for his papers), they cannot connect. Nor do they connect with Aston's brother, a mordant young entrepreneur who hardly says a word to Aston and who relates to Davies mainly by baiting him with cruel practical jokes. Following Aston's confession that shock treatments had addled his brain (a confession alien to the style of the play), Davies tries to form an alliance with Mick to evict Aston from the room. Mick first encourages Davies's scheme; then, smashing his brother's statue of Buddha for emphasis, ridicules it. After a petty altercation between the two room-mates over Davies's noisy sleeping habits — which climaxes when Davies, flourishing a knife, lets slip some unfortunate remarks about Aston's 'stinking shed' — Aston asks him to leave. Whimpering like a rebellious slave whipped into submission, Davies begs to be allowed to remain. That, apart from a wealth of equally mystifying details and a few comic epsodes, is the meat of the play; and I'm perspiring from the effort to extract this much coherence.

Robert Brustein, 'A Naturalism of the Grotesque',
Seasons of Discontent (London, 1966), p. 181-2,
reprinted from *New Republic*, 1961

I'd met a few, quite a few, tramps — you know, just in the normal course of events, and I think there was one particular one . . . I didn't know him very well, he did most of the talking when I saw him. I bumped into him a few times, and about a year or so afterwards he sparked this thing off.

Pinter, interview in *Theatre at Work*, p. 98

At the end of *The Caretaker*, there are two people alone in a room, and one of them must go in such a way as to produce a sense of complete separation and finality. I thought originally that the play must end with the violent death of one at the hands of the other. But then I realized, when I got to the point, that the characters as they had grown could never act in this way.

Pinter, 'Harold Pinter Replies',
New Theatre Magazine, Bristol, Jan. 1961, p. 10

On most evenings at the Duchess there is a sensible balance of laughter and silence. . . . As far as I'm concerned, *The Caretaker* is funny up to a

point. Beyond that point it ceases to be funny, and it was because of that point that I wrote it.

Pinter, 'Pinter Replies',
Sunday Times, 14 Aug. 1960, p. 21

[*Of the film.*] You can say the play has 'been opened out' in the sense that things I'd yearned to do, without knowing it, in writing for the stage, crystallized when I came to think about it as a film. Until then I didn't know that I wanted to do them because I'd accepted the limitations of the stage. For instance, there's a scene in the garden of the house, which is very silent; two silent figures with a third looking on. I think in the film one has been able to hit the relationship of the brothers more clearly than in the play. . . . Actors on the stage are under the delusion that they have to project in a particular way. There's a scene in the film, also in the play, when the elder brother asks the other if he'd like to be caretaker in the place. On film it's played in terms of great intimacy and I think it's extraordinarily successful. They speak quite normally, it's a quiet scene, and it works. But on stage it didn't ever work like that. . . . What I'm very pleased about myself is that in the film, as opposed to the play, we see a real house and real snow outside, dirty snow, and the streets. . . . In the play, when people were confronted with just a set, a room, and a door, they often assumed it was all taking place in limbo, in a vacuum, and the world outside hardly existed.

Pinter, 'Harold Pinter and Clive Donner',
in *Behind the Scenes*, ed. Joseph F. McCrindle
(New York: Holt, Rinehart and Winston, 1971),
from *Transatlantic Review*, No. 13 (Summer 1963)

All that happens is that they talk, fail to communicate with one another, and break into moments of violence which reflect all the despair in the world. I do not want to make this play sound glum or too consciously intellectual. It convulsed its audience, and sent them away thoughtful as well. It also showed Mr. Pinter as a master of silence. There are repeated moments of the utmost eloquence in which nothing happened except that Alan Bates moved his pupils or a handbag is silently thrown from one hand to another.

Alan Pryce-Jones, *The Observer*, 1 May 1960, p. 23

A riveting, uncompromising piece of egg-head Hitchcockiana . . . *The Caretaker* has all [Pinter's] now familiar ingredients — the atmosphere of hooded menace, the moments of dreadful revelation, the eve of the

thunderstorm tension, the grisly comic cryptograms which everyone is afraid to solve. But, for the first time, he has succeeded in adding the two ingredients I have always missed. His characters are now people rooted in a world of insurance stamps, and contemporary wallpaper, and mental asylums. They are still lost in mazes of self-deception, isolated behind barricades of private language, hungry at the smell of the next man's weakness — in other words, just like us. The second gain is in communication. *The Caretaker* has that final reel which fits the jigsaw together and explains everything which can be explained. . . .

[McWhinnie's] cast of three embody their roles with really rather uncanny self-absorption. Donald Pleasence has the part with most elbow-room — the wary mongrel of a tramp who bites the hand which feeds him and licks the boot which stamps on him. He thrashes about inside it with enormous skill like an insane Bisto Kid heady with the savoury sick smells of the lower depths. Alan Bates, as the teddy-boy with delusions of bourgeois grandeur, has a more ambiguous role which he interprets with a strong line in handsome shiftiness. But I think Peter Woodthorpe is the real triumph of the evening — you can almost see the bombed site of waste brain behind his eyes as he sits as quietly as a deaf child playing his secret, meaningless tiny games with himself.

Alan Brien, *The Spectator*, 6 May 1960

An elaborate network of ambiguity stretched tight over a simple little story. Although it is searingly accurate in its diction and characterization, it is too organized and surreal in effect to be called naturalistic. If Pinter uses tape-recorders to achieve such verisimilitude, he also edits his tapes poetically to avoid stale reproductions of life. It is painful and frustrating to coin definitions about the play. It is a kind of masterpiece, and will suffer the terrible consequences which critics inflict on all such works.

Charles Marowitz, *Confessions of a Counterfeit Critic*
(Eyre Methuen, 1973), p. 49, reprinted from *Village Voice*, 1960

What holds one, theatrically, is Mr. Pinter's bizarre use (some would call it abuse) of dramatic technique, his skill in evoking atmosphere, and his encyclopedic command of contemporary idiom. To take these qualities in order: where most playwrights devote their technical efforts to making us wonder what will happen *next*, Mr. Pinter focuses our wonder on what is happening *now*. Who are these people? How did they meet, and why? Mr. Pinter delays these disclosures until the last tenable moment; he teases us without boring us, which is quite a rare achievement. It is reinforced by his mastery of atmosphere. There is a special

belt of English suburbia, spectral in its dusty shabbiness, that exists in no other Anglo-Saxon country. . . . London is unique in the *déclassé* decrepitude of its western suburbs, with their floating population, their indoor dustbins, their desolate bed-sitters, their prevalent dry rot — moral as well as structural — and their frequent, casual suicides. Mr. Pinter captures all this with the most chilling economy. We come finally to his verbal gifts; and it is here that cracks of doubt begin to appear in the facade of my enthusiasm. Time and again, without the least departure from authenticity, Mr. Pinter exposes the vague, repetitive silliness of lower-class conversation. One laughs in recognition; but one's laughter is tinged with snobbism.

> Kenneth Tynan, *The Observer*, 5 June 1960,
> reprinted in *A View of the English Stage*
> (Davis-Poynter, 1975), p. 279-80

In Kevin Billington's direction the play is a little heavy, its tensions a touch too obviously displayed. Aston's monologue about his electro-convulsive therapy is sentimentalized by lighting and delivery; Mick's inner rage is all too outer, so that he seems madder than his brother can ever have been, hallucinations and all; and the old tramp is denied any element of sly delight in his self-induced predicaments. Still, the play retains all its eerie power — few members of the audience but will find themselves identifying, at one moment or another, with all three of these wretched men.

> J. W. Lambert, *Sunday Times*, 11 Apr. 1976, p. 37

I sat in amazement at the prodigality of the author's talent, his masterly technical skill, his impeccable ear and faultless deployment of varying speech-patterns and rhythms, his literally incomparable ability to suggest unlocatable fear — and the emptiness, weightlessness, and triviality of his entire play. This contrast between artifice and art struck me like a blow in the face. . . .

Nothing emerges. There is no sense of a view, however oblique, of these characters, no disclosure of a general truth based on particular conclusions, no comment, wise or otherwise, on anything. We come out exactly the same people as we were when we entered; we have been entertained, we have admired the author's ability, we have not been bored. But we have advanced our understanding and our humanity not a whit, and every experience we have had has been of an entirely superficial nature. The needle is sharp, the thread fine, the material sumptuous, the seamstress the best. But the Emperor's clothes do not exist.

> Bernard Levin, *Sunday Times*, 30 Oct. 1977, p. 38

Davies should begin abjectly, swell to a kind of authority, and fade away again, but [Max] Wall remains continuously on one level of affronted, slightly absent-minded dignity. With his sonorous gravel voice, his large frame, and that vaudevillian shuffle, he is a much more commanding presence than the other two actors. Both of these have individualized their parts — Peter Guinness's Aston by a tortoise-like gait and Anthony Higgins's Mick by a stagey, ferret-like springiness — and it is as if two small animals in a zoo are crawling about a sleepy, bored gorilla.

Victoria Radin, *The Observer*, 30 Oct. 1977

The quality of the laughter has changed. It's become the laughter, not of fear, but of familiarity. When Davies says 'If only I could get down to Sidcup', there's a fond, even cosy murmur of amused recognition from the audience. For all Pryce's alarming mannerisms, this is not a frightening *Caretaker*. It's difficult to decide whether this is because the characters are being too likeably played, whether the Lyttelton, which manages to be at once stuffy and deadening, swallows up all feeling; or whether twenty years have hardened the audience. Nothing that one's worst fears could imagine coming up from the basement, or into the boarding house, or knocking upon the door, hasn't come on to the stage in the last twenty years. . . . Only very rarely, in Mick's edgy reaction to the tramp's attacks on his brother ('What's funny about him?') or in Aston's final rejection of Davies is there a sense of deep fear in this *Caretaker*.

Hermione Lee, *Times Literary Supplement*, 21 Nov. 1980

Why has *The Caretaker* enjoyed two such successful decades? The truculent role of Davies is one answer. Another is the Pinterian unpredictability, the currents of threat, and the shifting allegiances between the trio. And yet in some respects the play seems faintly dated. Even Warren Mitchell's repertory of facial twists and turns, even Jonathan Pryce's arcane presence, don't quite mask the fact. It has dated in a way that the earlier *Waiting for Godot* (1955) has not. . . . Not that the tramps nowadays are any fewer, nor the derelict attics with their buckets to catch the drips. But the patina of social comment can almost be peeled off the play's core, leaving at most a wry proposition about the purgatory of sharing a bedroom with your neighbour.

What *The Caretaker* will remain is a virtuoso challenge, a text for prodigious performance. The climaxes are there, even if the story line, with its fadings in and out, betrays a certain looseness. Mick's contributions are essentially episodes in a manic key, from which we are returned to the tonic of his allegiance to his damaged brother. He is not so much a character as a playwright's tool for modulations of atmo-

sphere. And the piece is a sort of scherzo, its texture that of a fugue, a chase between three voices. Implied throughout is the impish idea of the intruder, half demon and half victim.

Kitty Mrosovsky, *Quarto*, Jan.–Feb. 1981, p. 2-3

In 1960 Donald Pleasence was Davies: a man who is charitably taken into another's house, exploits his position to his own advantage, and is then brutally expelled. Pleasence played the character as a blustering, belligerent, selfish impostor. It was a remarkable performance in that he seemed to inhabit the role completely. The voice was strident and cawing; the constant pounding of the left palm with the right fist suggested all the suppressed violence in the man; and yet the perennial stoop, as if he was all the time expecting someone to give him a deft blow between the shoulder-blades, evoked a lifetime of subservience and oppression. There was a complete blending of actor and role. Pleasence did not play Davies; he *was* Davies. And it came as no surprise to learn that, when the play was being filmed in Hackney, Pleasence went out on to the streets during breaks in the action and sold matches to passers-by. Twelve years later Leonard Rossiter played the same role, no less brilliantly, in a revival of the play at the Mermaid. . . . On this occasion the role was *presented* to us and the actor's identification was somewhat less than total. From the first one was acutely conscious of Mr. Rossiter's assumption of mock-gentility and refinement ('I've had dinner with the best', he announced, in terms suggesting many a nosh-up in Belgrave Square); of the way the mouth formed a repulsive rectangle rather like the aperture in a letter-box, with the tongue protruding against the lower-lip; and of the deferential gestures with two fingers raised to the brow in mock-salute. . . . This man was above all a skiver, a work-shy drop-out, a born malingerer. But whereas Pleasence seemed to be working from the inside out, Rossiter worked from the outside in, presenting the character to us through an accumulation of external detail.

Michael Billington, *The Modern Actor*
(Hamish Hamilton, 1973), p. 201-2

[*On the 1980 production, first filmed for television and then staged at the National Theatre.*] When the cast moved from the four walls of their television set into the three of the stage, they found the reaction of living, breathing, laughing spectators did much to reshape their performances. Until then they'd no idea the play was so funny. When Mick first meets the intruder Davies, he browbeats him with an odd, unsettling speech in which he compares the old man with a nut-loving relative of

his own: 'Peanuts, walnuts, brazil nuts, monkey nuts, wouldn't touch a piece of fruit cake.' The theatre audience collapsed at that point, and again and again afterwards, forcing Jonathan Pryce's Mick greatly to slow his delivery. On television such lines can be expected to rattle out, increasing the danger in the atmosphere. . . . Ives [the director] sees more than surprise and menace in Pryce's Mick: 'He brought out very strongly his love for his brother and his sadness at not being able to communicate with him.' He also believes that Kenneth Cranham brought unusual depth to the reclusive Aston, who feels betrayed by his experiences in a singularly hellish asylum and is now unable to talk easily to anyone, even Mick. Indeed, Ives regards the awkward, touching relationship between the two brothers as the very centre of the play, even though the only conversation the two of them actually have consists of a few desultory words about a leak in the roof. . . .

The tramp has always been popular with audiences, because his wheedling, suspicious, ignorant character gives rise to a good many funny lines. 'In fact, he has no saving grace', says Ives, 'not one atom of good in his make-up. He's a complete liar, bully and manipulator. He has absolute scorn for Aston's psychiatric troubles, and the moment he suspects he's weak, he turns into the cuckoo in the nest. He only respects strength, violence, the hitman, which is why he respects Mick, because he's stronger than him.' Some critics of the National production thought Warren Mitchell brought too much prankish charm to the part. Ives doesn't agree. 'I think he went for the insecurity of a tramp's life. What came across was a man enormously fearful of what might happen to him in that place. But he also had a considerable amount of aggression and pugnacity, a very strong bullying element, and a malicious sense of humour, shown in the way he manipulates Aston and thinks that he's manipulating Mick.' . . . Beaton should be less chirpy than Mitchell, and more evil. 'The play will still be about the loneliness of loving, caring', says Ives, 'but I'm hoping another aspect will come out more strongly. It's also about territory. About the ruthlessness of a man who comes in and stakes a claim to the place where another man lives.'

In other words, the simplicity of Pinter's story of three men in a room will once again be proved deceptive.

Benedict Nightingale, 'Taking Care',
Radio Times, 6-12 June 1981, p. 11-12

The Film

Pleasence has reproduced his stage performance as the elderly tramp without taking into account the difference between the two media. On the stage, he was generally thought to be superb — although even then

there were some who found his performance just a trifle over-acted, over-character-acted. As is so often the case, the cinema exaggerates any shade of falseness or melodrama, with the result that he is not very convincing on the screen. Alan Bates, too, plays the same role in the film as on the stage. In the process he has lost some of that mysterious authority which he so splendidly conveyed — probably because it is difficult to retain that hieratic presence in close-up and in two dimensions.

Richard Roud, *The Guardian*, 13 Mar. 1964

See also:
A. M. Aylwin, *Notes on Harold Pinter's 'The Caretaker'* (Methuen Study-Aid, 1976).
Gareth and Barbara Lloyd Evans, eds., *Plays in Review, 1956-1980* (Batsford, 1985), p. 96-9.

The Homecoming

Play in two acts.
First London production: Royal Shakespeare Co. at Aldwych Th., 3 June 1965, preceded by provincial tour (dir. Peter Hall; with Paul Rogers as Max, Ian Holm as Lenny, John Normington as Sam, Terence Rigby as Joey, Michael Bryant as Teddy, and Vivien Merchant as Ruth).
Revivals: Palace Th., Watford, Feb. 1969 (dir. Stephen Hollis; with Pinter as Lenny); Garrick Th., 2 May 1978 (dir. Kevin Billington; with Timothy West as Max, Michael Kitchen as Lenny, Charles Kay as Sam, Roger Lloyd Pack as Joey, Oliver Cotton as Teddy, and Gemma Jones as Ruth). Comedy Th., 12 Jan. 1991 (dir. Peter Hall; with Warren Mitchell as Max, Nicholas Woodeson as Lenny, John Normington as Sam, Douglas McFerran as Joey, Greg Hicks as Teddy, and Cherie Lunghi as Ruth).
First New York production: Music Box Th., 5 Jan. 1967 (London production, with Michael Craig as Teddy). *Revivals*: Bijou Th., 18 May 1971 (dir. Jerry Adler); CSC Repertory Th., Sept. 1972; Alive Th. Co., Wonderhorse, 6 Nov. 1975 (dir. Jack Chandler).
Film: released US 1973, Britain 1976 (dir. Peter Hall; with Rogers as Max, Holm as Lenny, Cyril Cusack as Sam, Rigby as Joey, Michael Jayston as Teddy, and Merchant as Ruth).
Published: Methuen, 1965; in *Plays: Three*.

Max, his sons Lenny and Joey, and his brother Sam live in a shabby old house in North London. Max once was a butcher. Now about seventy, he is retired. Sam is a chauffeur for a car-hire firm; Joey, who hopes to become a professional boxer, meanwhile works for a demolition firm. He is slow and plodding, exactly the opposite of the cocky and quick-witted Lenny, whose occupation goes unstated. They behave abominably to each other and talk of the boys' deceased mother, Jessie. Her role is left deliberately mysterious, their attitude toward her ambivalent. That night, Max's eldest son, Teddy, and his wife Ruth appear. They have stopped off on their way back from Italy to America, where Teddy teaches philosophy. Everyone else has gone to bed so Ruth's introduction to her father-in-law must be deferred. Eventually, she goes out for a walk and Teddy goes to bed. The woman Teddy introduces into their lair transforms their precarious, often embattled truce. Now, they must contend for her as well as for domination. The first to succeed — but not 'all the way' — is the oafish Joey. Teddy complaisantly accepts it; he is serenely, even smugly, above the battle. They invite Ruth to stay. But not simply as a guest: she must pay her way. Lenny, by now clearly established as a pimp, will set her up in business — a few hours a day should be sufficient. Perhaps Teddy, who is returning to his American campus, will even distribute her card to some of his London-bound colleagues.

Ruth's acceptance of the role at first seems inexplicable. It is less so when you consider the clues Pinter has dropped along the way. Before marrying Teddy, Ruth was a model 'for the body', clearly a euphemism for a prostitute. She is disenchanted with her life in America, bored with Teddy and their three children. Now she is back in her natural habitat, although Max insists that 'I've never had a whore under this roof before. Ever since your mother died.' Was Jessie, then, a whore? It all seems to fit; even to Lenny, now carrying on in his parents' footsteps, in the underground world of pimps, prostitutes, and petty criminals. In such a context, the proposal Max and Lenny make to Ruth seems, if anything, perfectly understandable. Obviously, such reasoning can be carried too far. There is much more to *The Homecoming* than an intellectual detective story. Its Oedipal undercurrents are strong. By the time the curtain falls Ruth's role is clear. She will be wife, mother, sex object. . . .

Pinter . . . is a much less 'obscure' writer than we give him credit for, more a realist than a dramatic metaphysician. A particular kind of realist, of course. His characters exist in their moments on the stage,

without announcing their motives or revealing more of themselves than those moments demand. They behave, if we stop to think about it, very much the way people behave. People, those we see every day, seldom provide us with the exposition, the motives for their actions. They appear, they speak, they act. It seems presumptuous to demand explanations. Pinter's characters do the same. It is only the fact that they are on a stage that causes us to think we must know all. All is something Pinter is not about to tell. What he is going to tell is enough. Enough for us to draw our conclusions, not necessarily reveal his own.

> Catharine Hughes, 'Pinter Revisited', *America*, 7 Aug. 1971, p. 70-1

It's about love and lack of love. The people are harsh and cruel, to be sure. Still, they aren't acting arbitrarily but for very deep-seated reasons. . . . I was only concerned with this particular family. I didn't relate them to any other possible or concrete family. I certainly didn't distort them in any way from any other kind of reality. I was only concerned with their reality. The whole play happens on a quite realistic level from my point of view. . . . There's no question that the family does behave very calculatedly and pretty horribly to each other and to the returning son. But they do it out of the texture of their lives and for other reasons which are not evil but slightly desperate. . . .

There are thousands of women in this very country who at this very moment are rolling off couches with their brothers, or cousins, or their next-door neighbours. The most respectable women do this. It's a splendid activity. It's a little curious, certainly, when your husband is looking on, but it doesn't mean you're a harlot. . . . If this had been a happy marriage it wouldn't have happened. But [Ruth] didn't want to go back to America with her husband, so what the hell's she going to do? She's misinterpreted deliberately and used by this family. But eventually she comes back at them with a whip. She says, 'If you want to play this game I can play it as well as you.' She does not become a harlot. At the end of the play she's in possession of a certain kind of freedom. She can do what she wants, and it is not at all certain she will go off to Greek Street. But even if she did, she would not be a harlot in her own mind.

> Pinter, quoted by Henry Hewes, 'Probing Pinter's Play',
> *Saturday Review*, 8 April 1967, p. 56, 58

The woman is not a nymphomaniac as some critics claimed. In fact she's not very sexy. . . . Certain facts like marriage and the family have clearly ceased to have any meaning.

> Pinter, quoted by Kathleen Halton,
> *Vogue*, 1 Oct. 1967, p. 245

The problem there is that the biggest bastard in a house full of bastards is actually the man who at first sight appears to be the victim — that is, Teddy, the brother who brings his wife home. He is actually locked in a battle of wills with his father and with his brothers, and, of course, with his wife, during which, in some sense, he destroys his wife, and his family, and his father, and himself, rather than give in. He is actually the protagonist. Now it's very easy for an actor to fall into the 'martyred' role in that part, because Teddy says so little — just sits there while all the other characters are speculating about his wife's qualities in bed. But this is the point — it's a tremendous act of will on his part to take it, and if he was actually feeling anything uncontrolled, he wouldn't be able to do it. It wasn't until Michael Jayston did it in the film that I realized how hard Teddy actually had to be, and how much in control he was. . . .

It sounds very fanciful, but the apples in *The Homecoming* had to be green — they could not be yellow or red, because they simply didn't disturb visually. The moment when Sam picks up the apple and eats it and says, 'Feeling a bit peckish' to the old man, is a kick in the crutch to him, and a soft yellow apple would not have had the effect.

> Peter Hall, 'Directing Pinter', *Theatre Quarterly*, No. 16
> (Nov. 1974–Jan. 1975), p. 6, 11, reprinted in Simon Trussler, ed.,
> *New Theatre Voices of the Seventies* (Methuen, 1981)

The phrase always on our lips when we were doing this play was 'taking the piss'. It's a cockney phrase meaning getting the better of your opponent by mockery. This play doesn't take the piss in a light or flippant way. It takes the piss in a cruel and bitter way. The characters are all doing this to each other. . . .

If there is a pause in the proceedings, for a small pause [Pinter] puts three dots; for a large pause he puts 'Pause'; for a very, very long pause he puts 'Silence'. Now of course it's not just enough to do that; because you have to *fill* those indications. But if one analyzes the scene, every time one of those three things happens there is a bridge which dramatists of the past have always verbalized. Now, Harold writes in silence as much as he does in words. . . . I did once have a dot and pause rehearsal. . . . It wasn't done to imprison the actor, but to add to his knowledge of the text. . . .

> Peter Hall, 'A Director's Approach', in John Lahr, ed.,
> *A Casebook on Harold Pinter's 'The Homecoming'*
> (New York, 1971), p. 14, 16, 17

[The family are] Jewish by descent, rather than by practice. . . . To an English actor, it leaps out of the text — the facility of speech, the quality

31

of speech, and the area: North London, Hackney. Far more important than this family being Jewish is their instinct for family, family unity. In Anglo-Saxon terms, this isn't part of the blood and being. This to an English audience would telegraph a Jewish heritage. . . . It's Ruth's homecoming right from the moment when she comes in through that door. It appears to be Teddy's homecoming, but he's long turned his back on that. . . . Teddy has not got the intelligence of Max, but he has got the family fibre which enables him to stand up to everything they throw at him. . . . His marriage was finished long before they left the States. . . . This is a very strange family. One important aspect which Harold kept hammering was that this is a very lovely family, his words were, 'It's a fine old mob.' And he was not being completely facetious. Indeed, they sit in the backyard on a fine summer's evening. . . . I would love to walk into Lenny's bedroom because I think Lenny has wall-to-wall carpeting and the most marvellous furniture. . . . Max has a wardrobe upstairs, I'm sure, of clothes that he can still get into and which are splendid and very expensive. . . . Stashed under the floorboards in my [Max's] bedroom is an enormous amount of money. . . .

There are two absolutely stark bastards in the play. The biggest bastard of all is Teddy, the other is Sam. Sam is a swine; when he appears to be defeated, he isn't. . . .

When Peter Hall was given the play to read by Harold, he met him, bubbling with excitement and said, 'What do you think of MacGregor?' He really wanted to know what Peter's feeling was about MacGregor. He's the leading character. . . .

[At the end, Ruth] is perfectly capable, after three days of quietly and completely dominating that household, of packing her case and following Teddy. On the other hand, she could stay put. . . . As far as I, Max, am concerned, the end of the play is far more shattering than it is to any audience.

Paul Rogers, 'An Actor's Approach', as above, p. 160-72

Their home is a vast open-plan North London living-room, working-class tat in epic concrete; a magnificent structure by John Bury, furnished with a Welsh dresser painted Berlin-black and a smoky-cut armchair. The whole thing is in monotone blacks and greys, the colours of mashed newspapers and cigarette ash and old socks. . . .

The drama in *The Homecoming* is not the plot. In Pinter it never is. It consists in the swaying of violent people as they gain minute advantages. A man who does the washing-up has the advantage over a man sitting in an armchair who thinks he can hear resentment is every swilling tea-leaf. . . . Pinter must stylize more than any writer in England apart from Ivy Compton-Burnett, which is why Peter Hall is right to

direct the play so anti-naturalistically. His people are entirely creatures of manoeuvre, hence the peculiar freezing mood of their moments of randiness. The sexual instinct in Pinter isn't at all emotional or even physical; it is practically territorial.

Penelope Gilliatt, The Observer, 6 June 1965
reprinted in Unholy Fools (London, 1973), p. 109-12

A young man, invited to a respectable house and mistaking it for a brothel, treats an innocent girl as a prostitute and her mother as the madame. Another young man, in a residence which he imagines to be an inn, yells at a dignified old man to pull his boots off. A conceited dandy is deluded into thinking that a lady is eager to sleep with him, then harshly disillusioned and mocked. Such incidents in classical English comedy do not shock us. We don't reflect on the cruelty with which the characters treat one another, on words that cut like whips into their feelings, on the brutality of the author; no, we laugh. We can feel no contrast between the play and real life in the seventeenth century, of which we have no experience. I don't think that Harold Pinter has ever been considered in relation to a writer like Wycherley, but the comparison may be illuminating. . . .

In *The Homecoming*, when someone claims to have taken part in the war, Max demands, 'Who did you kill?' Because most people we know don't talk with this savage candour, our laughter is uneasy. That uneasiness reflects a recognition that Pinter has driven deep into the unspoken realities amid which we live. . . .

The astonishing verbal candour of the loquacious characters — and Pinter's language has never been more compelling — shows that what one might take for an emotional desert is more like a primeval jungle. . . . The emotions are not pretty. Sexual in expression, they are rooted in violence. . . .

Mervyn Jones, Tribune, 11 May 1965, p. 15

Teddy is a pathetic figure, unable to cope with the animal aspects of his life, unbalanced. His wife is also pathetic: unable to control the animal. His brothers are doubly pathetic because what sex they want they have to draw up a contract for, and, at the same time, they share the woman's complete submission to sexuality. The nastiness in all this is that nowhere is there any mention of love. The characters, when seen out of the Pinter context, are pathetic; but they never emerge as pathetic on the stage. The only relationship feasible between them is on the Sade basis for the interhuman violence. They are in fact only partly real. But Pinter, in his own distinctive way, presents these characters as *the real*

thing. And he gets away with it because Pinter's peculiar way is so facilely attractive. It is important to note that this play is not a tragi-comedy, although it masquerades as one at times. Rather it is the tragic made comical, man held up to dispassion and consequently made to look ridiculous, coldly. For tragi-comedy there has to be a double awareness, of the absurdity of the human predicament and the pitifulness of it. Thus, although the audience was laughing when weeping might have been more appropriate, it was not because the playwright had shown the audience a way beyond the tears but because he had concealed the tears, distorted reality. . . . After all the surface layers have been removed, the various puzzles untied, it is clear that Pinter is saying, precisely, nothing. His play is his style. And his style is to dehumanize. . . . Look, Pinter is saying, this is how things are. They cannot be changed: you are all ridiculous creatures floundering in a vacuum you revere as human existence. You are absurd and ugly, nasty little creatures without a fibre of love in you. And while he is saying this, the audience is laughing and laughing, presumably unaware of the nihilist nonsense he is slipping over with the jokes. . . . Pinter is using the theatre to express a life-style, one that gives him comfort: he is trying to be *cool*. The kind of cold, fishy gaze he turns on the characters in his plays is the gaze he wishes he could turn on real life. What looks in his work like an almost Zennish detachment is, in fact, a disaffiliation, a refusal to be involved. And behind this refusal there is the fear of involvement and its *angst*-causing consequences. . . . *The Homecoming* is deceptive enough with its manipulation of human values and emotions to merit the label, obscene.

Tom McGrath, *Peace News*,
16 July 1965, p. 6-7

I would agree that Pinter's significance lies not in the content of his plays – which is always absurd or hopelessly enigmatic – but in the mood he creates on the stage: as McGrath puts it, a vision of dehuma-nized life, a projection of nothingness. But he seems to suggest that Pinter recommends this vision, or is cultivating complacency with it. Surely not. Isn't he rather obviously trying to make our skin crawl? The mood of depression McGrath took away from the play is clearly what Pinter is after.

Theodore Roszak, 'Letters',
Peace News, 30 July 1965, p. 11

Depending on one's mythopoeic faculty, a great deal might be made out of these events, but to do so entails much more effort than the author himself has gone to. If we are to take *The Homecoming* as something of

a parable, then I would recall how the most successful of modern parabolists, Kafka, while also basing his style on the method of self-contradiction — the assertion that at the same time and place A is and is not A — never left hold of the common notion of reality nor allowed existential anomalies to degenerate into mere caprices, unbuttressed by the very firm and specific narrative of his work. On the contrary, however nightmarish the situation, it always had enough *artistic* probability on its side to make it seem unexceptional and, therefore, truly terrifying. Pinter's disjoining of reality, on the other hand, is more of the funhouse variety than of *The Castle*. And if *The Homecoming* is not a parable? If it is no more and no less than the sum of itself? Well, then we are free to like or not like each moment of the play in isolation — in the same way as we have licence to tune in and out on a haphazard cocktail-party conversation. . . . The company that performs *The Homecoming* proves how effective sheer technique can be. English actors have always played well off language, trusting to the author for cohesiveness and justification of the attitudes the words lead them into. Even when these author's supports are not there, this very sensual verbal play can make it seem as though they are. . . . After all the tricks have been played, after the melodramatic codas to each act have been concluded, after the snippets of action have been juggled about, after all the sanguine acquiesence in the grotesque — after all of this, one is still left with the feeling that, in Harold Pinter, we have a writer who puts together loose fragments of highly actable scenes and then hopes that some part of life will conform to them.

Jack Richardson, *Commentary*, XLIII (June 1967), p. 73-4

I'm fairly sure I saw something last week at the Palace Theatre, Watford, which future generations of researchers into theatre history — cultural archaeologists, they'll probably be called by then — will want to know about. It was a performance by Harold Pinter in his own play, *The Homecoming*, playing the part of Lennie. . . . The first thing it demonstrated, predictably, is that Pinter is a superlative actor of Pinter. He gives first precedence to the words, spitting them out with a Cockney blend of malevolent gentility which makes you wonder whether Alf Garnett wasn't begotten at one remove by Pinterian rhetoric. His next emphasis is on giving force to those Pinter silences: charging them with formidable unspoken personality, eyes hooded or roving with dark, baleful intent. Apart from stabbing with his finger, a family characteristic underlining the basic hostility of everything said, he seemed to see Lennie as a personality expressing himself mainly through his feet, consciously displaying expanses of sinuous silk sock or padding about with neat, purposeful little steps like a cat, or jackal. The animal

overtones were there from the start, but muted, firmly embedded in the depths of a rounded human characterization. This was the great difference between Stephen Hollis's production and Peter Hall's original one at the Aldwych. Hall's was tuned like a Maserati, taut in every move and line, but I suspect now that it may have been too transparent in consequence, too overt. . . .

At Watford, recognition takes longer, never becomes so obvious that the surface of ordinary human wrestling for supremacy is broken by the zoo-patterns underlying its combat. You never lose sight of the fact that Ruth is not merely a sleek, docile mammal revelling in the male rivalry and display churning about her. She is also a woman cramped and stifled by an unsatisfactory possessive marriage. Her self-possession is not simply amoral acceptance of the fact that the strongest man will win her. It is a moral claim to freedom, to the right to possess herself. In the elaborate game of domination which ebbs and flows all evening over the stage, she is the winner.

Perhaps, you are left hoping, she will end the game for ever. Perhaps the whole point of it is to establish the woman as queen and peacemaker, holding the balance of hostilities which make up family life. For that now seems the point of the play. Instead of an arbitrary allegory about the beast in man, it seems a profound and penetrating exploration of the nature of family: its human possibilities as well as its bloody, tribal, biological roots.

Ronald Bryden,
The Observer, 9 Feb. 1969, p. 28

The least of *The Homecoming*'s troubles is that it does not make sense. This only stirs the interpreters, professional and amateur, to greater heights of interpretative madness. . . . The basic flaw . . . is that it is totally formulaic and predictable: every character, sooner or later, becomes the opposite of himself. . . . These instant contradictions extend to the whole play. . . . Now, people are often inconsistent, but they are not schematically self-contradictory. Nor are they, and this is the second big flaw here, all profoundly repulsive or utter nullities. But those are the only kind of characters you tend to find peopling (or, rather, insecting) a Pinter play. . . .

This leaves the language. But there hardly is any in Pinter: only commonplaces, repetitions, insults, *non sequiturs*, and pauses. This too is a language, I grant you, but is it a language for human beings? Take Ruth's speech: 'I was born quite near here. (*Pause*) Then . . . six years ago, I went to America. (*Pause*) It's all rock. And sand, it stretches . . . so far . . . everywhere you look. And there's lots of insects there. (*Silence. She is still*).' The words clearly mean very little; but the pauses,

ah, those famous Pinter pauses! How minimal can minimal art get? That is where you, dear spectator, fill in the play. . . .

Most noteworthy is the play's intense though latent homosexuality. Once again the motif of the same woman (and what a beastly woman!) shared by two or more men somehow involved with one another — in rivalry, kinship, or love-hate — appears; just as it did in *The Servant*, *Accident*, and *The Basement*, among others.

John Simon, *Uneasy Stages* (New York, 1975), p. 345-7,
reprinted from *The Hudson Review*, 1971

It ruptures the surface of more or less polite conversation like the eruption of a suboceanic earthquake. I have always found *The Homecoming* the most powerful as well as the most alarming of Pinter's plays. It is an absolutely stunning revelation of the terror that walketh at noonday, and lies in wait at night. Mr. Billington's production, and Oliver Cotton's performance, leave unexplained the strange passivity with which Teddy, the American professor, accepts his sleazy family's adoption of his wife into the commercial exploitation of sex by which they live. This, no doubt, is what Mr. Pinter intended. It has never been part of the Pinter ambition to make everything as clear as the ABC.

Harold Hobson, *Drama*, Summer 1978, p. 46

If this is Teddy's play, what does he want? Oliver Cotton, displaying a discreet transatlantic accent and occasional bursts of irritation and anxiety, succeeds no more than Michael Bryant did originally in clarifying the character's feelings or intentions: he remains a hole in the centre of the play, necessary only for things that happen to him.

Irving Wardle, *The Times*, 3 May 1978

Menace and ambiguity, which any second-year drama student will tell you are the playwright's especial stock-in-trade, hardly exist in *The Homecoming* at all: instead we have a logically plotted piece about the territorial imperative, dominated by the magnificent creation of Lenny . . . one of the great characters of the modern British theatre.

Sheridan Morley, *Shooting Stars* (Robson, 1983)

With an excellent set by Ellen Diss — an almost monochrome, bare, towering interior, suggestive of a prison — and with a notable performance from Timothy West as the ancient carp of a father, with downturned mouth, sagging belly, and glistening-grey skin, this

production shows that the play can still shock, chill, and elicit uncomfortable titters and squawks from an audience. . . . Those pregnant pauses abound; but too often; now that we have got used to them, the pregnancies seem to be phantom ones.

Francis King, *Sunday Telegraph*, 7 May 1978, p. 14

Warren Mitchell enters like a wounded bull, old and slightly out of control. It is a hugely powerful impersonation of somebody entirely powerless. This is how most men would like to see their fathers at one time or another: blustering, impotent, all wind and no muscle. In this sense, Harold Pinter's *The Homecoming* is like a dream of wish-fulfilment as well as a nightmare: I think Pinter knows most really important dreams are both. One of the reasons why Pinter's plays can seize your imagination is that in their world you recognize both the pernickety realism of life and the outrageous subversiveness of private fantasies. . . . There is the tension of failure about the place: egos are pushy but uncertain. There are rituals about everything: who has what, who sits where. Relationships have well-defined rules of engagement: insult, retort, resentful compromise pretending to be victory. . . . This family of men is like a hunting pack: all males, embattled and suspicious but mutually protective. . . .

When Peter Hall first directed it in 1965, the Aldwych stage had a cruel, hot-house air. Vivien Merchant played Ruth with a knowing and irresistibly erotic swagger, and Michael Bryant's Teddy let her go with a sense of dignified desolation and regret. Now Hall takes a wider and a harder view. For one thing, Hicks's Teddy is more recognizably a member of this predatory and defensive family: this excellent actor makes it clear that to Teddy his wife is less important than his freedom. . . . This is the true black comedy of the soul, both frightening and preposterously funny.

John Peter, *Sunday Times*, 13 Jan. 1991, p. 7

Even without listening to the words, you can tell *The Homecoming* is about a disconnected family. John Bury's black-and-grey set gives us a queer, dreamlike image of an old house in North London, the sort of picture that might turn up in sleep or in a 'fifties TV drama whose budget could run to only a few pieces of secondhand furniture and a floor lamp like a sinister shade tree. The stairway to the floor above is impossibly steep, and the only, jarring spot of colour is the poison-green apples in a bowl on the sideboard, a signal that a wicked woman is going to put in an appearance in this all-male household. . . . [Cherie Lunghi as Ruth] doesn't contribute to our understanding of a part that makes one

wonder whether Pinter is merely depicting male hatred of women, decrying it, or endorsing it. . . . Though it ends with Ruth's domination of her brothers-in-law, with one old man kneeling to her and another lying, possibly dead, at her feet, it degrades Ruth in the process of exalting her, by reducing her to a stereotype. Despite the lumpy treatment it gets here, this is still a disturbing, even sickening, play, as well as a funny and poetic one.

Rhoda Koenig,
Punch, 23-29 Jan. 1991

The revelation of this production is Cherie Lunghi's Ruth. Introduced as a stranger into this all-male household of unresolved sexual rivalries, myths, and fantasies, she seems immediately at home. Where other productions have made her the victim or object of male posturings and threats, this production presents her as Queen Bee, assuming from the start an inviolable composure and control. Her silence is not fear but self-possession. Dressed in a sleek black costume of severe allure, with movements precise, provocative, and poised, she exudes a sense of power.

David Nokes, *Times Literary Supplement*,
1 Feb. 1991, p. 16

Plays are not static objects. Their meaning is changed by time, place, and the chemistry of casting. Twenty five years ago at the Aldwych, Harold Pinter's *The Homecoming* offered an image of a domestic jungle filled with ferocious predators. Watching Peter Hall's magically precise new production at the Comedy, it becomes much more a play about triumphant female assertiveness. The play has changed; but then so have we. . . . What once seemed a Lorenz-like study in jungle law now becomes an image of self-fulfilment. In this production Ruth seems to be escaping from a patronizing academic chauvinist to rediscover her roots, her real identity, and a world that allows her to be a manipulative queen-bee. To call Pinter a feminist would be pitching it strong; but he certainly presents us with a female victory over masculine arrogance and sterility. . . . It is a sign of the richness of Pinter's play that it operates on several levels: as sexual myth, family drama, and social comedy. . . . This time round the family's crude, vituperative energy seems preferable to Teddy's philosophical detachment, and Ruth's final assumption of the roles of Madonna and Whore seem like a triumph of emancipation rather than a mark of captivity.

Michael Billington,
The Guardian, 12 Jan. 1991, p. 21

The Film

The camera seems always a sort of encumbrance, with nobody quite sure at any moment where to put it, so that we are more aware of what it is concealing, in its clumsiness, than what it is revealing and illuminating. The rhythm of the production, too, seems to have been affected by the fragmented construction of the film. The dialogue delivery tends to monotony; and the silences which are so articulate in the play often become in the film simply spaces. Still, the text is there; Roger's marvellous, menacing Max is there; and an imperfect record of a production of such importance is better than no record at all.

David Robinson, *The Times*, 23 Apr. 1976

Pinter's precise, sparing dialogue adapts naturally to the screen and is spoken by a cast quite good enough to make the most of it in any medium. . . .What one notices first about the film is how effectively it points up the humour.

Derek Malcolm, *The Guardian*, 23 Apr. 1976, p. 10

See also:

Denis Bablet, and Jean Jacquot, eds., *Les Voies de la Création Théâtrale*, IV (Paris: Editions du Centre National de la Récherche Scientifique, 1975), p. 319-60. [On the productions in London, Watford, Exeter, and Paris.]

John Elsom, ed., *Post-War British Theatre Criticism* (Routledge, 1981), p. 155-60.

Gareth and Barbara Lloyd Evans, eds., *Plays in Review, 1956-1980* (Batsford, 1985), p. 131-5.

John Lahr, ed., *A Casebook on Harold Pinter's 'The Homecoming'* (New York: Grove, 1971). [Includes useful and substantial interviews with Peter Hall, director; John Bury, designer; John Normington, and Paul Rogers, actors; and ten essays.]

Egil Tornqvist, *Transposing Drama* (Macmillan, 1991), p. 139-67. [Compares the film with a Dutch stage production and a Swedish TV production.]

Old Times

Play in two acts.
First London production: Royal Shakespeare Co. at Aldwych Th., 1 July 1971 (dir. Peter Hall; with Colin Blakely as Deeley, Dorothy Tutin as Kate, and Vivien Merchant as Anna).

Revival: Th. Royal, Haymarket, 24 Apr. 1985 (dir. David Jones;
   with Michael Gambon as Deeley, Nicola Pagett as Kate, and
   Liv Ullmann as Anna).
First New York production: Billy Rose Th., 16 Nov. 1971 (dir. Peter
   Hall; with Robert Shaw as Deeley, Mary Ure as Kate, and Rosemary
   Harris as Anna). *Revival:* Counterpoint Th. Co., 8 Oct. 1976
   (dir. Howard Green); Roundabout Stage, 12 Jan. 1984 (dir. Kenneth
   Frankel; with Anthony Hopkins as Deeley, Marsha Mason as Kate,
   and Jane Alexander as Anna); touring production, including St. Louis
   and Los Angeles, Autumn 1985–early 1986 (dir. Jones; with Pinter
   as Deeley, Pagett as Kate, and Ullmann as Anna).
Television: BBC-2, 22 Oct. 1975 (dir. Christopher Morahan; with Barry
   Foster as Deeley, Anna Cropper as Kate, and Mary Miller as Anna);
   BBC-2, 26 Oct. 1991 (with John Malkovich as Deeley, Kate Nelligan
   as Kate, and Miranda Richardson as Anna).
Published: Eyre Methuen, 1971; in *Plays: Four*.

Night in 'a converted farmhouse'; John Bury's set, spare yet
shadowy, shows the bones of the primitive supporting the
modish; his lighting unobtrusively moves from the everyday to
the near-abstract. Deeley, a middle-aged film-maker of sorts,
tough, tweedy, sits opposite his wife Kate. In their fragmentary
talk he exhibits by turns tenderness, complicity, bewilderment;
she lies utterly relaxed, like a swimmer floating idly in a warm
sea. Their thoughts are invaded by her friend Anna, with whom
she shared a flat in London twenty years before, when they were
both working girls with mild cultural aspirations. She is coming
to visit them; in a sense she is already with them. Suddenly a
waiting shadow at the back of the stage stirs, and she moves
down to join in. Now the apparent action of the play begins — a
duel between Deeley and Anna to decide which of them really
possesses Kate. Anna's weapon is reminiscence, of shared
experience in the days when Deeley did not yet exist for Kate —
the meals in cafés listening to the conversation of those the girls
took to be writers and artists, the long, intimate domestic
evenings in the flat, 'things that may never have happened — but
as I recall them, so they took place'. There is something creepy
about Anna (did she or did she not take a mysterious pleasure in
wearing Kate's underclothes without asking?). . . . Faced with
such an adversary, Deeley delves deep into himself, beyond the

41

genial drink-dispensing host, the possessive husband; soon the duel's the thing, not its ostensible object. First, he calls upon common memories of the past period — the contest takes on an air of jollity as they work their way haltingly through old popular songs. Then, with childlike cunning, which Colin Blakely stockily invests with sudden crinklings of suppressed glee, Deeley goes further. Who picked up whom at a fleapit showing of the film Odd Man Out? *Anna fights enigmatically back. Deeley takes off once more. If he cannot claim to have shared his wife's youthful past, he will — daring stroke — share Anna's. . . .*

These questions, and many others like them in the shadowy conflict, do not need precise factual answers: their unresolved resonances, as the tension between the two duellists mounts, speak for all our private fantasies, each with its kernel of forgotten fact. And while the duel has been flickering and blundering round the stage, the play's real action has been steadily developing, all unobserved. What has Kate to do with all this? Tiny, flower-faced, she sits relaxed as ever, with a quiet word here, a mild protest at being spoken of as though she were dead, a shared laugh there. Then up she gets. She will have a bath. Anna offers to run it for her. No, she will run it herself. She goes. In her absence the duel continues. And when she returns, all is changed. In a long white robe — a bathrobe, but what of that? — she commands the scene.

Of all the thousands of subtly contrived shifts and shades of emphasis which Peter Hall's direction has drawn from text and actors none is more remarkable than this unstressed transfiguration, for the passive object of a possessive combat between husband and old friend into a still passive yet all-embracing, all-devouring, radiantly indifferent force of nature. . . . Anna knows what has happened, gives up at once, retreats to lie silent as in death. Deeley, blundering, desperate by now, breaks down.

Once before he has burst out in near-despair, but still with enough force to express himself through anger. Now the despair is total: the genial middle-aged film-maker is a broken child. Sobbing, he burrows his way into Kate's arms as she kneels hieratically in her white robe: gently, gazing ahead, inexorably, she moves her protective arm away. Rejected, he stumbles back into the dark. The light fades from him as it has already left Anna. Alone, pulsing with merciless white calm, Kate remains, expressionless at the centre of perhaps the most piercing stage picture I have ever seen, creator and destroyer in one.

J. W. Lambert, *Drama*, No. 102 (Autumn 1971), p. 15-17

There's a section in the play where Deeley says to . . . the friend, that they met in this pub twenty years before. Well, the fact is they might have and they might have not. If you were asked to remember, you really cannot be sure of whom you met twenty years before, and in what circumstances. . . . It's true that in *Old Times* the woman is there, but not there, which pleased me when I managed to do that, when that came through to me. . . .

I wrote one new line in rehearsal. . . . The line is: 'Yes. I remember', and that affected all the brandy and the coffee. In this play, the lifting of a coffee cup at the wrong moment can damage the next five minutes. As for the sipping of coffee, that can ruin the act. [For New York] I did change a silence to a pause. It was a rewrite. This silence was a pretty long silence. Now it's a short pause.

> Pinter, quoted by Mel Gussow,
> 'A Conversation (Pause) with Harold Pinter',
> *New York Times Magazine*, 5 December 1971, p. 43, 131

[Anna's] not there, in actual naturalistic terms, but she is there, because she's been there for twenty years, in each of their heads. She's never left either of their heads, and she never will. She can't leave the room at the end. She tries to, it is impossible. Actually, the two of them would not stay married, they wouldn't stay related, they wouldn't almost exist, without the obsession of that third person in their heads, and the opening image illustrates that. It's a reaching towards a kind of imagery — an emblem in silence. . . .

What is remarkable about *Old Times* is that Deeley's own sexual insecurities, personal inadequacies, actually make him invent relationships and happenings which were not, in my view, true at all.

> Peter Hall, 'Directing Pinter', p. 12, 14

[*On playing Deeley in the first production.*] *Old Times* is a play about a certain time of life — the forties. Practically everyone concerned with that play was roughly the same age. It's a time when you do begin to re-evaluate — when you stand still for a moment and think about old times. Then you begin another plunge forward I suppose — I don't really know yet. . . . The first thing we were told by Peter Hall was that there are no victims in Pinter's plays. All the characters are aggressors. None of them surrenders an inch — they all finally attack each other. In *Old Times* there is a battle going on in the room, for life and death, for survival as a person. But it's all done through conversation. There are only two moments when the voice rises beyond normal conversation — when Deeley twice explodes in anger and frustration. . . .

When we started trying to 'move' the play we discovered we couldn't do it. We had to sit where we were (in fact Dorothy Tutin spends most of the first act just lying on a couch). Every slight movement began to suggest so much about the relationships that even puffing a cigarette would mean swinging an audience's attention onto your character. Everything you did would mean something. It boiled down to *doing nothing* at all — just sitting and feeling what was happening inside yourself, never in terms of what you might do. To sit in a chair for such a time, holding everything in, was quite an effort. In the interval and after a performance my body is literally shaking from all the mental energy spent holding back. When I finally do let go at the end of the play it is real *anger*, not an actor's energy. I'm blazing from having spent over an hour waiting to explode. . . .

We think it's a play about possession. Deeley thinks he loves Kate, his wife, but he doesn't. He just wants to keep her for himself. If you possess somebody then the person can't really exist — or only as part of you. Possessing your wife means destroying her. Deeley only learns twenty years after his marriage that his wife has in fact been her real self. Kate married him knowing that their whole relationship was a disaster from the start. She is as guilty as he is — the only way she has survived has been to withdraw from her husband's aggressivity completely — to remain silent.

It was pure chance that Anna arrived to visit Kate that night. A complete accident destroys Deeley's life. I think he had given up trying to draw Kate out — he went round the world making documentary films. I don't think he is a very good film-maker — he loses control too easily. But he could still kid himself that he had a home life worth returning for — so he's very threatened when this woman, Anna, turns up after twenty years for a visit. Why Anna comes we don't know — certainly not me! I think she is married but this is only a guess. I also believe she is a real person not a fantasy. We've never been told that for sure by Pinter. But we all think she's real. When Deeley claims that he has met Anna as well (at that party) I think he's making the story up. Either that or Deeley is determined to make their meeting real. He wants to possess Anna now as well as Kate. If he can turn her into a little bit he picked up in the pub one night, it will dispose of Anna as a threat. It's arguable that Deeley has fooled himself into thinking that he actually did know Anna.

Colin Blakely, interviewed in
Plays and Players, July 1971, p. 22, 24

Within the same triangular frame of memory as *Silence*, it mixes the sexual ambiguities of *The Collection* with the territorial wars of domi-

nance which underlay *The Homecoming*. . . . More clearly than before, it takes the form of a duel: a game of skill to the death. . . . As in *The Homecoming*, the final, devastating victory belongs to neither battler, but to the woman battled over. . . . Hall directs the comedy with a musician's ear for the value of every word and silence which exposes every layer of the text like the perspex levels of a three-dimensional chess-board. 'Do you drink brandy?' asks Deeley. Vivien Merchant's pause before replying that she would love some is just sufficient to remind you that, on Pinter territory, every question is an attempt to control and every answer a swift evasion.

Ronald Bryden,
The Observer, 6 June 1971

The goading, Pirandellian enigmas of memory and reality bump up against each other. Constantly we are being asked to reconcile the actual events of the past with those imaginary happenings which, in retrospect, are even more real — with the result that everyone's sense of reality is painfully undermined. The language of the play is structured with the kind of potent economy we associate with Beckett's most recent stage work. It creates a world of inference and innuendo which clings to its words like undertow. But the temperature of the evening is low. . . . If Wilde is right and the aim of art is simply to create a mood, then *Old Times* creates its mood perfectly. But we learn very little about the people generating that mood, and what we do learn has nothing of the particularity we've come to expect from the best art. . . . What *Old Times* gives us (and to a certain extent *Landscape* and *Silence* gave us the same) is a beautiful facsimile of the kind of play Beckett might have written if he were an East End English writer named Harold Pinter. The form of the artefact is concise and masterful, but the fabric is not made for such a high finish. . . . Pinter, little by little, has been tiring of the recognizable human ingredients which made up his best work, and in a writer who has done so much so well, it is an understandable tedium. But the more ambitious he becomes — and *Old Times* is highly ambitious — the more one feels he is demonstrating a knack rather than transmitting a personal experience.

Charles Marowitz, *Confessions of a Counterfeit Critic*, p. 186-8,
reprinted from *New York Times*, 13 June 1971

One could scarcely care less about this flaccid trio. The blood of life does not pump through them. They are reveries and idle speculations posing as people. Dramatically, the uses of the past are betrayed in *Old Times*. At the end of the play, nothing has been clarified or illuminated.

Nor has what Eliot called 'the present moment of the past' been reclaimed.

T. E. Kalem,
Time, 29 Nov. 1971, p. 43

The device of opening and closing the play with a sudden burst of very bright light photographically etches *Old Times* onto one's memory, like isolated moments from an old love affair. . . . The London and New York productions are noticeably different. In London . . . more of Pinter's ironic humour emerged, and the memories evoked a deeper nostalgic atmosphere. Here, the emphasis is on Deeley's intensely felt passion. As Robert Shaw portrays him, Deeley is not playing a casual game. He seems from the beginning to be a desperate man who resents the proceedings, and he expresses his vulnerability movingly both in short eruptive outbursts and in his copious weeping at the end.

Henry Hewes,
Saturday Review, 4 Dec. 1971

We care neither about the characters nor about the issues. . . . Of what consequence are these shadowboxing shadows? Why should anyone give a tinker's damn about such nebulous figures with wispy, indefinable, and probably illusory problems? Memory and oblivion, at any rate, do not work in this way. . . . *Old Times* suffers from what I can only call spiritual shallowness. It is of the greatest possible unimportance with whom one of these figurines spouting dim witticisms or pregnant silences (false pregnancies, as I once called them) has slept, is sleeping, or will sleep. . . . It is merely a question of ascendancies among puppets; we might as soon care about which horse on a merry-go-round will come to a halt ahead of another. . . . Hall knows how to stage these plays so that they assume a semblance of meaning. He gets from the actors all kinds of rubatos, crescendos, diminuendos, overtones, and soft-pedallings; he works out effects of movement in space worthy of a kinetic sculptor, of light and shadow to do an old Dutch master proud. John Bury executes the lighting plot as if it were a grand conspiracy (which it is), and designs his dependably brilliant sets — in this case, sparse modern furniture arranged somewhat bizarrely, proportioned a little discordantly, and surrounded with rather more space than customary. The colours, too, are a mite too coolly understated; the floor is raked; the walls given exaggerated foreshortening, so that our eye is fed more perspective than is its regular diet; one corner of the acting surface protrudes disquietingly from behind the curtain. The total effect is a refined malaise. . . . This is the exact visual equivalent of Pinter's

dramaturgy, and is managed rather better by the designer than by the author.

John Simon, *Uneasy Stages* (New York, 1975), p. 381-4,
reprinted from *The Hudson Review*, Spring 1972

We are in an extraordinary land straight away. Timothy O'Brien's set is first seen bathed in a white light, its mushroom-shaped window looking on to the sea, and the silent black-clad figure of the old friend, Anna, stands with her back to the husband and wife, while they discuss her imminent arrival. The room, with its dark cork walls, sterile furniture, and oddly shaped window, does not look real, and anything that happens in it also takes on an air of unreality. Instead of the original Peter Hall concept of an ordinariness that becomes out of joint, David Jones, the director, has chosen a setting that lends itself to enigma. . . .

Liv Ullmann, as Anna, takes the premise further away from the everyday. She has a hauntingly beautiful face and an accent which, by its foreignness, implies that she has come from a world elsewhere. The villa with marble floors on the cliffs of Sardinia may well not be a fantasy constructed jointly by her and Deeley, but her real home. She is an outsider in every sense. Nicola Pagett, as Kate, the elusive woman over which Anna and Deeley are striving for control, reveals nothing to the protagonists, nor to the audience, of her reactions under the surface. Her Kate is a doll-like figure, almost a marionette, the head turning towards whichever person is pulling the strings. Michael Gambon catches both the silly point-scoring irony and the bullying frustration that afflict a man who knows he cannot possess his wife, even by taking over her memories.

Clare Colvin, *Plays and Players*, June 1985, p. 25-6

[*Old Times*] is about two things. One is the capriciousness of memory, making now its merciful deletions and now its consoling additions, like an artist constantly rearranging the landscape before him. The other is jealousy in its most insidious form, not of a tangible rival but of the beloved's intangible past. . . . The work is extraordinarily tense and extraordinarily compact. It is also extraordinarily funny.

Francis King, *Sunday Telegraph*, 2 April 1985

The main problem facing a director of *Old Times* is the degree to which movements on stage should mime the remembered action. David Jones applies sensible restraint. For example, when Deeley is describing to the black-stockinged Anna the circumstances of looking up her skirt, the

two figures on sofas echo — perhaps suggest — the former posture, but he isn't made to stare (too crassly at least) in the same direction. For, as Deeley says of his own sexual and Anna's romantic 'gazing', 'that's all over now, isn't it?' Jones rightly sees that Deeley's jealousies are induced by pressures and images from the past (he is even made innocently anxious about his own relations with Kate). . . . Jones's only superfluous stroke of this kind is the airy blow he has Deeley aim at his wife in a moment of baffled frustration. Otherwise his intelligent reading is well served by the vigorous and amiable performance of Michael Gambon, a Deeley more angry than hurt, who lollops around the stage as if he owned it (he does).

Mick Imlah, Times Literary Supplement,
10 May 1985, p. 523

Jones's glittering revival reveals the play as an unsparing study in male insecurity. I've heard *Old Times* described as being obscure; but it should be crystal clear to anyone who has ever tried to re-think his own past to suit the present, or to anyone who is afraid of nightmares because they might come true. These are not things we're always conscious of. Writing like this harasses and tears at the soft underside of the mind.

John Peter, Sunday Times, 28 Apr. 1985

See also:
Gareth and Barbara Lloyd Evans, eds., *Plays in Review, 1956-1980* (Batsford, 1985), p. 177-80.

No Man's Land

Play in two acts.
First London production: National Th., 23 Apr. 1975, trans. Wyndham's Th., 15 July 1975 (dir. Peter Hall; with Ralph Richardson as Hirst, John Gielgud as Spooner, Michael Feast as Foster, and Terence Rigby as Briggs).
First New York production: Longacre Th., 9 Nov. 1976 (as London production, with Michael Kitchen as Foster).
Television: Granada, 3 Oct. 1978 (with New York cast).
Published: Eyre Methuen, 1975; revised ed., 1975; in *Plays: Four*.

The title No Man's Land *('icy and unchanging') refers to a*

powerful old man of letters [Hirst] who arrives at this elegant Hampstead home (semi-circular in John Bury's design to fit a reference to a lighthouse), accompanied by a gadfly [Spooner] he has picked up on the Heath. This creepy, crumpled acquisition startles Pinter aficionados by giving a detailed account of himself at the opening of the play; an account, moreover, couched in self-conscious poetic prose. Needless to say, the author is throwing sand in our eyes. By the end, we are not sure whether he writes poems or clears away glasses in a pub in Chalk Farm, or both. We do know that he has ousted as secretary-companion the youth and the thug who had been acting as bodyguards to the old man. The crucial bond between them is shared memories — but memories are notoriously unreliable. They seem to be old chums from Oxford, but a gushing exchange of reminiscences of the most intimate nature is punctuated by Richardson's gruff inquiry, 'Who is this man?' Pinter's refusal to answer this question, except by indicating a multiplicity of identities, is the core of his art.

Frank Marcus, *Sunday Telegraph*, 27 Apr. 1975, p. 14

I remember when I wrote *No Man's Land*. I was in a taxi one night coming back from somewhere and suddenly a line, a few words came into mind. I had no pencil. I got back to the house and wrote those lines down. . . . It was the very beginning of the play, and I didn't know who said them.

Pinter, quoted by Mel Gussow,
New York Times, 30 December 1979, Sec. II, 5

You'd rather expect me to play the other one, wouldn't you? I'm glad I'm not. I can't play drunk. And Ralph [Richardson] is so marvellous at that. I only met Auden twice, towards the end of his life. When I read the play I said to Pinter, 'What about Auden?' In a kind of way the suit, the cigarette, and the hair are the key to it. The socks and the sandals were my idea. . . . It is rather astonishing that nobody complains about the coarser passages in *No Man's Land*. . . . Perhaps such fans as I had have deserted me. . . . I was terrified that I'd be too sympathetic in this part. Spooner really is a monster, you know. I had to delve into the blackest parts of my character and draw on some of the most unpleasant people I know.

John Gielgud, quoted in 'Spooner Goes West',
The Observer, 13 July 1975

There is an icy preoccupation with time; and the long sustained speeches have a poetic validity which would have seemed incredible in the days of the brisk, hostile repartee of *The Birthday Party*. . . . It is extremely funny and also extremely bleak. A play about the nature of the artist: the real artist harassed by the phoney artist. . . . A feeling that I really know what it is about — opposites. Genius against lack of talent, success against failure, drunk against sobriety, elegance against uncouthness, smoothness against roughness, politeness against violence. . . . Spooner is the proudest and the most arrogant man you can imagine. If he ever plays humbly all the conflict has gone. . . . The truth is that Spooner is many things and changes his posture from second to second. . . . [Pinter said] *The Homecoming* and *Old Times* were primarily about sex and the pauses therefore reverberated with half meanings and suggested mean-ings. The pauses in *No Man's Land* are much more clearly a matter of threat and of tension. . . . At rehearsal this afternoon John [Gielgud] asked Harold what the Briggs-Spooner scene was for at the beginning of Act II. What did it give the audience? What did it convey? Harold paused. 'I'm afraid I cannot answer questions like that, John. My work is just what it is. I am sorry.' . . . John said to Harold that playing Pinter was like playing Congreve or Wilde. It needed a consciousness of the audience, a manipulation of them which was precisely the same as for high classical comedy. He thought it would be like playing Chekhov — where you must ignore the audience — but it wasn't.

Peter Hall, *Diaries*, ed. John Goodwin
(London, 1983), p. 119, 147, 157-60

No Man's Land is about precisely what its title suggests: the sense of being caught in some mysterious limbo between life and death, between a world of brute reality and one of fluid uncertainty. But although plenty of plays, from *Sweeny Agonistes* to *Outward Bound*, have tried to pin down that strange sense of reaching out into a void, I can think of few that have done so as concretely, funnily, and concisely as Pinter's. . . . In one way, the play is a masterly summation of all the themes that have long obsessed Pinter: the fallibility of memory, the co-existence in one man of brute strength and sensitivity, the ultimate unknowability of women, the notion that all human contact is a battle between who and whom. . . . Pinter's achievement, in fact, is to have treated comically a theme that most writers tackle with sententious gravity: that at any moment in time the 'real', tangible world may turn out to be an illusion. . . . Among the play's many themes, I suspect Pinter is also saying that the money, luxury, and privileges of literary success are themselves a death-in-life.

Michael Billington, *The Guardian*, 24 Apr. 1975

[Billington] sees it as a concrete and comic language game in which style is the means of attack in a battle of class and status. I saw it as a non-naturalistic time-play in which dislocation has set in for Ralph Richardson's Hirst. Old age becomes a shifting, disconcerting experience in which a hold upon memory is lost in fantasy and confusion. Either interpretation holds good at a second viewing. But it is the quality of bewildered suspense which now seems the most effective quality which Pinter brings to the play. . . .

Gielgud in the greatest character performance he has given in over a decade undergoes a complete physical transformation. Every limb of his body is arranged in a gesture of gauche ease: that lolloping tip-toe walk, that pursed lip scowl, those bent knees, a fluting voice, while Ralph Richardson with huge, terrified eyes magnificently achieves a transition between alcoholic eccentricity and voices and eyes aghast with memories.

Nicholas de Jongh, *The Guardian*, 23 July 1975

Sir John gives his most detailed and observant performance in years, one to amaze those who think of him as little more than a mellow cello, exquisitely played. With his baggy grey suit, orange shirt, sandals, rimless specs, and floppy, sandy hair, he's the sort of ragbag bohemian one can still sometimes see padding about Hampstead or Highgate, head full of memories of little magazines and the Spanish Civil War. But Sir John fills out this passé picture with tiny, mordant touches, reflecting diffidence or bravado or mockery or a sort of fastidious pique — his body bristling, wincing, teetering, and mildly writhing, like someone with ants in his armpits, and then sitting still, his mouth pinched into an inverted U, as if he'd just discovered his teeth were made of soap. His Spooner is precious, sour, not to be trusted, a piece of authentic characterization for which Pinter, too, obviously deserves our thanks. He has, in fact, written a part rather more memorable than the play that contains it.

Benedict Nightingale, *New Statesman*, 2 May 1975, p. 601

Plot there is none, only a sketch of the developing relationship between the two men, and that examined only as far as is required to summon up the spiritual wilderness in which the men live. The play is a concert piece for four actors. As Pinter has repeatedly demonstrated before, it is possible to create both music and tension on the stage without the need of an anecdote; he has created both in abundance in this play.

B. A. Young, *The Mirror up to Nature* (Kimber, 1982), p. 100, reprinted from *Financial Times*

Pinter is our greatest master of rhetoric. To the tingling tirades on drawing beer in *Landscape* and the public transport attractions of Dalston Junction in *The Caretaker* must now be added a beautifully architected oration in *No Man's Land* at the Old Vic on the baffling inaccessibility of Bolsover Street: which, surrounded by one-way streets, and complicated in its approach by a mews and a crescent, is almost impossible to reach by car, and quite impossible to leave. . . . [Hirst and Spooner] were friends at Oxford; one is wealthy, the other poor, and the rich man has seduced the poor man's wife. Or has he? Were they? Are they? These questions loom through the luxurious menace of the play's atmosphere, and the solution of them depends on Briggs, who has no intention of telling us the answers. Should we believe him if he did?

Harold Hobson,
Sunday Times, 27 Apr. 1975

No Man's Land, it seems to me, is the inner landscape of the old — when life has stopped but existence goes on. . . . Outer reality is a matter of politesse accelerating into shambolic anacoluthon. Hirst's incredible drinking is not an explanation of this condition, but the excuse for a complete fuddlement which would exist without alcohol. Banalities are the only safe currency, memories drift into dreams, the past must be clumsily improvised, pointless power-struggles take place. . . . The terminus has been reached. Briggs and Foster, the two young sinister helpers, with their threats, jokes, deliberate nonsense, and exaggerated politeness ('Doctor's orders') are surely the alien living, seen through the clouded retina and the failing mind.

Craig Raine, *New Statesman*, 1 Aug. 1975

Why should Hirst, who seems to figure at the centre of the pattern, be at least three completely different people in the course of the action? In the first part, he is an almost speechless drunk who exits through the door on his hands and knees. At the start of the second act, he is a comic old buffer of a club-man, who claims to recognize Spooner as a former acquaintance, Charles Wetherby, whom he once cuckolded, and Spooner responds to some extent as if this were true. Towards the end, he becomes a pseudo-poetic figure in a chair intoning a sort of chorus about time having to have a stop, with the help of Foster and Briggs. . . . And at no point does he correspond to his frequently stated character, which is that of an eminent and successful writer. He is neither held together by his unexplained drunkenness, nor convincingly shattered by it.

John Weightman,
Encounter, XLV (July 1975), p. 25-6

No Man's Land proved to be a new departure for Pinter, I thought — one which stepped back to make a flying leap forward. It is Pinter on Pinter, Pinter parodying Pinter, Pinter feeding on himself and his previous work for regeneration. . . . It is much more than that. Pinter's style, his particular poetic qualities, have always been allusiveness and ambiguity, silence and the unspoken — the concrete vagueness for which was coined the over-used epithet 'Pinteresque'.

While these qualities recur in *No Man's Land*, much of the previously covert is made overt. Spooner's homosexuality is blatant, not latent. Sexual innuendo, always in play between the lines in a Pinter play, bounces now like balls (that is typical!) along the surface of the racy dialogue, which is full of Shakespeareanly funny and earthily evocative punning. And it all worked wonderfully — the vulgar with the lyrical.

Catherine Itzin,
Tribune, 2 May 1975

If this last play is a picture of the world, there is a shallowness in it. Much that is apparently superficial *is* probably superficial, and even three or even seven ambiguities to a speech do not guarantee that any one of them is not shallow. To be thoughtful, even if portraying thoughts of others, is not to follow any predetermined formula — even one's own. I am worried that *No Man's Land* is too much the mixture as before. The manner is marvellous, both in craft and in comic relief, but is repetitive.

Bernard Crick,
Times Higher Education Supplement, 9 May 1975,
reprinted in *Essays on Politics and Literature*
(Edinburgh, 1989), p. 243-4

The play lacks the drama of *The Birthday Party*, the total comedy of his masterpiece *The Caretaker* (now dismissed by Pinter as wordy), and any new ideas, theatrical or otherwise. There's technique, but it's the technique of someone finding better ways of burying himself.

Steve Grant,
Time Out, 8-14 Aug. 1975

See also:
Gareth and Barbara Lloyd Evans, eds., *Plays in Review, 1956-1980*
(Batsford, 1985), p. 215-8.

Betrayal

Play in nine scenes, for performance with or without interval.
First London production: National Th. (Lyttelton), 15 Nov. 1978
(dir. Peter Hall; with Michael Gambon as Jerry, Penelope Wilton
as Emma, and Daniel Massey as Robert).
Revivals: Greenwich Th., 27 Apr. 1983 (dir. Gary Raymond;
with Raymond as Jerry, Susan Farmer as Emma, and
Edward Hardwicke as Robert); Almeida Th., 22 Jan. 1991
(dir. David Leveaux; with Bill Nighy as Jerry, Cheryl Campbell as
Emma, and Martin Shaw as Robert).
First New York production: Trafalgar Th., 5 Jan. 1980 (dir. Peter Hall;
with Raul Julia as Jerry, Blythe Danner as Emma, and Roy Scheider
as Robert).
Film: released 1983 (dir. David Jones; with Jeremy Irons as Jerry,
Patricia Hodge as Emma, and Ben Kingsley as Robert).
Radio: BBC Radio Three, 9 Oct. 1990 (dir. Ned Chaillet; with Gambon
as Jerry, Hodge as Emma, and Pinter as Robert).
Published: Methuen, 1978; revised ed., 1980; in *Plays: Four*.

In Betrayal *Pinter has gone straight. He tells the story of a wife's affair with her husband's best friend. We are given all the facts we need to comprehend the plot and the behaviour of the three characters; nothing gratuitous, mysterious, or menacing occurs offstage, although there lurks a man called Casey whom all three know at the periphery of their triangle and who seems to be waiting in the wings for Emma; moreover, the speech, middle-class for once, has become more stylized and elegant, although just as acutely heard. The three of them, publisher Robert, literary agent Jerry, and Emma, who is Robert's wife and for seven years Jerry's afternoon mistress. The story of their three-some begins at the end — the marriage breaking up, the affair over — and ends at the beginning with a drunken Jerry grabbing Emma in her bedroom while a party is going on and promising her 'They'll never know.' . . . The audience has the advantage over the characters and can ask itself the question: is knowing all that counts? Robert, after five years, finds out about his betrayal by Emma and Jerry; Jerry is in turn betrayed by Emma when she omits to tell him of Robert's discovery; Emma meanwhile discovers Robert's persistent betrayals of her.*

Betrayal is a completely unromantic account of infidelity, including the adultery of truth. A revolving stage enables us to see in clinically bare settings by John Bury the anxious reality of the lovers' flat — Emma worrying about the underutilization of the crockery and furnishings — and the scenes from married life in which the truth breaks slowly out in all of its banality. The chronological scheme of the play gives a marvellous tension to the scenes, which are mostly duets. The one in the Venetian hotel bedroom in which Robert discovers his wife's and his friend's affair together is made all the more dramatic by our prior glimpses into the stark intimacy of the Kilburn flat. The scene in which Robert and Jerry lunch together in an Italian restaurant in Soho . . . is made almost unbearable by our knowing that Robert believes Jerry knows that he knows.

Peter Jenkins, *The Spectator*,
25 Nov. 1978, p. 24

When I realized the implications of the play, I knew there was only one way to go and that was backwards. The actual structure of the play seemed to dictate itself. When I realized what was going on, this movement in time, I was very excited by it. It was evident more or less straightaway that there were only going to be three main characters, and that they'd been up to something. . . . In rehearsal in London I did three things. I cut one word, 'please'. I also took out a pause and I inserted a pause.

Pinter, quoted by Mel Gussow,
New York Times, 30 December 1979,
Sec. II, p. 5, 7

The marriage of Robert and Emma is actually kept going by her secret affair with Jerry and by the friendship of the two men. Once the betrayals cease, the marriage is over. . . . [Pinter has] written an absolutely enchanting, vigorous, life-enhancing woman with a keen appetite for life, a good intellect, a marvellous sense of humour, and little sense of morality — though an honourable sense of what is possible, which perhaps does less harm because it hurts others less. It is an advance for Harold, this play; the tension builds up at an enormous rate. It's not fanciful to think of Mozart. From my point of view there's the same precision of means, the same beauty, the same lyricism, and the same sudden descents into pain which are quickly over because of a healthy sense of the ridiculous.

Peter Hall, *Diaries*,
ed. John Goodwin (London, 1983), p. 378, 382

[Pinter's] picture of infidelity is bleak and relentless. His technique of showing the last scene of disillusionment first means that there is never a moment in the play when the audience thinks it possible that adultery will prove a profitable investment. . . . *Betrayal* is a play of very great power. . . . It has a unity of mood rare in English drama.

Harold Hobson, *Drama*,
No. 131 (Winter 1979), p. 42-3

What distresses me is the pitifully thin strip of human experience it explores and its obsession with the tiny ripples on the stagnant pond of bourgeois-affluent life. . . . Pinter has betrayed his immense talent by serving up this kind of high-class soap-opera (laced with suitable cultural brand-names, like Venice, Torcello, and Yeats) instead of a real play.

Michael Billington, *The Guardian*, 16 Nov. 1978

The story told in reverse order presents a new variation on one of Pinter's favourite motifs — the fallibility of memory. In other plays we are left to guess which version is correct. Here we are afterwards given the answer by actually seeing what happened. . . .

It is also by seeing the story in reverse sequence that the theme of the play indicated by its title gradually emerges: who betrayed whom . . . . Pinter is in fact drawing a horrifying portrait of a society, a way of life based on an infinite number of mutual betrayals; or is he, perhaps, saying that human life itself, of necessity, consists of such a web of lies, deceptions, and treasons?

Martin Esslin, *Plays and Players*, Jan. 1979

Their speech seems to consist of nothing but banalities — 'Oh, don't get upset. There's no point.' 'He's put on weight.' 'Yes, I thought that.' 'We used to like each other.' 'We still do.' They rattle devalued coinage exchanged a hundred times every day in mindless small talk. . . . And yet by some miracle of concentration, of rejection of everything that is not strictly relevant to the development of the situation, Pinter manages to provide it with an undercurrent of highly charged emotion that is almost Racinian. . . . The tempo is slow, deliberate, exact, and whichever of the three is speaking the tone seems monotonously right. It is not the voice so much as the face that has to express what is happening. Penelope Wilton as the wife/mistress has a wonderfully poignant moment when she is lying on a bed in a Venetian hotel room trying to read a novel and learns from her husband that he has discovered that she is in secret correspondence with his friend. Her voice continues more or

less normally answering his questions with complete matter-of-factness while her features start to flicker and then slowly to dissolve. She gives a very finished portrait of a woman whose essential honesty of mind and emotion is everywhere compromised by the situation in which she finds herself.

Anthony Curtis, *Drama*,
No. 131 (Winter 1979), p. 47-9

It suffers from two major flaws. First, it has a weak and undistributed middle: the central three scenes, where the principal development must occur, are repetitive and digressive, weak in language and gesture. Second, the characters and their petty, bourgeois concerns fail to suggest a significance wide enough or deep enough to justify sustained interest.

Dennis Kennedy, *Theater Journal*,
XXXI (Oct. 1979)

What were they like before that particular betrayal? Pinter very skilfully lifts off one layer of deceit, and finds another, although, all the time, the atmosphere surrounding the love and friendship perceptibly lightens. . . . Pinter can and has written sex-charged plays, but this is not one of them. It is about the loss of love; and at no time, during the ten years he describes, can any of the three afford, as it were, to let themselves go. . . .

[Hall's production] fails to make the most of the play. Over the past two or three years we have seen two Kevin Billington productions of Pinter's *The Caretaker* and *The Homecoming* which revealed how much was lost from the scripts in the pursuit of a kind of Ingmar Bergman high-style. Billington was down-to-earth, very direct in his approach to what had previously been regarded as tantalizing ambiguities, and the plays gained accordingly. The deceptive high-style has now returned to haunt *Betrayal*, where it is doubly ineffective, first because it looks old-fashioned and, secondly, because there are so few telling perplexities for it to exploit. The production does not explore, in particular, the changing atmospheres as the deceits are lifted. Each scene is paced in similar ways, with similar groupings, on similar shaped sets, within a smart-looking John Bury merry-go-round. Only Daniel Massey, of the three main actors, really tackled the problem of how to get not just younger, but more instinctive and innocent.

John Elsom, *The Listener*, 23 Nov. 1978

The London production had the benefit of actors with a pretty intimate knowledge of the kind of characters on whom the play is based, and

therefore with a clear understanding not only of what they were saying, but also of what they were keeping mum about. In the West Berlin production some of this notion survived, but a coarse sensuousness had infected the portrayal. Emma became at points almost something of a lush, while Jerry had turned alarmingly randy. . . . In the New York version, all the suavity of exterior has been faithfully copied, but the interior life was not quite so palpable. It was the comedy which held the evening together, not the suffering.

James Fenton, *Sunday Times*, 16 Mar. 1980

A black screen fills an enormous picture frame that contains the whole of the stage. To the sound of tinkly, silent-picture piano music, the title *Betrayal* is projected on to the screen, which lifts up, like the lid of an insect box. What is revealed is a blindingly white, antiseptic room, which, with minor alterations, becomes the setting for the restaurant, bar, house, hotel room, and rented flat in which Emma, her husband, and her lover enact, in reverse order, the beginning, disclosure, and end of her affair and the breakup of her marriage. I say 'enact' because the insects in Harold Pinter's chilly play have the air of people giving courtroom evidence rather than living a life of which we are invisible spectators. . . . There is a small problem with the tragedy of Robert, Jerry, and Emma's thwarted feelings and unhappy lives; it is that none of them is remotely interesting or sympathetic.

Rhoda Koenig, *Punch*, 30 Jan.–5 Feb. 1991

In a subtle and devious sense, the play is about the betrayal of art. Time was when Jerry and Robert lived for literature and said and felt things about it; now they deal in it, and their conversation has the laconic and unemotional efficiency of people in charge of a production line. . . . To betray is also to exclude. Pinter understands the clubby camaraderie of Anglo-Saxon men: the chummy, slightly adolescent team spirit to which the exclusion of women is essential. . . . *Betrayal* is about superficiality: it is about the way values and loyalties are undermined by social techniques, insecurity, and the need for self-assertion. . . . The final effect is nightmarish: as if you realized with a shudder that what you have just been through were only about to begin.

John Peter, *Sunday Times*, 27 Jan. 1991

The Film

The three actors all had the stricken look that is proper to a Pinter play; he doesn't bother writing about anyone who's alive. And there's nothing

else going on in this movie — once you've noticed how ugly the lamps are, you're left with the stiff, stilted talk that's so calculated it's a parody. . . . This story of adultery told backward is a perfectly conventional corpse of a play given a ceremonious funeral on the screen. It's from Beckett by way of Terence Rattigan.

Pauline Kael, *New Yorker*, 11 July 1983, reprinted in *State of the Art* (New York, 1985), p. 15

Hodge virtually steals the picture as the wife with a performance of cool sensuality that's all the more remarkable for giving precious little away. . . . [The characters] are, in a way, representative of a middle-class metropolitan society which seldom gives itself completely away and never gives itself completely, unattractive yet fascinating. Almost like Bunuel specimens, in fact. . . . It is a film which usually looks good and always sounds literate.

Derek Malcolm, *The Guardian*, 6 Oct. 1983

Most comic plays tell lies about adultery, but Harold Pinter's *Betrayal* presents painful truths that are even harsher in David Jones's movie than they were in Peter Hall's stage version. . . . Jones has treated the theatre text as if it were a screen play. He has approached it realistically, but he hasn't opened it out, or attempted to provide a larger social context than that encompassed in the dialogue.

Philip French, *The Observer*, 9 Oct. 1983

See also:
John Elsom, ed., *Post-War British Theatre Criticism* (Routledge, 1981), p. 249-56.

b: Shorter Plays

The Room

Play in one act.

First production: Bristol University Drama Department., 15 May 1957.

First London production: in double-bill with *The Dumb Waiter*,
Hampstead Th. Club, 21 Jan. 1960, transferred to Royal Court Th.,
8 Mar. 1960 (dir. Pinter at Hampstead; re-directed Anthony Page for
Royal Court; with Howard Lang as Bert, Vivien Merchant as Rose,
Henry Woolf as Mr. Kidd, and John Rees as Mr. Sands; in transfer,
Michael Brennan as Bert, John Cater as Mr. Kidd, and Michael Caine
as Mr. Sands).

First New York production: 14 Oct. 1961. *Revival:* in double-bill with
A Slight Ache, Writers' Stage Th., 9 Dec. 1964 (dir. Word Baker).

Television: Granada, 5 Oct. 1961 (dir. Alvin Rakoff; with Kenneth J.
Warren as Bert, Catherine Lacey as Rose, and J. G. Devlin as
Mr. Kidd); ABC (US), 26 Dec. 1987 (dir. Robert Altman; with Linda
Hunt as Rose, Donald Pleasence as Mr. Kidd, and Julian Sands as
Mr. Sands).

Published: with *The Dumb Waiter*, Methuen, 1960; in *Plays: One.*

---

*Rose Hudd chatters to her silent husband on a cold winter
afternoon, till he leaves in his van, despite icy roads. Mr. Kidd,
the elderly landlord, calls: he won't say where he lives and does
not know how many floors there are in the house. A couple call,
claiming they have been told that the flat in which Rose is living
is free. Mr. Kidd asks her to see the man from downstairs, though
she says that she does not know him. He comes, a blind Negro,
and tells her, 'Your father wants you to come home.' Bert
returns, describes his driving — 'I drove her back, hard' — then
knocks the Negro down. Rose clutches her eyes and the play ends
as she says, 'I can't see.'*

Pinter can convey the unease of modern society, the hidden
antagonisms, the anguish and gnawing worry of his characters, but he
can never resolve — or let the characters work out some kind of solution
to — their menacing problems. His implied philosophy — that violence

and conflict leave room for no counter-acting force — is pessimistic indeed.

The Stage, 12 Oct. 1961, p. 15

I did simply go into a room, which I'd never been into before, on one occasion and saw two people in this room. It was a rather odd image: a little man cutting bread and making bacon and eggs for a very big man who was sitting at the table quite silent, reading a comic. The big man never spoke — I was there about half an hour — the little man had a lot to say, and he was in the meantime cutting this bread and butter. It is only rarely that I have had an image like that in life which has started something going. When that does happen, the image itself — I mean the real thing — becomes dead very quickly. With those two characters, I changed the man, for instance, into an old woman, and so he was changed before he had hit the page almost. And then the play took another course which had nothing whatever to do with the two people.

Pinter, in conversation with Joan Bakewell,
The Listener, 6 November 1969, p. 630

The melodrama, enhanced by typically sinister music, extends beyond a cinematic presentation of menacing doom. Rose's interchanges with Riley become almost silly as she prances around the room mixing sexual innuendo with cruel sadism. . . . Altman gains time for alterations and theatrics by cutting one-fourth of the play's lines. Thus, there is time for repeated flashes of Mr. Kidd in the basement. The camera has time to linger on the Sands's car and Bert's van. . . . Hunt's performance as Rose is compelling. . . . Rose tries to sustain life, but her existence, like her tightly bobby-pinned hair, is constrained. Late in the play, as she removes the pins from her hair, it does not cascade about her shoulders in an ageless symbol of fertility. The hair merely sticks up out of her head. . . . Altman's alterations do not change Pinter's interest in displacement, in the paradox of simultaneous rejection and acceptance.

Anne Marie Drew, 'Robert Altman's *The Room*',
Pinter Review, No. 2 (1988), p. 74-5

The Dumb Waiter

Play in one act.
First production: Frankfurt am Main, Germany, 28 Feb. 1959.

First London production: in double-bill with *The Room*, Hampstead Th. Club, 21 Jan. 1960, transferred to Royal Court Th., 8 Mar. 1960 (dir. James Roose-Evans; with Nicholas Selby as Ben and George Tovey as Gus).

Revival: Soho Poly, 11 Dec. 1973 (dir. Paul Joyce; with John Hurt as Ben and David Warner as Gus).

First American production: Guthrie Th., Milwaukee, 22 July 1962.

First New York production: in double-bill with *The Collection*, Cherry Lane Th., 26 Nov. 1962 (dir. Alan Schneider).

Television: Granada, 8 Aug. 1961 (dir. Paul Almond; with Kenneth Warren and Roddy McMillan); BBC-2, 23 July 1985 (dir. Kenneth Ives; with Colin Blakely as Ben and Kenneth Cranham as Gus); ABC (US), 12 May 1987 (dir. Robert Altman; with John Travolta as Ben and Tom Conti as Gus).

Published: with *The Room*, Methuen, 1960; in *Plays: One*.

Two killers wait in a room in an apparently deserted house to carry out a contract. They bicker and fret and respond in agitation to repeated written demands from a dumb waiter for sago pudding or 'One Char Siu and Beansprouts'. Ben, the dominant one, makes contact with an unseen presence by means of an old speaking-tube. But when Gus, the troubled partner, already expressing unease about their recent killing of a girl, leaves the room for a moment, he returns to find himself looking down the barrel of his companion's gun. He is to be the victim. They stare at each other. Curtain.

At that moment, fatal to the expansion of mystery or metaphysics, everything is explainable. Even the bizarre carry-on with the dumb waiter and the speaking-tube. When the intended victim is out of the room this tomfoolery stops and we see Ben, obviously in the know, using the tube to get confirmation of his orders. The play is explainable in the genre of the traditional short story with a twist in its tail, or a Hemingway anecdote.

Peter Lennon, *The Listener*, 18 July 1985

What strikes one about Pinter is how much his early work owed to traditional music-hall techniques. . . . The rapid-fire cross-talk about the propriety of saying 'light the kettle', the panic reaction every time the dumb waiter zooms down the chute, the slow-burn reaction to loaded words like 'ball-cock' all convince me early Pinter owes as much to the Shepherd's Bush Empire as it does to Sam Beckett. . . . The difference

is, of course, that Pinter adds an element of irony and genuine fear: two pro killers are, in fact, being subjected to the menace they themselves employ.

Michael Billington, *The Guardian*, 12 Dec. 1973

A Slight Ache

Radio play.

Radio: BBC Third Programme, 29 July 1959 (dir. Donald McWhinnie; with Maurice Denham as Edward and Vivien Merchant as Flora).

First London stage production: Arts Th., 18 Jan. 1961, in triple-bill entitled *Three*, transferred to Criterion Th. (dir. McWhinnie; with Emlyn Williams as Edward, Alison Leggatt as Flora, and Richard Briers as the Matchseller).

Revivals: Ashcroft Th., Croydon, Apr. 1973, restaged, Royal Shakespeare Co. at Aldwych Th., 17 Oct. 1973, in double-bill with *Landscape* (dir. Peter James; with David Waller as Edward and Peggy Ashcroft as Flora); in double-bill with *The Lover*, Young Vic, 24 June 1987 (dir. Kevin Billington; with Barry Foster as Edward and Jill Johnson as Flora).

First New York production: in double-bill with *The Room*, Writers' Stage Th., 9 Dec. 1964 (dir. Word Baker).

Television: BBC-2, Feb. 1967 (dir. Christopher Morahan; with Maurice Denham as Edward and Hazel Hughes as Flora).

Published: A Slight Ache and Other Plays, Methuen, 1961; in *Plays: One*.

An elderly couple, Edward and Flora, chat about which flowers are in bloom and trapping a wasp in the marmalade. Then Flora brings in the silent, dirty old matchseller, who has been standing for two months at the gate without selling any matches. Edward succeeds in persuading the matchseller to sit down, in his own chair. Flora grows more and more sympathetic to the matchseller. Edward returns and is slowly reduced to gibbering, inexplicable terror. Flora goes off with the matchseller, whom she names Barnabas, giving his tray of matches to Edward, now on his knees.

It was hard to know, in spite of the sharp clarity of the performance and

63

the sure speech formations of Mr. Denham and Miss Merchant, what the play was really about. Perhaps Pirandello could help us, for he, I feel, had something to do with the beginnings of Mr. Pinter's genre. Perhaps he would observe that no amount of brilliance in dialogue makes up for the dearth of a clear plot.

Ian Rodger, *The Listener*, 6 Aug. 1959

I could have done with more production-pointing [from McWhinnie's direction]. When a play can mean a number of things it seems to me the producer is obliged to show a preference for one meaning against another.

Charles Marowitz, *Encore*, No. 30 (Mar.–Apr. 1961)

We follow this study in capitulation with fascinated attention but, as far as I am concerned, without much belief. Why should Flora give herself, and why should Edward give himself away, the one so freely, the other so crassly? What's in a matchseller? Unless we can credit their reactions to him as a human being, he can only be an author's convenience, the laziest of symbols.

Robert Cushman, *The Observer*, 21 Oct. 1973

[On television] the matchseller was no more than a shadowy figure clipping the frame. On the stage, he is incontrovertibly *there*. . . . He has a fierce grey moustache and looks, in his balaclava, like a battered old warrior in chain-mail. . . . I regret the matchseller (no reflection on Peter Schofield) because I regret that explicitness. I can't help wondering why Edward and Flora should react as they do to *him*, to this particular person whom I can see and, therefore, to whom I react. In my reading of the play, each section of Edward's address to the matchseller, sub-divided by pauses, is different in tone, almost as though each section is a reaction to a different stimulus. . . . [David Waller] is an Edward who relishes the orotund pronouncements ('Horseflies suck') and the perfunctory orders ('Tilt') and he does some peculiar ducking and weaving movements, like a seized-up boxer. This approach means that the undermining of Edward comes over as a bit of a giggle, whereas Maurice Denham on telly made it really unnerving. . . . [When Peggy Ashcroft emerges] she's rather mousy, nervy, and devoted, given to little smiles and starts. At last revealing the appetites beneath, she finds a measured poise that stills the house, and then zaps us with seductiveness.

W. Stephen Gilbert, *Plays and Players*, Dec. 1973

The purist Pinter school argues that the play works best on radio where the matchseller seems a figment of the married couple's imagination. I profoundly disagree. The physical presence of this pitiable relic enhances both the comedy and the anxiety.

Michael Billington, *The Guardian*, 26 June 1987

The tramp who stands under a tree selling mouldy matches every day is sure of his place in the world — the cushy ageing couple aren't. To one he represents excitement, to the other philosophical strength.

John Connor, *City Limits*, 2 July 1987

[*A Slight Ache*] opens with comic dialogue worthy of Pinter's best revue sketches and degenerates into a cumbersome symbolic parable of a leisurely writer hounded in his country house den by a sinister matchseller who could be an angel of death or a parody of an Ibsenite eccentric.

Michael Coveney, *Financial Times*, 25 June 1987

A Night Out

Play for radio and television.

Radio: BBC Third Programme, 1 Mar. 1960 (dir. Donald McWhinnie; with Barry Foster as Albert, Mary O'Farrell as Mrs. Stokes, Pinter as Seeley, and Vivien Merchant as the Girl).

Television: 'Armchair Theatre', ABC-TV, 24 Apr. 1960 (dir. Philip Saville; with Tom Bell as Albert, Madge Ryan as Mrs. Stokes, Pinter as Seeley, and Vivien Merchant as the Girl); BBC-2, 13 Feb. 1967 (with Tony Selby as Albert and Avril Elgar as the Girl).

First London stage production: as part of triple-bill entitled *Counterpoint*, Comedy Th., 2 Oct. 1961, transferred from Gate Th., Dublin (dir. Leila Blake).

Published: A Slight Ache and Other Plays, Methuen, 1961; in *Plays: One.*

Albert Stokes . . . is Pinter's Albert Herring: a mother's boy who is almost persuaded to stay at home and eat a cottage-pie instead of attending an office party. The party, a disaster for him, culminates in a scene in which he is wrongfully accused of 'taking a liberty' with one of the female guests — in fact the guilty party is the old codger whose imminent retirement has been the occasion

of the gathering — has an undignified scuffle with a bragging bully of a colleague, and rushes out into the night. The inane repetitions of the exchanges between devouring mother and resentful but docile son and the meaningless politenesses of the dreadful little party show a high degree of mimetic skill on Mr. Pinter's part. . . . Eventually Albert, having threatened his mother and dashed out of the house, finds himself in the sleazy bed-sitter of a middle-aged tart. Here the pace quickened; and Avril Elgar's assumption of the part of the woman — the walk at once jaunty and wobbly, the muscles of the face twitching with suppressed hysteria beneath the tight-stretched skin, the voice perpetually striving for the upper-middle-class inflections it could never quite achieve — was so successful that the remainder of the play was riveting. . . . The moment when Albert, having been nagged by her as mercilessly as he has been nagged for years by his mother, at last rebels, threatens her with her alarm clock, and then forces her to put on his shoes for him, was splendidly dramatic.

Francis King, *The Listener*, 23 Feb. 1967

[*On the radio production.*] We had some superb windbag dialogue, a sense of situation, and a feeling of excitement that leaked away steadily, till by the finish the play had lain down and gone to sleep.

Paul Ferris,
The Observer, 6 Mar. 1960,

You were left with the impression of a box of tricks, a scenario for a ballet rather than a play. . . . His characters came alive when he presented them, but as soon as they started interacting with each other they seemed to turn into puppets.

Maurice Richardson,
The Observer, 1 May 1960

I remember the impact made by the play when first shown in 1960. It seemed true to life then, as opposed to true to art. The surface naturalism covered disturbing implications. . . . Our attention is held by the author's use of words. The famous Pinter pauses were not yet in evidence, but a discussion of a football game assumed the quality of poetry.

Frank Marcus, *Plays International*, Apr. 1987

A Night Out said a great deal in properly placed silences and well-timed hesitations. It had just enough plot for its duration of an hour and moved through three or four moods surely and in a neat pattern. . . . The concentration and completeness of the script of *A Night Out* was excellently served by professionally quiet radio acting and unobtrusive production.

Frederick Laws, *The Listener*, 10 Mar. 1960

Night School

Play for radio and television.
Television: Associated-Rediffusion, 21 July 1960 (dir. Joan Kemp-Welch; with Vivien Merchant as Sally and Milo O'Shea as Walter).
Radio: BBC Third Programme, 25 Sept. 1966 (dir. Guy Vaesen; with Prunella Scales as Sally and John Hollis as Walter).
Published: in *Tea Party and Other Plays,* Methuen, 1967; television version in *Plays: Two,* 1979.

Walter returns from jail to his home with his two old aunts, and finds that while he was away they have let his room to Sally, a teacher, who goes out three evenings a week to night school. Walter talks to her, claiming to be a 'triple bigamist' and a 'gentle gunman'. The landlord, Solto, who claims to be only a pensioner, is having income tax troubles. Solto — urged by Walter — seeks Sally in a nightclub and finds out that she actually works as a 'hostess'. After this, Sally leaves her lodging suddenly, at night.

It is superficially more direct than his earlier plays. . . . The characters now genuinely interact, instead of existing in separate worlds. . . . Here we are left in no doubt about the characters or their motives. Walter has really been to prison (in another play we should surely also have been given reason to suppose the contrary); his lies are easily distinguishable from truth. Solto is a disreputable old scrap-dealer whose boasts are probably not true but are left uncontradicted. . . . One is relieved here when the aunts are on the scene, considering the temperature of a glass of milk, or when Walter suddenly begins obsessively ordering Sally to cross and uncross her legs. The play was at its weakest in the traditional Jewish humour of the scenes with Solto and Tully . . . at its strongest in those least connected with the plot. Perhaps it is in fact the plot which is

the trouble. Mr. Pinter seems happier developing a situation than constructing a story.

'Mr. Pinter's Concession', The Times, 22 July 1960

The Dwarfs

Radio play, based on Pinter's novel of the same name (written earlier, but not published until 1990: see page 99).

Radio: BBC Third Programme, 2 Dec. 1960 (dir. Barbara Bray; with Richard Pasco as Len, Jon Rollason as Pete, and Alex Scott as Mark).

First London stage production: in double-bill with *The Lover*, Arts Th., 18 Sept. 1963 (dir. Pinter; with John Hurt as Len, Philip Bond as Pete, and Michael Forrest as Mark).

Revival: in double-bill, Young Vic, July 1972 (dir. Peter James).

US Television: Public Broadcasting, Boston, 28 Jan. 1968.

Published: in *A Slight Ache and Other Plays*, Methuen, 1961 (revised twice: minor changes between editions of 1961, 1966, and 1968); in *Plays: Two*.

Pinter puts three characters before us: Pete, Mark, and Len, all thirtyish, in an interacting situation in which two jockey for dominance and the third, Len, escapes the power struggle through his private fantasy world. Each of the characters has built his identity, in varying ways and degrees, on illusion and self-deception. 'Where does actuality leave off and hallucination begin?' Pinter asks. Len, the imaginative activist, hallucinates openly: he perceives himself as beleaguered by dwarfs. Mark, the aesthete, has his illusory world, too, erected largely on the putative admiration of Pete. When Len tells Mark that Pete thinks him a fool, that world is shattered. Pete, less self-deceiving, is yet somewhat so. A parasitic intellectual-of-sorts, Pete feeds on Mark's dependence. . . . By the end of the play, Len has begun to move away from the squalid world of the dwarfs, for him an agony of relinquishment. . . . Like other Pinter dramas, The Dwarfs *can be read allegorically, imposing on it Freudian, Christian, Marxist, Existentialist, models.*

John McLaughlin, America, 10 Feb. 1968

I had only the very faintest glimmering of a notion of what was happening to whom and why. . . . The three people in *The Dwarfs* were at any given moment lucid enough, . . . but they were dealing with subconscious matters into which my subconcious had no insight.

Frederick Laws, *The Listener*, 8 Dec. 1960

The tragedy [of isolation], if it is a tragedy, is presented ready-made at the very beginning. Len is handled with admirable virtuosity, but he remains desperately tedious and unimportant.

Paul Ferris, *The Observer*, 11 Dec. 1960

As it happens, Pinter's own production, though it does not altogether hide the untheatrical nature of the material, does manage to hit on just the right tone. . . . The result is that one does not finally care about whether the play is or is not in theory 'theatrical'; it is a riveting experience in the theatre.

John Russell Taylor,
Plays and Players, Nov. 1963

As a picture of a state of mind *The Dwarfs* convinces but doesn't involve me. The germs are given no fable to breed in. Len merely recites his fears in a stream of poetic prose, much of it magnificent on the printed page; but in the theatre I found the images soon became muffled and blurred by boredom.

Bamber Gascoigne, *The Observer*, 22 Sept. 1963

The Collection

Play for television.
Television: Associated-Rediffusion, 11 May 1961 (dir. Joan Kemp-Welch; with Griffith Jones as Harry, Anthony Bate as James, Vivien Merchant as Stella, and John Ronane as Bill); Granada, 5 Dec. 1976 (dir. Michael Apted; with Laurence Olivier as Harry, Alan Bates as James, Helen Mirren as Stella, and Malcolm McDowell as Bill).
First London stage production: in double-bill, Royal Shakespeare Co. at Aldwych Th., 18 June 1962 (dir. Peter Hall and Pinter; with Michael Hordern as Harry, Kenneth Haigh as James, Barbara Murray as Stella, and John Ronane as Bill).

First New York stage production: in double-bill with *The Dumb Waiter*, Cherry Lane Th., 26 Nov. 1962 (dir. Alan Schneider).
Radio: BBC Third Programme, 12 June 1962.
Published: The Collection and The Lover, Methuen, 1963; in *Plays: Two.*

The dominant character . . . is a mysterious intruder who, in typical Pinter fashion, forces his way into a house where a middle-aged homosexual, Harry, lives with his protégé, Bill, a young man from the slums who has talent as a dress designer. The intruder turns out to be an injured husband. He accuses Bill of sleeping with his wife in Leeds, and finally browbeats him into admitting it; but after this admission he begins to savour his power over the young man and makes a habit of dropping in to see him, on quite a friendly basis. Harry, understandably jealous, puts the same operation into reverse. He goes to see the wife and browbeats her into admitting that she made the whole story up. The husband apologises to Harry and Bill, and returns to his wife; and, with a quizzical smile from her, the play ends. If anyone is the victor it is she. And what did happen in Leeds? We don't know. These tangles of doubt, jealousy, and domination provide some excellent moments for actors.

Bamber Gascoigne, *The Spectator*, 29 June 1962

For the audience, part of the problem was to keep the enigma intact — I mean, of course, what actually happened in Leeds in *The Collection*. All you can do for the actors is to discover what needs to have happened in Leeds for each of them, so that their behaviour will make human and emotional sense. And if you ask Pinter what happened in Leeds, he does say, 'What needs to have happened in Leeds? What does it say?' Well, that's fair enough, I think. Pinter productions which remove the ambiguous, the contradictory, the enigmatic, actually become very simplistic and boring. The image lacks complexity, and is then *unlike* memory because it is uncontradictory.

Peter Hall, 'Directing Pinter', p. 5

The gratuitous mystification of this desultory episode, adding up to what might be called *La Semaine Dernière à Leeds* is acceptable enough if you accept this kind of thing at all; and the portentousness is well timed

and highly polished. . . . Some people find this kind of thing 'simply fascinating' (I thought so myself of *Marienbad*). But a critic is apt to feel like a busy GP called to the bedside of a bland hypochondriac who has not the slightest intention of divulging any real symptoms or running the risk of a cure.

Philip Hope-Wallace, *The Guardian*, 19 June 1962

[*The Collection*] abounded in ambiguities, many of which were quite arbitrary, and some of which seemed to me silly. . . . Too often [Pinter] exploits the difficulties and limitations of the [radio] medium, not in order to surmount them but to mystify. . . . It is played all the time for ambiguities: ambiguities of time and place and phrasing and repartee which, in the end, defeated themselves and muffled the central ambiguity of the theme. This, at the deepest level, was probably their purpose. For the theme, at bottom, was not all that ambiguous. It was pretty clear that she did sleep with him but neither she, nor her husband, nor her lover, nor his lover, were human enough for it really to matter, to anyone who turned on the wireless, how they organized their couplings. For Pinter is not really interested in character. For him drama is always a leap into the dark, but the dark fascinates him for trifling reasons: his excursions into it titillate, even chill sometimes, but his plays, like those of the lesser Jacobeans, lack significant construction. They have the air but not the substance of ironic works of realist art. Their small, closely chiselled narratives are dexterously made. But so are the waxworks at Madam Tussaud's.

Martin Shuttleworth, *The Listener*, 21 June 1962

The Lover

Television play.
Television: Associated-Rediffusion, 28 Mar. 1963 (dir. Joan
    Kemp-Welch; with Alan Badel as Richard and Vivien Merchant as
    Sarah).
First London stage production: in double-bill with *The Dwarfs*,
    Arts Th., 18 Sept. 1963 (dir. Pinter; with Scott Forbes as Richard and
    Vivien Merchant as Sarah).
Revivals: King's Head, Aug. 1985 (with Robert Morris as Richard and
    Karin MacCarthy as Sarah); Young Vic, 24 June 1987 (dir. Kevin
    Billington; with Simon Williams as Richard and Judy Buxton as
    Sarah).

First New York production: in double-bill, Cherry Lane Th., 5 Jan. 1964
(dir. Alan Schneider).
Published: The Collection and The Lover, Methuen, 1963; in
Plays: Two.

The Lover *was an off-white comedy, an optimistic study in
marriage between two happy perverts whose perversions fit.
Theirs were mild though elaborate — a convention that she had
a lover and he a mistress. When he, a prosperous intellectual-
looking Home Counties commuter, left the house, his sleek young
wife would dress up and wait quivering for his return in the
afternoon, under another name. Morning and evening they would
discuss, philosophically rather than clinically, their pseudo-
adulterous experiences. The situation was immediately hinted at,
and then slowly and steadily revealed to the audience with the
carrot-in-front-of-the-donkey technique that is the essence of
what is called 'theatre'. There was an occasional titillation, such
as a late visit from the milkman, to keep up suspense. And the
husband gave out a powerful current of sinister brooding right
until the final uxorious ecstasy. . . . It was a little silly, as
perversions are apt to be, but quite pleasing and entertaining.
The extent to which they are meant to be conscious or
unconscious of thier play-acting and identity-juggling, and its
deeper significance if any, were left as a bone for you to chew
over.*

Maurice Richardson, *The Observer*, 31 Mar. 1963

Most people seemed to regard *The Lover* as a weird piece of mumbo-
jumbo to be interpreted with cunning and with symbol-detectors. In fact,
it was a straightforward and engaging slice of domestic fetishism. . . .
Pinter's dialogue was as crisp and brittle as a piece of papyrus; while the
play itself must be brightening up marriages from Pimlico to Pock-
lington, and doing wonders for the sales of hip-hugging skirts and sky-
scraper heels.

Hugh Leonard, *Plays and Players*, June 1963

[In the 1963 stage production] the serious aspect of the game of
identities husband and wife play with each other, separating out the
husband-wife and lover-mistress sides of their marriage into lust in the

afternoon and domesticity in the evening, are accentuated to a point where the biting wit is almost entirely overlaid. This is a great pity, since the play can be, and I think should be, funny and disturbing at the same time.

John Russell Taylor, *Plays and Players*, Nov. 1963

In a longer play Mr. Pinter might have created a cyclic continuum in which the forces of separation and integration kept battling each other. Instead . . . *The Lover* emerged as a good extended revue sketch.

Henry Hewes, *Saturday Review*, 25 Jan. 1964

The Lover makes sense to anyone in what you might call a long-stay relationship who fantasizes about someone else. Since this must include about 99 per cent of those eligible, it probably helps to account for the play's success.

Ros Asquith, *The Observer*, 25 Aug. 1985

The Lover is a cunningly inflected play in which a suburban marriage is spiced up with erotic games-playing. Richard departs for the office only to return as his own wife's gum-chewing leather-clad lover. Sarah, in turn, discards her Laura Ashley dress for a clingy pink miniskirt, and battle is joined with bongoes and touch-ups under the table.

Michael Coveney, *Financial Times*, 25 June 1987

Pinter's account of a couple aspiring to sexual sophistication and finding only unhappiness is among his most expressionist texts. Thus it seems very wrong that Simon Williams as the husband puts his considerable charm into creating a character where there should only be a type. Judy Buxton gives the words more room, but remains too sharply individual and too querulous. They are amusing and sexy. . . . But what was a Pinter pronouncement on the aridity of organized adultery is mere light comedy.

Alex Renton, *The Independent*, 27 June 1987

Judy Buxton and Simon Williams give an icily brilliant account of the tortured puritanical mind in which fantasy is both the cure and the justification of dullness, and marital war is simply the continuation of marital peace by other means. These are gripping performances in which every movement and glance carries huge weight: the true language of secret anguish.

John Peter, *Sunday Times*, 28 June 1987

Tea Party

Television play, based on a short story written in 1963 (first published
    1965, in *Poems and Prose*, and in *Plays: Three*). The TV play was
    commissioned by the BBC for broadcast in all countries of the
    European Broadcasting Union. (Pinter comments in *Poems and
    Prose*, 'in my view, the story is the more successful' treatment of the
    subject.)
Television: BBC, 25 Mar. 1965 (dir. Charles Jarrott; with Leo McKern
    as Disson and Vivien Merchant as Wendy).
First London stage production: in double-bill with *The Basement*,
    Duchess Th., 17 Sept. 1970 (dir. James Hammerstein; with Donald
    Pleasence as Disson, Vivien Merchant as Wendy, and Barry Foster
    as Willy).
First New York stage production: in double-bill with *The Basement*,
    Eastside Playhouse, 15 Oct. 1968 (dir. James Hammerstein).
Published: Tea Party and Other Plays, Methuen, 1967; in *Plays: Three*.

---

*This, though devilish clever, was a simple, rather shallow piece,
with a story that a fly could follow. You might call it a
dramatized case-history: crack-up, over a period of a year, of
Robert Disson, middle-aged, self-made, over-protesting tycoon
(sanitary engineer and bidet specialist) who has married above
himself. He becomes paranoid, has attacks of hysterical blind-
ness, and finally takes refuge in total blackout. . . . Disson's chief
imaginary persecutor was his smooth young brother-in-law,
Willy, whom he took into his business and seemed half-inclined
to dote on; soon he was suspecting him of incest. An additional
complication was the weird personality of his new secretary,
whose arrival coincided with his marriage. Her peculiar blend of
primness and provocation was perfectly suggested by Vivien
Merchant looking like a pretty snake — one who hasn't lost her
legs. She was the occasion for several of those titillatory fetishis-
tic capers, favourite TV specialities of Pinter's, with his sharp
eye for camera possibilities: high-heel displays, a ludicrous
game of football with a lighter — 'tackle me'. More conspicuous,
symbolically, was a frightful blind-man's-bluff, fumbling ritual
which they evolved when they used her scarf to bind up his tired
eyes. . . . You saw a lot of the action through his distorted view,
and shared when he was blindfolded at the end his deluded*

fantasies about the tangle of Willy, wife, and secretary on the sofa.

Maurice Richardson, *The Observer*, 28 Mar. 1965

[Pleasence's] Disson is a rasping, embattled marvel, a noble (and sometimes touching) monster, a sort of Caliban of the boardroom. *Tea Party* also offers an appropriately tantalizing, and tantalizingly brief, glimpse of Vivien Merchant — all crackling loin and slithering stockings, an escalator ad come to life. Is any actress, anywhere, able to express so much lubricity with so little effort?

Benedict Nightingale, *New Statesman*, 25 Sept. 1970

The Basement

Television play (adapted from script for a short film which was not made).

Television: BBC-2, 20 Feb. 1967 (dir. Charles Jarrott; with Pinter as Stott, Kika Markham as Jane, and Derek Godfrey as Law).

First London stage production: in double-bill with *Tea Party* , Duchess Th., 17 Sept. 1970 (dir. James Hammerstein; with Barry Foster as Stott, Stephanie Beacham as Jane, and Donald Pleasence as Law).

First New York stage production: in double-bill with *Tea Party*, Eastside Playhouse, 15 Oct. 1968 (dir. James Hammerstein).

Published: in *Tea Party and Other Plays*, Methuen, 1967; in *Plays: Three*.

The Basement *deals with two young men, Law and Stott, who were once close friends, but who have lost touch. One rainy evening Stott turns up at his former friend's cosy basement apartment and asks if he may spend the night (at the moment, he says, he is looking for a place to live). Law assures him that he can stay as long as he likes. Stott then asks if he can bring in a girl who has been waiting outside in the rain. Law, only slightly puzzled, politely consents. The girl enters. Stott and the girl immediately undress, get into bed, and proceed to make love with no embarrassment at Law's presence. The arrangement appears to develop into a permanent one, till the girl 'seduces' Law; this irregular triangle in turn seems to become fixed, but then*

75

animosity between the men mounts to the point of violence. Law disappears and Stott occupies the basement. At the final curtain, we see Law return as Stott had previously done in a downpour, but with no girl, and ask to stay over. There may be a homosexual inference in the plot, but what is much more relevant to it is that the two fellows are more eager to enjoy the comforts of the basement apartment than of the girl. Most of Pinter's work comes to this: bereft of all but a residual animal instinct and no firm moral or intellectual objectives, man loses his human identity. He can be or do anything without any clear consciousness of his behaviour.

Harold Clurman, 'Theatre',
The Nation, 4 Nov. 1968

Infuriatingly tedious and impossible to switch off. Tedious because all three characters remained dim shadows; impossible to switch off in the way in which it is impossible to put down a crossword with difficult clues. Pinter is a disturbing playwright — but not in the traditional sense that he reveals something new and unexpected about his characters. He is disturbing in that he expects his audience to create a picture for themselves out of a series of blobs and splotches on the canvas.

Rudolf Klein,
The Listener, 2 Mar. 1967

The tale is told in a series of abrupt scenes which, though presented with considerable dexterity and ingenuity on a very small stage, still betray their origins too clearly. It is as though one were present at a recording for television, watching the action from somewhere on the studio floor.

Sheridan Morley, *Review Copies* (Robson, 1975), p. 48,
reprinted from *The Tatler*

The Basement struck me as sort of parody Pinter. All menacing pauses, which somehow never for me became menacing. The outline of the play was either too familiar or too predictable. . . . What to me made it a very tepid experience was that Mr. Pinter had not tried — or anyhow hadn't succeeded — in making anything precise or personalized of his two young men. Each was a cypher.

T. C. Worsley, *Television: the Ephemeral Art*
(Alan Ross, 1970), p. 50,
reprinted from *Financial Times*

See also:
Christopher C. Hudgins, 'The Basement: Harold Pinter on BBC-TV', Modern Drama, March 1985, p. 71-82. [A full description of what is seen on television.]

Landscape

Play in one act, written for the stage. (Radio production followed Lord Chamberlain's refusal of a licence. The play was staged following the abolition of his powers of censorship.)

Radio: 25 Apr. 1968 (dir. Guy Vaesen; with Peggy Ashcroft as Beth and Eric Porter as Duff).

First London stage production: in double-bill with *Silence*, Royal Shakespeare Co. at Aldwych Th., 2 July 1969 (dir. Peter Hall; with Peggy Ashcroft as Beth and David Waller as Duff); this production revived, 17 Oct. 1973.

First New York production: in double-bill with *Silence*, Forum Th., Lincoln Centre, 2 Apr. 1970 (dir. Peter Gill; with Mildred Dunnock as Beth and Robert Symonds as Duff). *Revival:* in double-bill with *Silence*, Forum Th., Lincoln Centre, 9 Feb. 1971 (dir. Jules Irving).

Television: BBC-2, 4 Feb. 1983 (dir. Kenneth Ives; with Dorothy Tutin as Beth and Colin Blakely as Duff).

Published: Landscape and Silence, Methuen, 1969; in *Plays: Three*.

A middle-aged couple, chauffeur and housekeeper, sit in the huge, bare kitchen of a country house pursuing their own thoughts aloud in a ghastly semblance of conversation. He tries, without much conviction, to get through to her with his gossip of walks with the dog, pub encounters, and the Scottish trip with their master when he was unfaithful to her. But she, who once studied drawing, is withdrawn in composition of an internal landscape: a memory of the beach where she once lay with a man she loved, and asked if he did not want a child. Just possibly, he may have been her husband; but, if so, his past self has become a dream lover with whom she revenges his infidelity. Their separation is total, but oddly companionable. Their mono- logues echo each other distantly — when he talks of his pub, she remembers the seaside hotel where she went for a drink; when he brutally imagines violating her in the empty hall, she recalls love. . . . Landscape is a play, developing through every second

of its duration, the amount of life it contains always pressing against its limits.

Ronald Bryden, The Observer, 6 July 1969

Ives [director for television] convinced [the actors] that Duff's sexual infidelity, mentioned by him at one point, explains the marriage's collapse. 'He confessed', says Blakely, 'and from that moment she clammed up completely. What made it worse, you see, is that he seems to have told her the day after going to bed with her. That made the whole thing horrendous in her mind. She gave him a kiss goodbye, a Judas kiss, and hasn't spoken to him for five, ten years.' Dorothy Tutin thinks the time-scale rather different; she suspects it all happened more recently. Beth and Duff still live in a house that belonged to a Mr. Sykes, whose servants they were; and it is, she thinks, since the old man's death that the barrier between them became total. 'He kept a balance between them, and she had her job to do, she cooked for him. But now she doesn't seem to work. She does nothing but cling on to her memories.'...

The critics couldn't agree whether the lover Beth evokes with such tenderness was Sykes, Duff as a younger man, someone else altogether, a figment of her imagination. . . . It was, in fact, Duff himself, remembered by his wife sometimes at or just after his big confession, sometimes long before. 'Both memories mean a great deal to her, one happy, one very painful, both intermingled', explains Tutin. 'And in the end she is left with the earlier memory, because it is the more pleasant. There she is, saying "my true love" about the man who has abused her.'

Meanwhile, Duff rages internally and, finally, externally. 'He is a masculine kind of man', says Blakely, 'and she is a very remote lady. They're opposite ends of the spectrum as far as personality is concerned. Occasionally he says tender things to her, but mostly he uses language as a weapon against her, talking of beer, piss, shit — animal things compared to her rarefied words, and either way he gets nowhere. Every time he tries to get back to her, she deflects him. And he can't leave because there is some sort of love, some bond, between them. So there she sits dreaming of the man he was, he sits there talking, and it will go on until they die.'

Benedict Nightingale, 'Landscape with Figures',
Radio Times, 29 Jan. 1983

There are secret ways of escaping from the disillusionment of everyday existence; and in *Landscape* Mr. Pinter shows us one of them. Dame Peggy Ashcroft's Beth lives entirely in the transfiguring memory of an

encounter she once had with an unnamed man by the seashore. Against the impregnable armour with which this clothes her the common chatter of her rough but not unkindly husband beats in vain, and the confession of unfaithfulness on which he sets regretful store is powerless to darken even by a shade or for a moment the brilliant light of her remembered joy. His cheerful affection for her, his desire, even at the end his surging and good-humoured lust, are wonderfully counterpointed and rebuked into irrelevance by her last devoted and ecstatic cry of 'Oh my true love', to a presence not there but which nevertheless fills the house.

Harold Hobson, *Sunday Times*, 9 July 1969

Since this is Pinter country, no certainty, no definitive information emerges from these two fragmented versions of a married life. . . . Why does this pair of retainers still live in a house denuded of its lonely owner? What was his relationship to the woman? Why does the husband try so desperately to engage her attention with his coarse and sex-filled memories? The answers are not important since it is the conjuring of mood and emotion which is pre-eminent. Dame Peggy Ashcroft . . . now plays the woman with a more pronounced proletarian accent and does not supply quite the same degree of reminiscent anguish and joy.

Nicholas de Jongh, *The Guardian*, 13 Oct. 1980,
on 'Platform Performance' at Lyttelton Theatre,
to mark Pinter's fiftieth birthday

The production, as far as I am concerned, is admirable, characterized in all its aspects by an emphasis on simplicity, economy, and clarity which I find especially rewarding.

Pinter, letter to *New York Times*, 26 Apr. 1970,
on 1970 Lincoln Centre production

Silence

Play in one act.
First London stage production: in double-bill with *Landscape*, Royal Shakespeare Co. at Aldwych Th., 2 July 1969 (dir. Peter Hall; with Frances Cuka as Ellen, Anthony Bate as Rumsey, and Norman Rodway as Bates).
First New York production: in double-bill with *Landscape*, Forum Th., Lincoln Centre, 2 Apr. 1970 (dir. Peter Gill). *Revived:* in double-bill

with *Landscape*, Forum Th., Lincoln Centre, 9 Feb. 1971 (dir. Jules Irving).
Published: Landscape and Silence, Methuen, 1969; in *Plays: Three*.

Silence *has the curtain rise on three seated people, their shadows misty giants on the grey screen behind them. Their spoken reminiscences constitute the short thirty-minute drama. If drama it can be called, this quiet pastel of three entangled lives. They hardly move, they hardly ever speak to each other. Their interlocking soliloquies are for themselves. At first they seem young. Ellen, seated between them, was apparently as a child loved by both men. One, a countryman of some substance [Rumsey], egocentric and philosophic by nature, recalls their country walks. But perhaps her naivety, her common voice, irritated him. Advising her to find a husband, he is now old and enjoys riding alone. The other man [Bates], a blustering farm hand, has tried to coax the girl to stay with him. They had known each other well, but now he only remembers her persistent refusals. He is old now, bullied by his land-lady, hating young people, suffocated by memories, rebellious and alone. The girl who, like the others, lives by herself now, half shares their thoughts and, unmarried, in old age pretends to her 'friendly drinking companion' that she can recall her non-existent wedding day. When she sees people now she passes through them, noticing nothing, alone. . . A muted reverie, scored from themes stored in the rag-and-bone shop of memory. Infinitely sad, because, as between long pauses the trio grow older, their memories fade until all they have left are recapitulated fragments, half-sentences, a few old bones.*

John Barber,
Daily Telegraph, 3 July 1969

The play is essentially undramatic, and Pinter is only erratically capable of the poetry, the language beyond language, that would compensate, and the production is not capable of really insinuating itself into the subconscious. One listens, but the silence does not really speak.

Catharine Hughes,
Plays and Players, June 1970

Family Voices

Play for radio and stage (broadcast in advance of stage production, with same cast, by arrangement with National Theatre).

Radio: 22 Jan. 1981 (dir. Peter Hall; with Michael Kitchen as Voice 1, Peggy Ashcroft as Voice 2, and Mark Dignam as Voice 3).

First London stage production: Lyttelton Th., 13 Feb. 1981 (director and cast as radio production).

Revival: in triple-bill, *Other Places*, with *Victoria Station* and *A Kind of Alaska*, National Th. (Cottesloe), 14 Oct. 1982 (dir. Peter Hall; with Nigel Havers as Voice 1, Anna Massey as Voice 2, and Paul Rogers as Voice 3).

Published: in *Other Places*, Methuen, 1982; in *Best Radio Plays of 1981*, Methuen, 1982; in *Plays: Four*

The young man on whose (unuttered?) thoughts or (unwritten?) letters addressed to his mother we eavesdrop throughout Family Voices *has chosen his other place. It is a substitute home, with all the glamour that burgeoning fantasy can confer: the social glamour of the scarlet Lady Withers and her icily familiar patronage, the sexual glamour of Jane, and the mother-comforts of the boozily grieving Mrs. Withers, her romantic past and penchant for a cuddle. Throughout the bulletins, the abandoned mother of 'real life' moves from desolation to piqued possessiveness in her replies, and her son's old dependency steadily reasserts itself; not, it is clear, out of sympathy for her plight, but out of growing unease with his own set-up. The young man may be getting his Withers wrong; or so the shift of real tension and inventiveness, away from this comedy of ambivalence in his dealings with the ladies, onto his encounters with the even more alarming menfolk, would imply. . . . In the face of such grotesque passion and conviction the young man's jauntily-affected knowingness melts away: he will return to the fold, the venomous ministrations of his mother, the vengeful shade of his father who died 'in lamentation and oath'.*

Alan Jenkins, *Times Literary Supplement*, 29 Oct. 1982

Essentially this is a *radio* play, and it is, I think, a mistake to stage it. After all, the point of the piece is that it takes place within the young man's consciousness; *he* imagines the letters he might write to his

mother, *he* imagines his mother's possible appeals to him, and in the end it is he who wonders whether his father might now be dead. By putting the son and the mother visibly in front of our eyes — however stylishly silhouetted against brilliantly lit screens — and by letting the father's voice come out of a black region between them, there is a clear indication that the mother and son are more real than the father; there is no more room to wonder whether the mother actually utters these sentiments, or whether they are merely within the son's imagination.

Martin Esslin, *Plays and Players*, Dec. 1982

As their monologues circle in, getting shorter until they have the shape of a church response, the characters grow further apart, with the mother expressing hate for the son and the son gleefully announcing his homecoming.

Ned Chaillet, *The Times*, 19 Feb. 1981

Does the old lady have an objective existence, or is she just a 'family voice', nagging away at the back of her son's mind? The answer, perhaps, is both at once.

Benedict Nightingale,
New Statesman, 20 Feb. 1981

A Kind of Alaska

Play in one act.
First London production: in triple-bill, *Other Places*, with *Family Voices* and *Victoria Station*, National Th. (Cottesloe), 14 Oct. 1982 (dir. Peter Hall; with Judi Dench as Deborah, Paul Rogers as Hornby, and Anna Massey as Pauline).
Revival: in triple-bill, *Other Places*, with *One for the Road* and *Victoria Station*, Duchess Th., 7 Mar. 1985 (dir. Kenneth Ives; with Dorothy Tutin as Deborah, Colin Blakely as Hornby, and Susan Engel as Pauline).
First New York production: in triple-bill, *Other Places*, with *One for the Road* and *Victoria Station*, Manhattan Th. Club, 3 Apr. 1984 (dir. Alan Schneider)
Television: Central, 16 Dec. 1984 (dir. Kenneth Ives; with Dorothy Tutin as Deborah, Paul Scofield as Hornby, and Susan Engel as Pauline).
Published: in *Other Places*, Methuen, 1982; *Plays: Four* (Faber, 1991).

['Inspired by' the case of Rose R, as described in Oliver Sacks's
Awakenings *(1974). Sacks tells how in the late 'sixties, by giving
the drug L-DOPA to sufferers from sleeping sickness* (encepha-
litis lethargica)*, he awoke patients who had been asleep as long
as thirty years.] Deborah's traumatic return to health is com-
pressed into just one hour of theatre. In the first moments of her
awakening she tries to relive her childhood, but then —
prompted by the gentle refusals of her doctor — she turns to
more daring, often impossible collations of the past and present.
She crashes around in her mind, grabbing at images and
metaphors to envelop her experience. She makes her first attempt
to walk and then, as though passing to an easier form, dances in
slow motion. It is only when she feels the unavoidable reality of
her sister Pauline, the tangible difference of the person from the
memory, that Deborah is stunned. Finally she does reach a sort
of accommodation. In her last lines she recapitulates what she
has learnt, states the factual things she is sure of, and concludes:
'I think I have things in proportion now.'*

Michael Stewart, *Tribune*, 10 Dec. 1982

As interesting — more interesting, though kept on too tight a rein — are
the reactions of her doctor and her sister: 'It is we who have suffered.'
They are married. The sister calls herself a 'widow', since the doctor has
given his life to his patient. Isn't it unlikely that she would wax
insistently metaphorical at such a time? Isn't there enough in the play
about the borderline of life and death already? And if it's mystification,
who needs it?

Robert Cushman,
The Observer, 17 Oct. 1982

[We have] two simultaneous dramas: the Pirandellian drama of the great
yawning gap at the very centre of Deborah's life; and the existential
drama created by the confrontation with the unknown, with the
documentary reportage about life in the distant planet of nothingness.
Pinter does not play on the fairy tale element and refuses to grant the
patient the magical status of a Sleeping Beauty, immune to the biological laws which regulate the ageing process. Deborah's only mythical
dimension is the long experience of lethargic absence.

Guido Almansi,
Literary Review, Jan. 1983

[*A Kind of Alaska* is about] the sorrow of growing old. For Pinter's Deborah, the past is not barren or desiccated, but packed with love, hope, clamour, conflict, *life*; and Judi Dench's gaping dismay as she begins to realize she's lost it, her numb, grey face under her cropped, grey hair will surely set off echoes in many, and not just in the nostalgic or immature, those who would clamber back into the womb if they could. The play is an admittedly extreme metaphor for a feeling we must all have at times. Where did time go? What did I do while it was passing? Why did I make so little of it? It is Pinter's version of Hopkins's marvellous poem, 'Margaret, Are You Grieving?', and ends on a not-dissimilar note of resignation, acceptance.

Benedict Nightingale, *New Statesman*, 22 Oct. 1982

Where Ms. Dench conveyed the miracle of re-birth, Ms. Tutin creates a teenage tomboy uncannily preserved into middle age (she highlights the dated slang like 'flibbertigibbet'), and also someone cruelly distanced from those who have cared for her. . . . First time round, the play struck me as being about the common experience of feeling that those closest to us are phantoms in some dream. In Kenneth Ives's production it emerges as a much more Beckettian study of human solitude.

Michael Billington, *The Guardian*, 8 Mar. 1985

[*A Kind of Alaska*] received a chilly, reverential production from Peter Hall at the National Theatre. . . . Ives's version . . . was far more urgent and compassionate; more perhaps than the play deserved. Pinter's script is highly accomplished, but he isn't interested in 'sleeping sickness' as much more than a dramatic device for a play about memory and growing old.

Sean French, *Sunday Times*, 23 Dec. 1984

One for the Road

Play in one act.
First London production: in double-bill with *Victoria Station*, Lyric Th., Hammersmith, 13 Mar. 1985 (dir. Pinter; with Alan Bates as Nicholas, Roger Lloyd Pack as Victor, and Jenny Quayle as Gila).
Revival: in triple-bill, *Other Places*, with *Victoria Station* and *A Kind of Alaska*, Duchess Th., 7 Mar. 1986 (dir. Kenneth Ives; with Colin Blakely as Nicholas; Roger Davidson as Victor, and Rosie Kerslake as Gila).

First New York production: in triple-bill, *Other Places*, with *Victoria Station* and *a Kind of Alaska*, Manhattan Th. Club, 3 Apr. 1984 (dir. Alan Schneider).
Television: BBC-2, 25 July 1985 (dir. Kenneth Ives; with Bates as Nicholas, Pack as Victor, and Kerslake as Gila).
Published: Methuen, 1984; with an interview, Methuen, 1985.

It is as necessary and inevitable a twentieth-century work as Koestler's Darkness at Noon. *There are four scenes, resembling in power and intensity some of Francis Bacon's more disturbing canvases. Mr. Pinter's use of language — words, sentences, the pauses between syllables — is as scrupulous as ever, but what, perhaps, is new is a devastating moral force. Alan Bates plays Nicholas, head of the secret — or maybe not so secret — police in a country that could be, and probably is, anywhere; which is not to say nowhere, but everywhere. In the first scene the smooth brute interrogates Victor, in the second his wife Gila, in the third their seven-year-old son Nicky, and in the fourth Victor again. Husband and wife are hideously tortured, but not in the neurotically tidy office in which they are interviewed. The only suggestion in Tim Bickerton's set that this isn't an ordinary room is the window high up in the wall. The torture we witness is entirely verbal. The crime is not stated, less an accidental or devious omission than to emphasize Mr. Pinter's view that the world is increasingly a police state, that if those in control don't like your face, your politics, or your style, you're better off dead. . . . Mr. Bates's lounge-suited policeman mostly chats away to the prisoners as if he's conducting job interviews. He drinks an infinite number of whiskies for the road, and is utterly, discreetly ruthless without showing emotion except the occasional facial twitch. . . . It is the most terrible play, at times nearly unbearable to sit through. Unlike so much of the work of Edward Bond, which just disgusts, it floods the mind with despair, the eyes with tears, the stomach with sickness, the heart with dread.*

Giles Gordon, *The Spectator*, 24 Mar. 1984

It's to do with my fascination with our separation between reality and our interpretation of it. Our human experience can be totally dislocated by these facts and it happens every day of the week. But it's not

dislocated for people having drinks at a cocktail party. It's exactly the same as when people talk about nuclear war. The words have simply become abstractions — people can't face them. . . . This play comes out of my life and of my understanding of life. What we are encouraged to think in the West is that we have a moral advantage, that we inhabit a superior moral position. But the United States brought down the Chilean regime and they're doing the same in Nicaragua. They are supporting the most fiendishly appalling system in El Salvador. If you shake hands with murderers you have no moral position.

> Pinter, quoted by Bryan Appleyard,
> 'The New Light That Burns within Harold Pinter',
> *The Times*, 16 Mar. 1984

One for the Road as a metaphor. For anything. It describes a state of affairs in which there are victims of torture. You have the torturer, you have the victims. And you can *see* that two of the victims have been physically tortured. . . . There are at least ninety countries that practise torture now quite commonly — as an accepted routine. With any imprisonment, with any arrest, torture goes with it. And on both sides of the fence, Communist and non-Communist.

> Pinter, in conversation with Nicholas Hern,
> *One for the Road* (Methuen, 1985), p. 8

One for the Road — whose extremely raw material makes Pinter's craftsmanship look incongruously showy — emerges as too slick and contrived, too spick and span for its lacerated and lacerating subject. . . . Things keep degenerating into mere staginess: contrived frisson, cunning showmanship, Gothic outbursts such as Nicholas's purring aria, 'I love death . . . the death of others'. As a result *One for the Road* doesn't so much disturb you by authentic insights into the world of a torturer as leave you slightly uneasy at having watched a piece of elegant juggling with vileness.

> Peter Kemp, *Times Literary Supplement*, 9 Aug. 1985

Mountain Language

Short play in one act.
First London production: National Th. (Lyttelton), 20 Oct. 1988
    (dir. Pinter; with Michael Gambon as Sergeant, Miranda Richardson

as Young Woman, Eileen Atkins as Elderly Woman, and Tony
Haygarth as Prisoner).
First New York production: in double-bill with *The Birthday Party*, CSC
Rep, 31 Oct. 1989 (dir. Carey Perloff).
Television: BBC-2, 11 Dec. 1988 (director and cast as for National Th.).
Published: Faber, 1988; *Plays: Four* (Faber, 1991).

---

*At a gruesomely functional camp, a handful of women wait to
visit their imprisoned men. The oldest speaks only the banned
'mountain language', so cannot communicate with her son when
at last they're permitted to meet. A young woman walks into a
corridor, only to see her husband collapse, hooded and beaten.
Pinter satirizes the vernacular of official terror with characteristic acerbity, as when an officer demands the name of the
Dobermann Pinscher which has bitten the old woman, and when
the Sergeant jokes grimly that the 'computer' has allowed the
wife through the wrong door: 'The computer's got a double
hernia.' But Pinter's chief theme is the alliance of physical
brutality with violence toward language.*

Jim Hiley, *The Listener*, 3 Nov. 1988

In 1985 I went to Turkey with Arthur Miller, on behalf of International
PEN, to investigate the situation of writers in Turkey. . . . One of the
things I learned while I was there was about the real plight of the Kurds:
quite simply that they're not really allowed to exist at all and certainly
not allowed to speak their language. . . . When I got back from Turkey
I wrote a few pages of *Mountain Language*, but I wasn't at all sure about
it and put it away. . . . I did nothing for three years with it and then one
day, earlier this year, I picked it up and suddenly wrote it. The spring-
board . . . was the Kurds, but this play is not about the Turks and
the Kurds. I mean, throughout history, many languages have been
banned — the Irish have suffered, the Welsh have suffered, and Urdu
and the Estonians' language banned; the Basques' language was banned,
you know, at various times. . . .

I have no aim in writing other than exploring the images that come
into my mind. I find some of those images really quite shocking, so they
shock me into life and into the act of writing. The image is there and you
attempt to express it. I was jolted by the images and by the state of
affairs they refer to, which I think are serious facts most people prefer,
understandably, to remain indifferent to, ignore, pretend don't exist. One
thing, when you meet people who've been through these appalling

deprivations and assaults on their system, you realize that they're exactly the same as you and I. . . .

I'm not writing a play simply about Turkey; in fact the play isn't about Turkey at all. I think the play is very much closer to home and I believe it reflects a great deal that's happening in this country. . . . My own view is that the present government is turning a stronger and stronger vice on democratic institutions that we've taken for granted for a very long time. It's embodied in things like Clause 28, the Official Secrets Act, police powers, and it's happening quite insidiously, but happening nevertheless in a very strong and purposeful way. I believe most people don't seem to realize that the dissenting voice and the minority are in great danger in this country.

Pinter, in conversation with Anna Ford,
'Radical Departures', *The Listener*, 27 Oct. 1988, p. 4, 6

'Mountain language' is very much a double-edged metaphor. It is on the one hand a metaphor of enforced silence, the remote language of remote hill people which remains unrecognized, which does not officially exist. On the other hand it appears to be a metaphor for the self-censorship which Pinter has subconsciously effected in his own play, cutting down on dramatic development with such brutal severity that the whole enterprise falls through the floor. . . . No amount of political pleading conceals the unacceptable face of minimalism. . . . The Pinter of fragments is trying to have it both ways. He shows us persecution without suggesting its origin or its spurious rationale. His political precision cannot match his linguistic precision.

John Orr, *Literary Review*, Dec. 1988

Party Time

One-hour play.
First London production: in double-bill with *Mountain Language*,
    Almeida Th., 31 Oct. 1991 (dir. Pinter; with Barry Foster as Gavin,
    Roger Lloyd Pack, Nicola Pagett, and Dorothy Tutin).
Unpublished.

Party Time *consists of a back-slapping get-together of the super-rich who evidently have something to celebrate. Some of the guests have had a hard time reaching Gavin's house; and it*

*gradually emerges, amid the braying laughter, that outside this
secure room the streets are in turmoil. 'Between ourselves',
Gavin acknowledges, 'we've had a bit of a round-up this
evening.' One of the wives almost spoils things by asking what
has happened to her brother; but she is forcefully shut up by her
spouse, and the party-goers resume their gushing compliments
and carefree chat about health clubs and island holidays until
darkness abruptly descends on them, and out of a brilliantly lit
doorway steps their first victim.*

You will not learn anything new about tyranny from this piece; what it
does is to reawaken what you know already. The message is simple: the
manner of presenting it extremely cunning. The characters are undefined
but a clear pecking order emerges from the leader (Gavin) through the
representatives of new and old money, down to the barely tolerated
Terry, a brute on his best behaviour, who is there to carry out his betters'
dirty work. They all exchange small talk; but in Pinter no talk is small,
and it encodes an electrifying range of cajolements, insults, threats,
occasionally splitting open into verbal assaults of insensate savagery. . . .
He has at last constructed a bridge between his dramatic world and the
world of his political conscience. *Party Time* may be unlocalized, but it
reflects the reported iniquities of Africa and Latin America in the
perspective of a London he knows inside out.

Irving Wardle, *Independent on Sunday*,
10 Nov. 1991, p. 23

What [Pinter] offers is an image of a style-conscious, narcissistic, bourgeois society cut off from and culpably indifferent to the intolerance and
squalor of the outside world. . . . Pinter's point is surely that our lives are
increasingly governed by an apolitical materialism in which it is uncool
to get het up about injustice and corruption.

Michael Billington, *The Guardian*, 7 Nov. 1991

c: Revue Sketches and Playlets

Black and White *and* Trouble in the Works

First London production: in *One to Another*, Lyric Th., Hammersmith, 15 July 1959.
Published: in *A Slight Ache and Other Plays*, Methuen, 1961; in *Plays: Two*; 'The Black and White' also published as a short story in *Poems and Prose*.

Last to Go, Request Stop, *and* Special Offer

First London production: in *Pieces of Eight*, Apollo Th., 23 Sept. 1959.
Published: in *A Slight Ache and Other Plays*, Methuen, 1961; in *Plays: Two*.

Applicant

Excerpt from *The Hothouse*.
Radio: BBC Third Programme, Feb.-Mar. 1964.
Published: in *A Slight Ache and Other Plays*, Methuen, 1961; in *Plays: Three*.

That's Your Trouble, That's All, Interview, *and* Dialogue for Three

Radio: BBC Third Programme, Feb.–Mar. 1964.
Published: in *Plays: Three*.

Night

Short dialogue.
First London production: as one of eight short plays in *Mixed Doubles*, Comedy Th., 9 Apr. 1969 (dir. Alexander Doré; with Vivien Merchant as the Woman and Nigel Stock as the Man).
Revival: in double-bill with *Monologue*, Orange Tree, transferred to Bush Th., Autumn 1973 (dir. Sam Mendes).

Published: in *Mixed Doubles*, Methuen, 1970, p. 41-4; in *Landscape and Silence*, Methuen, 1969; in *Plays: Three*.

Night is an elegiac duologue in which a long-married couple, making an elegant picture in the romantic lamplight, cast their minds back to their first meeting. Initially it suggests an advertisement for expensive chocolate, with dialogue amounting to a classy variation on 'Oh yes, I remember it well', as he recalls fondling her on a bridge while she distinctly recalls having her back against the railings. For so short a piece, Pinter takes his time to cut short this irrelevant association; but when he does the piece comes beautifully into focus as a stratagem by which the couple preserve their relationship by ascribing all their most treasured erotic memories to each other. A minor-key echo of Pinter's The Lover.

Irving Wardle,
The Times, 10 Apr. 1969

Monologue

Twenty-minute piece for television.
Television: BBC, 13 Apr. 1973 (dir. Christopher Morahan; with
Henry Woolf).
First London stage production: in double-bill with *Night*, Orange Tree,
Richmond, transferred to Bush Th., Autumn 1973 (dir. Sam Mendes;
with Henry Woolf).
Published: Covent Garden Press, 1973; in *Plays: Four*.

Woolf, in seedy room, gas fire, gloomy light, tea pot and milk bottle on table beside him, talking to an empty chair in which is seated — we learn at the end — his brother. The talk to the chair concerns mostly bits of their relationship, rivalry, matyness, and the black girl they seemed to share. The image of the unseen character spans a time-warp age from leather-clad motorbike kid to balding decline in Notting Hill Gate. There are times when you could think he was talking to his other self — or was this just a false move by director Christopher Morahan (brave lad) switching Woolf's right-facing face suddenly to the reverse image? . . . Did I like it? Did you? Why should we commit ourselves?

Peter Fiddick,
The Guardian, 14 Apr. 1973

The Examination

Short prose piece, written 1959.

First London stage production: Ambiance at Almost Free Th., 12 Mar.
1978 (dir. Jack Emery; with Derek Godfrey).

Published: in *The Collection and The Lover*, Methuen, 1963; in
Plays: One; in *Ten of the Best*, ed. Ed Berman (Inter-Action Imprint,
1979), p. 199-205, with stage-directions added.

Victoria Station

Sketch.

First London production: in triple-bill, *Other Places*, with *Family
Voices* and *A Kind of Alaska*, National Th. (Cottesloe), 14 Oct. 1982
(dir. Peter Hall; with Paul Rogers as Controller and Martin Jarvis as
Driver).

Revived: with *One for the Road*, Lyric Th., Hammersmith, 13 Mar. 1984
(dir. Pinter; with Roger Lloyd Pack as Controller and Alan Bates as
Driver); in triple-bill, *Other Places*, with *One for the Road* and
A Kind of Alaska, Duchess Th., 7 Mar. 1985 (dir. Kenneth Ives; with
Colin Blakely as Controller and Roger Davison as Driver).

First New York production: in triple-bill, *Other Places*, with *One for the
Road* and *A Kind of Alaska*, Manhattan Th. Club, 3 Apr. 1984
(dir. Alan Schneider).

Published: in *Other Places*, Methuen, 1982; *Plays: Four* (Faber, 1991).

*A mini-cab driver languishing by the side of 'a dark park' in Crystal
Palace, and his increasingly demented controller wrestling over the air-
waves with the former's stunned incomprehension and his own raging
loneliness, sketch the outlines of a mutual dependency so desperate and
so charged with misunderstanding that the controller's promise to
'come down there' sounds like a death-threat and the driver's plaintive
'don't leave me' gasped into his car-radio sounds like the cry of a
helpless child. The one in his darkened office, the other in his darkened
cab, exchange the counters of their trade less and less convincingly, and
both eventually give way to escapist fantasy. . . . Has [the driver] a
passenger on board, a sleeping girl with whom he has fallen in love, as
he says he has, and will he stay in Crystal Palace for ever? Has he
perhaps killed the girl?*

Alan Jenkins,
Times Literary Supplement, 29 Oct. 1982

Precisely

Sketch.
First London stage production: in anti-nuclear weapons show, Victoria
   Apollo, 19 Dec. 1983.
First New York production: New York University, Dec. 1984 (in reading
   by Pinter).
Published: in *The Big One*, ed. Susannah York and Bill Bachle,
   Methuen, 1984; *Harpers* (New York), May 1985, p. 37.

---

*Two men discuss numbers: it emerges that they are agreeing that the
people of Britain would accept twenty million dead in a nuclear war, but
that those who argue that the figure could be thirty million or even forty
million are 'actively and wilfully deceiving the people'.*

The New World Order

Ten-minute play.
First London stage production: preceding *Death and the Maiden*, by
   Ariel Dorfman, Royal Court Th. Upstairs, July 1991 (dir. Pinter; with
   Michael Byrne as Lionel and Bill Paterson as Des).
Published: in *Granta*, No. 37 (1991), p. 251-4.

---

*Three men are in a cell-like room. One, blindfolded and barefooted,
twitches, but never speaks. Christian names discreetly differentiate the
social class of his interrogators. . . . For the moment they are content
merely to brutalize their victim with words, but a reference to the need
to defend western democracy hints at the violence that is to come. . . .
[Pinter] has moved from the generalized menace of his early work to
more specifically political tones.*

Robert Hewison,
Sunday Times, 28 July 1991

There is a frisson of something here — disharmony amid the ranks of
torturers? buddy-buddy fascism? — but this passionless, pretentious
fragment is over before it has begun to intrigue.

Katharine Way,
City Limits, 1-8 Aug. 1991, p. 58

The New World Order lasts ten nerve-wracking minutes and gets closer to the nerve of torture than any play I know.

Robert Cushman, *Independent on Sunday*,
21 July 1991, p. 20

The prisoner's silence is dramatically effective, but politically enigmatic. Is Pinter telling us that now, in the time of the New World Order, the world simply does belong to the men with the immaculately ironed white shirts? . . . The very existence of the prisoner, the fact that some opposition continues, resists the more totally pessimistic and politically simplistic response this brief play evokes.

Michael Gilsenan, *Times Literary Supplement*,
26 July 1991, p. 16

d: Film scripts

Pinter's adaptations of novels for film (and twice for television) have had an unusual amount of attention – indeed, two of his published screenplays are for films never made, which is exceptional. For certain of these screenplays (notably The Servant, Accident, *and* The French Lieutenant's Woman) *it may be said that Pinter brought the original material close to his own preoccupations: and he sees all the screenplays as part of his oeuvre, in contrast to certain other dramatists (such as Edward Bond and Tom Stoppard) who view their film scripts as written to make money to support more serious work. None of the published scripts states whether it is a final draft before the film was made, or a post-production script, which conforms with the film as released. For a discussion of Pinter's earlier screenplays, see Joanne Klein,* Making Pictures: the Pinter Screenplays *(Columbus: Ohio State University Press, 1985).*

The Servant

Adapted from the novel by Robin Maugham.
Released: 1963 (dir. Joseph Losey; with Dirk Bogarde as Hugo, James
    Fox as Tony, Wendy Craig as Susan, Sarah Miles as Vera, and Pinter
    as 'Young Man in Restaurant').
Published: in *Five Screenplays* (Methuen, 1971); in *The Servant and
    Other Screenplays* (Faber, 1991).

The Pumpkin Eater

Adapted from the novel by Penelope Mortimer.
Released: 1964 (dir. Jack Clayton; with Anne Bancroft as Jo,
    Peter Finch as Jake, and James Mason as Conway).
Published: in *Five Screenplays* (Methuen, 1971); in *The Servant and
    Other Screenplays* (Faber, 1991).

The Quiller Memorandum

Adapted from the novel, *The Berlin Memorandum*, by Adam Hall.
Released: 1966 (dir. Michael Anderson; with George Segal as Quiller,
    Alec Guinness as Pol, and Max von Sydow as Oktober).

Published: in *Five Screenplays* (Methuen, 1971); in *The Servant and Other Screenplays* (Faber, 1991).

Accident

Adapted from the novel by Nicholas Mosley.
Released: 1967 (dir. Joseph Losey; with Dirk Bogarde as Stephen, Stanley Baker as Charley, Jacqueline Sassard as Anna, Michael York as William, and Vivien Merchant as Rosalind).
Published: in *Five Screenplays* (Methuen, 1971); in *The Servant and Other Screenplays* (Faber, 1991).

The Go-Between

Adapted from the novel by L. P. Hartley.
Released: 1971 (dir. Joseph Losey; with Julie Christie as Marian, Alan Bates as Ted Burgess, Edward Fox as Trimingham, Dominic Guard as Young Leo, Michael Redgrave as Leo, Michael Gough as Mr. Maudsley, and Margaret Leighton as Mrs. Maudsley).
Published: in *Five Screenplays* (Methuen, 1971); in *The Servant and Other Screenplays* (Faber, 1991).

The Proust Screenplay

Adapted from the novel *A la Récherche du Temps Perdu*, by Marcel Proust.
Written: 1972; not made as film.
Published: Eyre Methuen, 1978; Faber, 1991.

The Last Tycoon

Adapted from the novel by F. Scott Fitzgerald.
Released: 1977, in Britain (dir. Elia Kazan; with Robert De Niro as Monroe Stahr, Tony Curtis as Rodriguez, Robert Mitchum as Pat Brady, Jeanne Moreau as Didi, Jack Nicholson as Brimmer, Donald Pleasence as Baxley, and Ray Milland as Fleishacker).
Published: in *The French Lieutenant's Woman and Other Screenplays* (Methuen, 1982; Faber, 1991).

Langrishe, Go Down

Adapted from the novel by Aidan Higgins.
Television: 'Play of the Week', BBC-2, 20 September 1978 (dir. David
    Jones; with Jeremy Irons as Otto Beck, Judi Dench as Imogen,
    Annette Crosbie as Helen, and Pinter as Barry Shannon).
Published: in *The French Lieutenant's Woman and Other Screenplays*
    (Methuen, 1982; Faber, 1991).

The French Lieutenant's Woman

Adapted from the novel by John Fowles.
Released: 1981 (dir. Karel Reisz; with Jeremy Irons as Charles and
    Meryl Streep as Sarah).
Published: in *The French Lieutenant's Woman and Other Screenplays*
    (Methuen, 1982; Faber, 1991).

Victory

Adapted from the novel by Joseph Conrad.
Written: 1982; not made as film.
Published: in *The Comfort of Strangers and Other Screenplays*
    (Faber, 1990).

Turtle Diary

Adapted from the novel by Russell Hoban.
Released: 1985 (dir. John Irvin; with Glenda Jackson as Neaera Duncan,
    Ben Kingsley as William Snow, Michael Gambon as George
    Fairbairn, and Pinter as 'Man in Bookshop').
Published: in *The Comfort of Strangers and Other Screenplays*
    (Faber, 1990).

The Heat of the Day

Television adaptation of novel by Elizabeth Bowen.
Televised: Granada, 30 Dec. 1989 (dir. Christopher Morahan; with
    Patricia Hodge as Stella, Michael Gambon as Harrison, and
    Michael York as Robert).
Published: Faber, 1989.

The Handmaid's Tale

Adapted from the novel by Margaret Atwood.
Released: 1990 (dir. Volker Schlondorff; with Natasha Richardson as
    Kate, Robert Duvall as the Commander, Faye Dunaway as
    Serena Joy, and Aidan Quinn as Nick).
Unpublished.

Reunion

Adapted from the novel by Fred Uhlman.
Released: 1990 (dir. Jerry Schatzberg; with Jason Robards as Hans in
    Old Age, Christien Anholt as Young Hans, and Samuel West as
    Konradin).
Published: in *The Comfort of Strangers and Other Screenplays*
    (Faber, 1990).

The Comfort of Strangers

Adapted from the novel by Ian McEwan.
Released: 1990 (dir. Paul Schrader; with Rupert Everett as Colin,
    Natasha Richardson as Mary, Christopher Walken as Robert, and
    Helen Mirren as Caroline).
Published: in *The Comfort of Strangers and Other Screenplays*
    (Faber, 1990).

Collected Poems and Prose

Published: Methuen, 1986; Faber, 1991.

Contains 39 poems and ten prose pieces, two of which, 'The Black and White' and 'Tea Party', are closely linked with plays. Two reveal Pinter's passion for cricket; while 'Mac' (first published separately by Pendragon Press in 1968) is a reminiscence of touring in Ireland in the early 1950s with the Anew McMaster company. 'Mac' and 'Tea Party' also appear in Plays: Three. *The 1986 edition adds five poems and one prose piece to the volume published by Eyre Methuen in 1977 under the same title. Both include* Poems *(Enitharmon Press, 1968).*

The Dwarfs

Novel, written in the mid-1950s.
Published: Faber, 1990.

Pete, a cerebral and neurotic misanthropist, stands roughly centre stage surrounded with images of death. Beside him sits Mark, a down-to-earth actor with an unswerving libido, while Len — a frail railway porter with a fetish for geometry — scuttles around behind. Virginia, Pete's long-suffering girl-friend, stands a little way off, secretly admired by Mark. The action shuffles conversations around various drab rooms in a London desolate à la T. S. Eliot. As the characters slowly begin to sniff the truth about each other, a triangle of disaffection emerges. Pete falls out with both Mark and Virginia (who fall into bed) while Len looks on, a non-playing observer, accompanied by the Dwarfs — figments of his imagination that personify his predatory voyeurism. Central to the novel, a vivid hotchpotch of

styles, is the idea that perception, truth, and morality are dependent on the perspective of the subject.

Michael Wright, 'Life Shown as Mirror Fragments',
The Times, 4 Oct. 1990, p. 24

See also:

'The Knight Has Been Unruly; Memories of Sir Donald Wolfit', *The Listener*, 18 Apr. 1968, p. 501

'The US Elephant Must be Stopped', *The Guardian*, 5 Dec. 1987. [Defends Nicaragua and attacks US policy towards the country.]

Two poems in *Soho Square, II*, ed. Ian Hamilton (Bloomsbury, 1989).

Pinter has a reputation for reticence. It is indeed the case that he has only once talked at length biographically (in the New Yorker *in 1967), and has made only two substantial statements on his work — a speech in 1962 and an interview with* Paris Review *in 1966, both early in his career. He was laconic both in dismissing the Common Market ('I have no interest in the matter and do not care what happens',* Encounter, *Dec. 1962, p. 59) and in opposing the Vietnam War ('The Americans should not have gone in, but they did. They should now get out, but they won't ',* Authors Take Sides on Vietnam, *ed. Cecil Woolf and John Bagguley, London, 1967, p. 41). However, the total number of comments is considerable, and in the 'eighties he was prepared to discuss the political issues which increasingly concerned him.*

My situations and characters aren't always explicit. Well, I don't see life as being very explicit. Our personalities are too complex to be cut and dried and labelled. Then the dialogue — I don't see myself doing anything uncommon. It's not Pinter. It's people. I don't mine it, like gold. It's there all the time. You only need to listen to people, listen to *yourself.* I catch my wife saying to me at breakfast, 'Do you like the cornflakes? Are they nice this morning?' and I say 'Yes, they're very nice. How's the tea? Is that nice?' — because I've made the tea — and she says, 'Yes, the tea's very nice', and on we go.

Critics talk a lot about the problem of non-communication amongst my characters, as if they can't understand each other. It's not really that. I'm interested in people who have *chosen* not to communicate, not to understand each other. . . .

I like comedy. I enjoy amusing myself when I write and it's nice to know I amuse others. But the comedy has to spring from character and situation. It's no good me *trying* to be funny.

> Interviewed by Philip Purser,
> 'A Pint with Pinter Helps to Dispel the Mystery',
> *News Chronicle,* 28 July 1960

The explicit form which is so often taken in twentieth-century drama is . . . cheating. The playwright assumes that we have a great deal of information about all his characters, who explain themselves to the audience. In fact, what they are doing most of the time is conforming to the author's own ideology. They

don't create themselves as they go along, they are being fixed on the stage for one purpose, to speak for the author, who has a point of view to put over. When the curtain goes up on one of my plays, you are faced with a situation, a particular situation, two people sitting in a room, which hasn't happened before, and is just happening at this moment, and we know no more about them than I know about you, sitting at this table. The world is full of surprises. A door can open at any moment and someone will come in. We'd love to know who it is, we'd love to know exactly what he has on his mind and why he comes in, but how often do we know what someone has on his mind or who this somebody is, and what goes to make him and make him what he is, and what his relationship is to others?

> Interviewed by John Sherwood, BBC European Service,
> 3 March 1960, as quoted in Martin Esslin,
> *Pinter the Playwright*, p. 31

There is no question that Beckett is a writer whom I admire very much and have admired for a number of years. If Beckett's influence shows in my work that's all right with me. You don't write in a vacuum; you're bound to absorb and digest other writing; and I admire Beckett's work so much that something of its texture might appear in my own. I myself have no idea whether this is so, but if it is, then I am grateful for it. However, I do think that I have succeeded in expressing something of myself.

> Interviewed by Harry Thompson, 'Harold Pinter Replies',
> *New Theatre Magazine*, Bristol, II, No. 2 (Jan. 1961), p. 8-9

The germ of my plays? I'll be as accurate as I can about that. I went into a room and saw one person standing up and one person sitting down, and a few weeks later I wrote *The Room*. I went into another room and saw two people sitting down, and a few years later I wrote *The Birthday Party*. I looked through a door into a third room, and saw two people standing up and I wrote *The Caretaker*. . . . I'm convinced that what happens in my plays could happen anywhere, at any time, in any place, although the events may seem unfamiliar at first glance. If you press me for a definition, I'd say that what goes on in my plays is realistic, but what I'm doing is not realism. . . . I like writing for sound radio, because of the freedom. When I wrote *The Dwarfs* a few months ago, I was able to experiment in form — a mobile, flexible structure, more flexible and mobile than in any other medium. And from the point of view of content I was able to go the whole hog and enjoy myself by exploring to a degree which wouldn't be acceptable in any other medium. I'm sure the

result may have been incomprehensible to the audience, but it isn't as far as I'm concerned, and it was extremely valuable to me.

'Writing for Myself', *Twentieth Century*,
CLXIX (Feb. 1961), p. 174, 175

I'm not a theorist. I'm not an authoritative or reliable commentator on the dramatic scene, the social scene, any scene. I write plays when I can manage it, and that's all. . . .

I've had two full-length plays produced in London. The first ran a week and the second ran a year. Of course, there are differences between the two plays. In *The Birthday Party* I employed a certain amount of dashes in the text, between phrases. In *The Caretaker* I cut out the dashes and used dots instead. So that instead of, say: 'Look, dash, who, dash, I, dash, dash, dash', the text would read: 'Look, dot, dot, dot, who, dot, dot, dot, I, dot, dot, dot, dot.' So its possible to deduce from this that dots are more popular than dashes and that's why *The Caretaker* had a longer run than *The Birthday Party*. The fact that in neither case could you hear the dots and dashes is beside the point. You can't fool the critics for long. They can tell a dot from a dash a mile off, even if they can hear neither. . . .

I suggest there can be no hard distinctions between what is real and what is unreal, nor between what is true and what is false. A thing is not necessarily either true or false: it can be both true and false. . . . Apart from any other consideration, we are faced with the immense difficulty, if not the impossibility, of verifying the past. I don't mean merely years ago, but yesterday, this morning. . . .

To supply an explicit moral tag to an evolving and compulsive dramatic image seems to be facile, impertinent, and dishonest. Where this takes place it is not theatre but a crossword puzzle. . . .

So often, below the word spoken, is the thing known and unspoken. My characters tell me so much and no more, with reference to their experience, their aspirations, their motives, their history.

Speech of 1962, as 'Introduction: Writing for the Theatre',
in *Plays: One* (Eyre Methuen, 1976), p. 9-13

Ultimately, politics do bore me, though I recognize they are responsible for a good deal of suffering. I distrust ideological statements of any kind. . . . I'll tell you what I really think about politicians. The other night I watched some politicians on television talking about Vietnam. I wanted very much to burst through the screen with a flame-thrower and

burn their eyes out and their balls off and then inquire from them how they would assess this action from a political point of view.

> Interview in *Paris Review*, Fall 1966, reprinted in
> *Theatre at Work*, ed. Charles Marowitz and Simon Trussler
> (Methuen, 1967), p. 104

Writing becomes more and more difficult as I apply more rigorous standards to myself. When I was younger, my writing was free — words poured out of me onto the paper. Now my writing tends to be careful — constipated. I try to do a lot of things without any success at all.

> Interviewed by Patricia Bosworth,
> 'Why He Doesn't Write More',
> *New York Times*, 27 Oct. 1968, Sec. V, p. 3

Once, many years ago, I found myself engaged uneasily in a public discussion on the theatre. Someone asked me what my work was 'about'. I replied with no thought at all and merely to frustrate this line of enquiry: 'The weasel under the cocktail cabinet.' That was a great mistake. Over the years I have seen that remark quoted in a number of learned columns. It has now seemingly acquired a profound significance, and is seen to be a highly relevant and meaningful observation about my own work. But for me the remark meant precisely nothing. . . .

Sometimes, the director says to me in rehearsal: 'Why does she say this?' I reply: 'Wait a minute, let me look at the text'. I do so, and perhaps I say: 'Doesn't she say this because he said *that*, two pages ago?' Or I say: 'Because that's what she feels.' Or: 'Because she feels something else, and therefore says that.' Or: 'I haven't the faintest idea. But somehow we have to find out.' Sometimes I learn quite a lot from rehearsals. . . .

I am not concerned with making general statements. I am not interested in theatre used simply as a means of self-expression on the part of the people engaged in it. . . . I can sum up none of my plays. I can describe none of them, except to say: That is what happened. That is what they said. That is what they did.

> 'Speech: Hamburg, 1971', *Theatre Quarterly*,
> I, No. 3, (July-Sept. 1971), p. 3, 4

What it all comes down to is time. . . . The whole question of time and all its reverberations and possible meanings really does seem to absorb me more and more. . . .

I have very strong objections to all sorts of things — South Africa, for instance. I'm a member of the anti-apartheid organization. . . . The

trouble is that things that are said and are put down in print really stare you in the face for the rest of your life. So much surely depends on how you feel on a particular day. I might say something totally different tomorrow. . . .

Do you know which play took the longest time to write? *Silence*. . . . The structure was so different.

In conversation with Mel Gussow, *New York Times Magazine*,
5 Dec. 1971, p. 133, 134, 136

I in common with a great body of people have been sleepwalking for many years, really, and I remember years ago I regarded myself as an artist in an ivory tower — really when it comes down to it a rather classic nineteenth-century idea. I've now totally rejected that and I find that the things that are actually happening are not only of the greatest importance but [have] the most crucial bearing on our lives, including this matter of censorship of people and writers' imprisonment, torture, and the whole question of how we are dealt with by governments who are in power . . . and essentially to do with the nuclear situation.

Quoted by Ronald Knowles, 'Harold Pinter, Citizen',
Pinter Review, 1989, p. 25, from Channel 4 TV, 9 Jan. 1984

The military coup in 1973 in Chile which overthrew a democratically elected government was brought about, I believe, by the United States. . . . [This] told me without any further ado that I could not sit back and not take responsibility for my own actions, my own thoughts, and act upon them, which I've been doing ever since, making a bit of a nuisance of myself, in fact.

Quoted by Ronald Knowles, as above, p. 25,
from interview with John Tusa, *Saturday Review*,
BBC-2 TV, 28 Sept. 1985

I made a fatal mistake in the early part of my career when, to my eternal regret, I wrote the word 'pause'. All I was talking about was a natural break, when people don't quite know what to do next. Or even less important than that, when the breath goes out. It was a slight pause. But this damn word 'pause' and those silences have achieved such significance that they have overwhelmed the bloody plays. Which I find a bloody pain in the arse. The problem with certain productions of my plays is that they have seen them as abstract and boring; a lot of waffling around. I prefer them to be much more immediate, much quicker. . . .

My mind has changed so much with my political concerns that I can't quite get it together on the page. I'd love to, but I just can't find the way to do it. I hope it's not a permanent state.

> In conversation with Sue Summers, 'Breaking the Silence',
> *London Daily News*, 19 June 1987, p. 19

The plays like *The Birthday Party*, *The Dumb Waiter*, and *The Hothouse* are metaphors, really. When you look at them, they're much much closer to an extremely critical look at authoritarian postures — state power, family power, religious power, power used to undermine, if not destroy, the individual, or the questioning voice, or the voice which simply went away from the mainstream and refused to become part of an easily recognizable set of standards and social values.

> In conversation with Anna Ford, 'Radical Departures',
> *The Listener*, 27 Oct. 1988, p. 5-6

I understand your interest in me as a playwright. But I'm more interested in myself as a citizen. We still say we live in free countries, but we damn well better be able to speak freely. . . . My attitude toward my own playwriting has changed. The whole idea of a narrative, of a broad canvas stretching over a period of two hours — I think I've gone away from that forever.

> In conversation with Mel Gussow,
> *New York Times*, 6 Dec. 1988, Sec. III, p. 17, 22

a: Primary Sources

Collections of Plays

Plays: One, Plays: Two, Plays: Three, and *Plays: Four*
   (Methuen, 1976, 1977, 1978, 1981; Faber, 1991).

All Pinter's stage plays with the exception of Party Time *are
collected in these volumes. Individual editions as first
published by Methuen are noted under their titles in Section 2:
all have now been reissued by Faber. Twelve of Pinter's
screenplays have been collected in* The French Lieutenant's
Woman and Other Screenplays, The Servant and Other
Screenplays, *and* The Comfort of Strangers and Other
Screenplays: *for full particulars, see under 'Film Scripts',
pages 95 to 98.*

Articles and Essays

'Writing for Myself', *Twentieth Century*, CLXIX (Feb. 1961),
   p. 172-5; reprinted in *Plays: Two* (1977).
'Introduction: Writing for the Theatre', *Plays: One* (1976),
   p. 9-16. [Speech of 1962.]
'Speech: Hamburg, 1970', *Theatre Quarterly*, I, No. 3
   (July-Sept. 1971), p. 3-4; reprinted in *Plays: Four* (1981).

Interviews

Philip Purser, 'A Pint with Pinter Helps to Dispel the
   Mystery', *News Chronicle*, 28 July 1960.
Harry Thompson, 'Harold Pinter Replies', *New Theatre
   Magazine* (Bristol), II, No. 2 (Jan. 1961), p. 8-10.
Peter Lewis, 'Fascinated by Unsatisfactory People', *Time and
   Tide,* 21 June 1962, p. 16-17.
John Russell Taylor, '*Accident*', *Sight and Sound*, XXXV,
   No. 4 (Autumn 1966), p. 178-9.
'Harold Pinter', *Theatre at Work*, ed. Charles Marowitz and
   Simon Trussler (Methuen, 1967), p. 96-109. [Reprinted
   from *Paris Review*, Fall 1966; also appears in *Writers at
   Work: Paris Review Interviews*, Third Series; and in *The
   Playwrights Speak*, ed. Walter Wager.]

'Two People in a Room', *New Yorker*, 25 Feb. 1967, p. 34-6.

William Packard, 'An Interview with Harold Pinter', *First Stage*, No. 6 (Summer 1967), p. 82.

Kathleen Halton, 'Funny and Moving and Frightening Pinter', *Vogue*, 1 Oct. 1967, p. 194, 236, 239, 245.

Patricia Bosworth, 'Why He Doesn't Write More', *New York Times*, 27 Oct. 1968, Sec. IV, p. 3.

Judith Crist, 'A Mystery: Pinter on Pinter', *Look*, 24 Dec. 1968, p. 77-78, 80, 83.

'Harold Pinter Talks to Michael Dean', *The Listener*, 6 Mar. 1969, p. 312.

Joan Bakewell, 'In an Empty Bandstand', *The Listener*, 6 Nov. 1969, p. 630-1.

Richard Roud, 'Take Three on the Go-Between', *The Guardian*, Mar. 1971.

Mel Gussow, 'A Conversation (Pause) with Harold Pinter', *New York Times*, 5 Dec. 1971, Sec. VI, p. 42-3, 126-9, 131-6.

Jack Emery, 'Just a Simple Little Love Story?', *Radio Times*, 16-22 Sept. 1978, p. 80-3, 85. [On *Langrishe, Go Down*.]

Mel Gussow, 'Harold Pinter: "I Started with Two People in a Pub" ', *New York Times*, 30 Dec. 1979, Sec. II, p. 5, 7.

Miriam Gross, 'Pinter on Pinter', *The Observer*, 5 Oct. 1980, p. 25, 27.

Bryan Appleyard, 'The New Light That Burns within Harold Pinter', *The Times*, 16 Mar. 1984.

Nick Hern, in *One for the Road* (Methuen, 1985), p. 7-23.

Sue Summers, 'Breaking the Silence', *London Daily News*, 19 June 1987, p. 19.

Anna Ford, 'Radical Departures', *The Listener*, 27 Oct. 1988, p. 4-6.

Mel Gussow, 'Pinter's Plays Following Him out of Enigma and into Politics', *New York Times*, 6 Dec. 1988, Sec. III, p. 17, 22.

Michael Ciment, 'Visually Speaking', *Film Comment*, XXV, No. 3 (May-June 1989), p. 20-2. [On *Reunion*.]

Stephen Schiff, 'Pinter's Passions', *Vanity Fair*, Sept. 1990.

b: Secondary Sources

Because of the vast amount of commentary on Pinter's works, this list is confined to books in English wholly devoted to Pinter. Some of the best of the many articles can be found in the five collections listed below, edited by Lahr (1971), Ganz (1972), Scott (1986), Bloom (1987) and Gordon (1990).

Arnold P. Hinchliffe, *Harold Pinter* (Boston: Twayne, 1967; revised ed., 1981).

Walter Kerr, *Harold Pinter* (New York: Columbia University Press, 1967). ['Columbia Essays on Modern Writers' series.]

Ronald Hayman, *Harold Pinter* (Heinemann, 1968).

Lois G. Gordon, *Stratagems to Uncover Nakedness: the Dramas of Harold Pinter* (Columbia: University of Missouri Press, 1969).

John Russell Taylor, *Harold Pinter* (Longmans, for British Council, 1969). ['Writers and Their Work' series.]

James R. Hollis, *Harold Pinter: the Poetics of Silence* (Carbondale: Southern Illinois University Press, 1970).

John Lahr, ed., *A Casebook on 'The Homecoming'* (New York: Grove, 1971).

Katharine H. Burkman, *The Dramatic World of Harold Pinter: Its Basis in Ritual* (Columbus; Ohio State University Press, 1971).

Arthur Ganz, ed., *Pinter: a Collection of Critical Essays* (Englewood Cliffs, N.J.: Prentice-Hall, 1972).

William Baker and Stephen Ely Tabachnick, *Harold Pinter* (Edinburgh: Oliver and Boyd, 1973).

Simon Trussler, *The Plays of Harold Pinter: an Assessment* (Gollancz, 1973).

Austin E. Quigley, *The Pinter Problem* (Princeton, N.J.: Princeton University Press, 1975).

Bernard F. Dukore, *Where Laughter Stops: Pinter's Tragicomedy* (Columbia: University of Missouri Press, 1976).

Lucina P. Babbard, *The Dream Structure of Pinter's Plays: a Psychoanalytic Approach* (Rutherford, N.J.: Farleigh Dickinson University Press, 1976).

Steven H. Gale, *Butter's Going Up: a Critical Analysis of Harold Pinter's Work* (Durham: Duke University Press, 1977).

Bernard F. Dukore, *Harold Pinter* (Macmillan, 1982; revised ed., 1988).

Martin Esslin, *Pinter the Playwright* (Methuen, 1982; fourth ed. of book originally published as *The Peopled Wound*, 1970).

Guido Almansi and Simon Henderson, *Harold Pinter* (Methuen, 1983).

Alan Bold, ed., *Harold Pinter: You Never Heard Such Silence* (Vision, 1985).

Elin Diamond, *Pinter's Comic Play* (Lewisburg, Pa.: Bucknell University Press, 1985).

Joanne Klein, *Making Pictures: the Pinter Screenplays* (Columbus: Ohio State University Press, 1985).

David T. Thompson, *Pinter: the Player's Playwright* (Macmillan, 1985).

Steven H. Gale, ed., *Harold Pinter: Critical Approaches* (London: Associated University Presses, 1986). [Original essays.]

Michael Scott, ed., *Harold Pinter: 'The Birthday Party', 'The Caretaker', and 'The Homecoming': a Casebook* (Macmillan, 1986).

Harold Bloom, ed., *Harold Pinter: Modern Critical Views* (New York: Chelsea House, 1987).

J. M. Bordewijk-Knotter, *Pinter Appeal: a Comparative Study of Responses to 'The Homecoming'* (Leiden: Quick Service, 1988).

Ronald Knowles, *'The Birthday Party' and 'The Caretaker'* (Macmillan, 1988). ['Text and Performance' series.]

Elizabeth Sakellaridou, *Pinter's Female Portraits* (Totowa, N.J.: Barnes and Noble, 1988).

Volker Strunk, *Harold Pinter: Towards a Poetic of His Plays* (New York: Peter Lang, 1989).

Lois Gordon, ed., *Harold Pinter: a Casebook* (New York: Garland, 1990).

Susan Hollis Merritt, *Pinter in Play* (Durham, North Carolina: Duke University Press, 1990).

Penelope Prentice, *Harold Pinter: Life, Work, and Criticism* (Fredericton, New Brunswick: York Press, 1991).

Journal

Pinter Review, annual since 1987, University of Tampa, Florida.

Bibliography

Steven H. Gale, *Harold Pinter: an Annotated Bibliography* (Boston: G. K. Hall, 1978).

CONCORDIA UNIVERSITY LIBRARY

3 9371 00048 6423

PR 6066 .I53 Z65 1993

File on Pinter